PRAISE FOR *SAVING FREUD*

"Nagorski tells a riveting new story, one that shows just how narrow Freud's escape from the Nazi genocide was. . . . The narrative pace and Nagorski's fluid writing give this book the character of an adventure story."

—Rachel Newcomb, *The Washington Post*

"Andrew Nagorski's absorbing chronicle of Sigmund Freud's harrowing escape from Nazi occupied Vienna is an insight-filled group portrait of the founder of psychoanalysis and his followers. It is also a psychobiographical thriller about the limits of genius. . . . Their audaciously valiant effort makes for compelling reading."

—Diane Cole, *The Wall Street Journal*

"Thrilling . . . as edge-of-your-seat gripping as any heist movie."

—Kathryn Hughes, *The Guardian*

"Nagorski mixes the pacing of a historical thriller (think Alan Furst, but non-fiction, and starring therapists instead of spies) with a meditation on the limits of insight and what it means to be attached to a specific place and to live in a given moment in time. . . . The result is hard to put down, poignant, and distressingly timely."

—Patrick Blanchfield, *The New Republic*

"Astonishing . . . In the American journalist Andrew Nagorski this tale has found its ideal narrator: clear, objective and keen to keep things moving. . . . It tells its story with a propulsive urgency."

—Sebastian Faulks, *The Sunday Times* (London)

"*Saving Freud* is a must read for anyone interested in biography and history, Nagorski shows how one of the brightest minds of modern history could be lulled by wishful thinking and denial of Hitler's all-out war against his fellow Jews nearly cost him what was left of his life."

—Robert A. Cohn, *St. Louis Jewish Light*

"As exciting and suspenseful as a spy novel, Andrew Nagorski's masterful narrative reveals how an eclectic group of Sigmund Freud's friends came together to do the seemingly impossible: engineer his rescue from Nazi-controlled Austria as the Gestapo were closing in. Their successful efforts underscore how powerful love, loyalty, and friendship can be, even in the midst of overwhelming evil."

—Lynne Olson, author of *Madame Fourcade's Secret War: The Daring Young Woman Who Led France's Largest Spy Network Against Hitler*

"An intimate, touching portrait of a genius as an old man. Ill, myopic, in denial, and terribly vulnerable, this Freud is more human than any I've encountered before. Andrew Nagorski has an artist's eye for revealing detail and a novelist's ability to bring to life a long-lost world and its myriad denizens."

—Sylvia Nasar, author of *A Beautiful Mind*

"Andrew Nagorski has written a gripping masterpiece about one of the greatest figures in history, whose insights about human beings as 'savage beasts' could not be more timely."

—Professor Brett Kahr, Honorary Director of Research, Freud Museum London, and author of *Freud's Pandemics: Surviving Global War, Spanish Flu, and the Nazis*

"Part engrossing biography of the father of psychoanalysis, part vivid group portrait of the circle of notables who rescued Freud from the Nazis, *Saving Freud* pulses with urgent life. Nagorski captures the power of self-delusion and denial even among the most brilliant minds."

—Kati Marton, author of *The Chancellor: The Remarkable Odyssey of Angela Merkel*

"With his characteristic clarity and meticulous research, Nagorski has once again produced a masterful work. *Saving Freud* is a page-turner, mixing biography and escape narrative, with a powerful reminder that historians need to pay attention not just to words, but to relationships."

—Rebecca Erbelding, historian and author of *Rescue Board: The Untold Story of America's Efforts to Save the Jews of Europe*

"Crackles like a novel and sparks with the razzle-dazzle of a big-screen extravaganza: an unforgettable cast of characters (think *The Dirty Dozen*), spine-tingling suspense (*The Day of the Jackal*), a death-defying savior (maybe *Mephisto*), and Nazis—the epitome of evil."
　　　　　　　—Kitty Kelley, *Washington Independent Review of Books*

"I am a longtime fan of Andrew Nagorski's work and his phenomenal talent for personalizing history, allowing the reader to witness events through the eyes of those who lived them. *Saving Freud* is one of his finest—a spectacularly engaging and entertaining account of an incredible rescue. Do not miss this one."
　　　　　　　—Seth MacFarlane, executive producer of *Family Guy* and *The Orville*

"Nagorski delivers a riveting page-turner. . . . Excellent."
　　　　　　　—*Kirkus Reviews* (starred review)

"Sigmund Freud's vibrant life in Vienna and narrow escape from the Gestapo are recounted in this entertaining history. . . . An invigorating look at a lesser-known chapter of Freud's well-documented life."
　　　　　　　—*Publishers Weekly*

SAVING FREUD

THE RESCUERS
WHO BROUGHT HIM
TO FREEDOM

ANDREW NAGORSKI

SIMON & SCHUSTER PAPERBACKS

NEW YORK LONDON TORONTO SYDNEY NEW DELHI

Simon & Schuster Paperbacks
An Imprint of Simon & Schuster, Inc.
1230 Avenue of the Americas
New York, NY 10020

First Simon & Schuster trade paperback edition August 2023

SIMON & SCHUSTER PAPERBACKS and colophon are registered trademarks
of Simon & Schuster, Inc.

For information about special discounts for bulk purchases, please contact Simon &
Schuster Special Sales at 1-866-506-1949 or business@simonandschuster.com.

The Simon & Schuster Speakers Bureau can bring authors to your live event. For
more information or to book an event, contact the Simon & Schuster Speakers
Bureau at 1-866-248-3049 or visit our website at www.simonspeakers.com.

Interior design by Carly Loman

Manufactured in the United States of America

10   9   8   7   6   5   4   3   2   1

Library of Congress Cataloging-in-Publication Data has been applied for.

ISBN 978-1-9821-7283-1
ISBN 978-1-9821-7284-8 (pbk)
ISBN 978-1-9821-7285-5 (ebook)

For Isabel,
And, as always,
For Krysia

"It is an iron law of history that those who will be caught up in the great movements determining the course of their own times always fail to recognize them in their early stages."

—STEFAN ZWEIG, *The World of Yesterday*

CONTENTS

SAVING
FREUD

1.

"TO DIE IN FREEDOM"

On March 15, 1938, three days after German troops had crossed into Austria, about 250,000 people greeted Adolf Hitler when he appeared on the balcony of the Hofburg, Vienna's imperial palace, to announce the elimination of a separate Austrian state. "The oldest eastern province of the German nation shall from now on be the youngest bulwark of the German nation," he declared. The Anschluss, his oft-proclaimed dream of incorporating the country of his birth into the Third Reich, was now a reality—and the crowd appeared deliriously happy. From the moment Hitler's troops had marched across the border, most Austrians had responded with similar outbursts of jubilation.

But not all. The new arrivals launched mass arrests of anyone categorized by the Gestapo as anti-Nazi, while simultaneously triggering a wave of anti-Semitic violence. Jews were beaten and killed, their stores looted, and dozens committed suicide. According to German playwright Carl Zuckmayer, who was in Vienna at the time, "The city was transformed into a nightmare painting by Hieronymus Bosch . . . What was unleashed upon Vienna was a torrent of envy, jealousy, bitterness, blind, malignant craving for revenge . . . It was the witch's Sabbath of the mob. All that makes for human dignity was buried."

Ensconced in his longtime residence and office at Berggasse 19, Sigmund Freud had written a terse note in his diary as soon as the German takeover began: *"Finis Austriae"* (the end of Austria). For all but the first four years of his life, the founder of psychoanalysis had lived in the Austrian capital—and now, as he was approaching his eighty-second birthday, he found himself right in the middle of the unfolding nightmare. As a Jew, he was automatically in danger; as the undisputed public face of what most Nazi officials denounced as a Jewish pseudoscience, there was no telling what the new masters had in store for him.

Freud was an immediate target. On the same day that Hitler delivered his speech nearby, Nazi thugs invaded both Freud's apartment and the International Psychoanalytic Press, the publishing house for the works of Freud and his colleagues, which was situated just up the street at Berggasse 7. At the apartment, Freud's wife, Martha, had the presence of mind to throw the "visitors" off balance by playing the polite hostess. She pulled out the cash she had on hand and asked, "Won't the gentlemen help themselves?" Anna, the couple's youngest daughter, then took their "guests" to another room where she emptied the safe of 6,000 shillings, the equivalent of about $840, offering that sum to them as well.

The stern figure of Sigmund Freud suddenly appeared, glaring at the intruders without saying anything. Visibly intimidated, they addressed him as "Herr Professor" and backed out of the apartment with their loot, announcing they would return another time. After they left, Freud inquired how much money they had seized. Taking the answer in stride, he wryly remarked, "I have never taken so much for a single visit."

But there was nothing amusing about the unfolding drama there or, nearby, at the site of the International Psychoanalytic Press, where

Martin, the Freuds' oldest son, had gone to destroy documents that the Nazis could use against his father. When about a dozen "shabbily dressed" thugs burst into the premises, as Martin recalled, they pressed their rifles against his stomach and held him prisoner for several hours. One of the men ostentatiously pulled out a pistol and shouted, "Why not shoot him and be finished with him? We should shoot him on the spot."

During that chaotic first day, the invaders looked confused about their mission and it was unclear who was giving them orders. They missed several documents that Martin, while pleading a stomach ailment, managed to flush down the toilet. By the end of the afternoon, all of the Nazis retreated, promising a full investigation later.

Back at the apartment, where Martin joined his parents and sister, there was little sense of relief. Anna was especially despondent. "Wouldn't it be better if we all killed ourselves?" she asked her father. Freud's pointed response indicated that he was not about to contemplate anything of the sort. "Why? Because they would like us to?" he said.

But his predicament—with its very uncertain outcome—raised troubling questions: Why had Freud allowed himself to be trapped in this extremely perilous situation? Why had he failed to leave Vienna earlier when it would have been relatively easy for him to do so?

And why, even after the Nazi raiders left his premises on March 15, vowing to return soon, was Freud still reluctant to act? Once Martin was released from the publishing house, he had immediately gone home to check on his parents. "In spite of this trying ordeal, I do not think father had yet any thought of leaving Austria," Martin wrote. Instead, he hoped "to ride out the storm," expecting "that a normal rhythm would be restored and honest men permitted to go on their ways without fear."

The irony was that Freud should have been uniquely qualified to understand the dark forces propelling his world to mass murder and destruction. In his famed 1930 essay "Civilization and Its Discontents," he discussed man's "aggressive cruelty," which "manifests itself spontaneously and reveals men as savage beasts to whom the thought of sparing their own kind is alien." He specifically noted how often Jews had "rendered services" to others by serving as the outlet for such primal impulses.

During a life that spanned the last decades of the Austro-Hungarian Empire, World War I, and the interwar period, Freud was no stranger to political turmoil and anti-Semitism, which was less of an undercurrent than a regular feature of his immediate surroundings. On one level, he knew that this made for a combustible mix that could explode at any time, threatening him and his family. But on another level, he was in denial. He was struggling with the cancer that had developed in his jaw as a result of his long addiction to cigar smoking, and he was acutely aware that his allotted time was running out, prompting him to hope desperately that he could spend whatever was left of it in relative peace, without the upheaval of settling elsewhere.

It was more than the combination of old age and illness that was holding him back, however. Freud felt a deep attachment to the Vienna that had been a major center of cultural—and Jewish—life in Europe for centuries. Its thriving Jewish community included composers like Gustav Mahler and Arnold Schoenberg, writers like Stefan Zweig, Franz Werfel, and Joseph Roth, along with physicists, physicians, and, of course, many of the other leading psychologists of the era. Freud knew or had at least encountered most of them.

The center of Freud's universe was Berggasse 19, where he and Martha had raised six children. It was also where he saw his patients, wrote his essays and books, and met on Wednesday evenings with the members of the Vienna Psychoanalytic Association. He was wedded to rituals like his evening walks on the Ringstrasse and visits to the city's famed cafes, where he would smoke his cigars and read newspapers. In short, he was a revolutionary thinker who also subscribed to the German saying *"Ordnung muss sein,"* which roughly translates as "There must be order." In the Third Reich, those words would take on a much more sinister meaning, but in prewar Vienna they could coexist with generally tolerant social norms—and Freud's relentless exploration of once taboo subjects.

Vienna was also the stage where Freud had transformed himself from a self-described outsider who was often scorned by the medical establishment into the city's widely acclaimed practitioner of his new science. He was the king of his realm, attracting apostles and patients from all across Europe and the United States. By the 1920s and 1930s, he was Vienna's most famous resident, and his appearance anywhere drew immediate attention.

John Gunther, a foreign correspondent for the *Chicago Daily News* and subsequently the author of *Inside Europe* and a string of other popular histories, penned a novel about Vienna called *The Lost City.* Loosely based on his experiences in the Austrian capital in the early 1930s, the book includes a description of a diplomatic party thrown by the Polish embassy where Freud shows up. It demonstrates Freud's already mythic stature.

A guest spots the celebrity and exclaims: "Now, ah, we have a true rarity. Enters Freud!" Gunther then writes:

And indeed Dr. Sigmund Freud, no less, with his gleaming violet eyes, his hard carved beard, his note of tense and even exasperated superiority, was advancing gravely to host and hostess. A hush came over the room as he moved forward like a boat through bulrushes; guests crammed to watch, but were bent back by the force of his slow, majestic passage. "Freud!" people whispered. The whole assembly became silent in awe.

That kind of fame could have meant ruination or salvation for Freud. Once the Anschluss was completed, the Nazi overlords could have decided to demonstrate that no Jew, no matter how prominent, was safe from their wrath. Or they could have calculated that, at this early stage of Hitler's triumphs, it would be better to allow Freud out of the trap he had, to a large extent, set for himself. In reality, though, they had made no firm decision about what to do with Freud when they took over. His fate was still in play, and it would take the concerted efforts of an ad hoc rescue squad to arrange his escape from Vienna.

Those rescuers were an improbable mix of colorful personalities of divergent backgrounds and nationalities. What they had in common was their devotion to Freud and his theories and, in the tense final period, their determination, first of all, to overcome his remaining reluctance to leave Vienna. Then, when he finally bowed to the necessity of doing so, they took on the task of making the frantic arrangements to convince the Nazi authorities to let him go. And at a time when Jewish emigrants were finding it increasingly difficult to find a country to accept them, they were charged with convincing the British government to accept Freud and his large entourage, a total of sixteen people, including family members, in-laws, and his doctor and family. It was a complex operation, with no guarantee of success—and no possibility of success at all if the rescue squad had not risen to the occasion.

The main members of that team:

Ernest Jones, a Welsh physician who first met Freud in 1908 and learned German to study his works. Jones became his most fervent disciple in the English-speaking world. He served as president of the British Psychoanalytical Society and the International Psychoanalytical Association, which propagated Freudian ideas. He would play a key role both in convincing Freud to leave Vienna and in convincing the British government to grant entry to him and his party.

Anna Freud had five older siblings but developed the closest personal and professional relationship with her father, devoting herself to his care until the end of his life. During most of that time, she was involved in what she called a "precious relationship" with Dorothy Tiffany Burlingham, the American granddaughter of Charles Tiffany, the founder of Tiffany & Co. Anna became a leading child psychoanalyst, applying her father's theories as she treated her young patients.

William Bullitt, the U.S. ambassador to France and earlier the Soviet Union, was Freud's patient in 1926, when his marriage was falling apart and he was possibly contemplating suicide. Their sessions did not save his marriage but did help him with his depression and led to an unexpected collaboration between the two men on a biography of a statesman they both despised, President Woodrow Wilson.

Marie Bonaparte represented Europe's high society. She was Napoleon's great-grandniece and was married to Prince George of Greece and Denmark. Although she conducted a long-running affair with the prime minister of France, Aristide Briand, she started her analysis with Freud in 1925 to overcome her "frigidity" and soon became an analyst in her own right. Like Jones and Bullitt, Bonaparte was a gentile.

Max Schur specialized in internal medicine but, even in his student days, he was fascinated by Freud and underwent analysis himself. During Marie Bonaparte's stays in Vienna, she was one of his patients. Intrigued by this "psychoanalytically oriented internist," Bonaparte introduced him to Freud, who took him on as his physician in 1929. Schur, who like Freud was Jewish, was far more alarmed by the looming Nazi threat than his patient. Although he had made arrangements for his family to emigrate to the United States, he stayed on in Austria to care for Freud right up until his departure—and then made sure he had proper care in London as well.

Anton Sauerwald was the member of Freud's rescue squad who was totally out of place. No one would have predicted that a Nazi bureaucrat, who was assigned the task of overseeing the extortion of Freud's assets, would play a critical role in the final chapter of his life in Vienna. But that was exactly what happened.

The famous old man in Vienna had to rely on all these people—along with others who helped them—to make it possible for him to spend the final fifteen months of his life in London, granting him his wish "to die in freedom."

———

During the 1980s and 1990s, I served as *Newsweek*'s bureau chief in Moscow, Rome, Bonn, Berlin, and Warsaw. Vienna was often part of my beat. I had first visited the city as a teenager, and I was delighted to return there again and again. It is a place drenched in history, magnificent art, architecture, music, and literature, and it still offers many of the same views and pleasures as it did in Freud's time.

You can replicate his regular walks around the Ringstrasse, the horseshoe-shaped grand boulevard that was constructed on orders from the Habsburg emperor Franz Josef in the second half of the nineteenth century. As it takes you around the town center, you can admire the Vienna State Opera, the Parliament, City Hall, the university, and other stately buildings and gardens.

Like Freud, you can stop at any number of cafés, including his favorite, Café Landtmann, which is situated next to the Burgtheater. There, you can sit on the velvet banquettes or original Thonet chairs from the imperial era while gazing at the mirrors from the 1920s and exquisite inlays on the wooden walls. Before I fully appreciated this Belle Époque ambience, I discovered that almost everyone I wanted to meet in Vienna—political scientists, sociologists, writers, artists—would suggest that we meet there.

But for anyone who lives in Vienna for any length of time, or even visits often, the city arouses strong conflicting emotions. John Gunther described it as a city that is "so seductive, so oppressive, but possessed of an enigmatic charm."

Some of that charm was noticed even by the victims of the Nazi era. In the early days of the German occupation of Poland, sixteen-year-old Weronika Kowalska was among a large group of teenage girls in Czestochowa who were abruptly ripped away from their families and dispatched to Vienna as forced laborers. They spent most of the war working in an Ericsson factory producing field telephones for the German army while living in an austere barracks nearby. Much later, when I knew her as my mother-in-law, Kowalska never minimized the hardships she and the others endured. But she also vividly remembered the occasional glimpses she caught of a city that looked completely dazzling to her.

The stories I covered on my trips to Vienna frequently involved explorations of the same sinister past. I often visited the famed Nazi hunter Simon Wiesenthal, who was based in the Austrian capital, to report on his efforts to bring the criminals to justice. During the early postwar period, many Austrians successfully portrayed themselves as the first victims of the Third Reich, a sanitized version of events that was bolstered in the popular imagination by the immense success of the movie *The Sound of Music*. The fact that Austrians were among Hitler's most fervent supporters—and, as Wiesenthal repeatedly pointed out, were disproportionately represented as commandants and other functionaries in the death camps—was largely overlooked.

It wasn't until former United Nations Secretary General Kurt Waldheim emerged as the leading candidate in the 1986 Austrian presidential election that the country began a long overdue reckoning with its recent past. In official biographies, he had acknowledged his early wartime service on the Eastern Front, but "forgot" to mention his subsequent tour of duty in the Balkans on the staff of General Alexander Löhr, who was later convicted and hanged in Yugoslavia as a war criminal. When Waldheim's omissions were exposed, the schaden-freude of some of my German friends was all too evident. "The Austrians have convinced the world that Beethoven was an Austrian and Hitler was a German," they joked. (Hitler was born in Upper Austria, while Beethoven was born in Bonn.)

While I was reporting on this story, I found Waldheim's reaction to the allegations about his wartime role as disturbing as anything he may have done as an intelligence officer at the time. Seizing on the fact that the World Jewish Congress was in the forefront of those accusing him of war crimes, he resorted to barely veiled anti-Semitic rhetoric to mobilize his supporters, who rewarded him with a bitter victory. Austria's reputation had been tarred again, but a new generation of Austrian educators took advantage of the controversy to try to introduce more honest programs about history into the schools and public forums.

I have continued to return to Vienna whenever possible. I find the pull of the city to be strong, its appeal hard to resist, no matter what shadows it continues to cast. Perhaps for that reason, Freud's attachment to it feels completely understandable to me, despite his increasingly fractured emotions. It was an ambivalence he held on to right up until he lapsed into his final sleep in London.

"LABORATORY OF THE APOCALYPSE"

DURING THE FINAL PERIOD OF ITS EXISTENCE, WHICH SPANNED the latter part of the nineteenth century and the first part of the twentieth until the cataclysm of World War I, the Austro-Hungarian Empire was home to fifty million people who represented at least nine major nationalities and numerous minorities. Vienna was the glittering imperial capital for everyone, but the Habsburg rulers granted their diverse subjects and regions limited yet impressive autonomy, allowing them to set many of their own rules while trading and traveling freely. By and large, this looked like a recipe for political and economic success.

But it was a recipe that also depended on a built-in willingness, by rulers and subjects alike, to tolerate the ambiguities, contradictions, and tensions inherent in such a relatively enlightened multinational, multicultural arrangement. This was particularly true for that somewhat amorphous group of people who identified as Austrians—and not simply as Germans who happened to live in Vienna or elsewhere.

Dorothy Thompson, the famed American newspaper correspondent who reported from Vienna, Berlin, and the rest of Central Europe in the 1920s and 1930s, pinpointed what that meant in practice. "Insofar as a man thought *nationally* in the old Empire, he thought of himself as a Hungarian, a Pole, a Czech, an Italian, a Croat, or a German," she wrote. "When he thought of himself as an Austrian, he thought of something quite different: allegiance to a monarch; a certain form of life; a curious culture, compounded of many clashing and complementing elements."

Although Sigmund Freud rarely thought of himself in terms of national identity, he almost perfectly fit that description of an Austrian. Depending on an observer's perspective and prejudices, his Jewish roots were "clashing" or "complementing." Either way, this did not alter the fact that he was a product of an empire that was both dying and still vibrant right up until World War I and the subsequent Treaty of Versailles that decreed its demise. Freud's personality, drive, and contradictions were forged in the era when "Golden Vienna" reigned supreme. This was the Vienna that shaped his Weltanschauung, his world view, and this was the Vienna that he refused to leave until it was almost too late.

Appropriately enough, Vienna could look and feel schizophrenic at times—showcasing its dazzling displays of high culture, artistic verve, and scientific accomplishment; alternatively, it could reveal its dark side of sordid hostels for the homeless, abject poverty, and widespread prostitution, along with the political intrigues and unrest that inevitably flourished in such conditions. It could feel like the peak of cosmopolitan sophistication or like a provincial backwater suffocating in its staid, bureaucratic ways. This divide roughly defined what could be called Freud's Vienna and Hitler's Vienna.

While the future ruler of the Third Reich spent only about five years in the Austrian capital, they constituted a critical chapter in his young life. It is no exaggeration to say that Vienna shaped both Freud and Hitler. Nor was it an exaggeration when Karl Kraus, a popular turn-of-the-century writer and editor of the magazine *Die Fackel* (The Torch), declared: "Vienna is the laboratory of the apocalypse."

It was also Freud's laboratory where he invented the term "psychoanalysis" and developed the theories and practices that still largely define it today. Just as Copernicus and Darwin shocked their contemporaries with their startling discoveries, Freud shocked his world with what biographer Peter Gay called "his portrait of man, the insatiable animal pushed and pulled by unrespectable, largely unconscious, desires and aversions." Heavily emphasizing the role of childhood sexuality, repressed memories, dreams, fantasies, and narcissism, he offered what appeared to be a bewildering glimpse into the previously uncharted subconscious territory of the human mind.

Yet Freud boldly asserted: "Psychoanalysis simplifies life. Psychoanalysis supplies the thread that leads a man out of the labyrinth." Coining novel concepts, he explained the interplay among them: the id, which is driven by inherent instincts; the ego, which tries to control the instincts for the sake of avoiding what he called "unpleasure"; the superego, which is shaped by parental and other early influences on a person's development that extend into adulthood. The psychoanalyst's task, he explained, was to discover the often deeply buried reasons for a patient's behavior and neuroses.

Freud was not born in that Vienna laboratory; in fact, he would frequently express diametrically opposite feelings about the city that would become his home for almost all his life. He was born on May 6, 1856, in the Moravian town of Freiberg situated 175 miles northeast of Vienna. (Today called Pribor, it is now in the Czech Republic.) His father, Jacob Freud, was a forty-year-old wool merchant who had been married twice before he wed Amalia Nathansohn, who was half his age, in 1855. By then, he had two grown sons from his first marriage, along with a one-year-old grandson. Sigmund was technically the grandson's uncle, but they played together as if they were brothers.

Amalia favored her first child, calling him *"mein goldener Sigi,"* but she had little time to dote on him. She soon gave birth to a second son, who died at seven months, and then to five daughters followed by another son. The family struggled financially and, as Sigmund recalled later, his father was "always hopefully expecting something to turn up." Vienna was a magnet for many Jews of the empire seeking to improve their lot, and Jacob moved the family there when Sigmund was almost four, settling in the heavily Jewish quarter of Leopoldstadt. But initially he did not find much more success as a merchant there, and the family name was tainted by a scandal involving one of Jacob's brothers who was jailed for dealing in counterfeit rubles.

Not surprisingly, Sigmund, who would become a prolific writer, was hardly eager to dwell on the tribulations of his family in Vienna. "Then came long hard years," he noted tersely. "I think nothing of them was worth remembering." As for the young boy who had left the overwhelmingly Catholic town with less than five thousand inhabitants surrounded by woods and meadows for the sprawling capital of a multicultural empire, he added, "I never felt really comfortable in the city."

That discomfort only reinforced the rosy memories Sigmund claimed to have of the first years of his life. So did his first trip back to Freiberg at the age of sixteen. He stayed with the Fluss family, who had been friendly with his parents; he quickly struck up a friendship with the son Emil and was briefly infatuated with the daughter Gisela, who was a year younger than him. Upon his return to Vienna, Freud wrote to Emil that the city was "disgusting to me," complained about "the abominable steeple" of St. Stephen's Cathedral, and insisted that his spirits lifted only whenever he could travel elsewhere.

Some of those feelings remained with him even after he had achieved fame and, to a degree, fortune. In 1931, when the mayor of Pribor unveiled a bronze tablet marking the place where Freud was born seventy-five years earlier, the honoree waxed poetic in his letter of thanks. "Deep within me, covered over, there still lives the happy child from Freiberg, the first-born son of a youthful mother, who had received the first indelible impressions from this air, from this soil," he wrote. This was no pro forma letter; it expressed his long-held idyllic view of his earliest years.

Despite his frequent complaints about Vienna, Freud flourished there. The city attracted Jews who, unlike many of their counterparts in small towns and villages, assimilated quickly. Under Emperor Franz Josef, who ascended to the throne in 1848—the year that popular revolutions challenged old regimes across the continent—Austria eliminated special taxes on Jews and other restrictions, including on what jobs they could hold, as well as such measures as a ban on Jewish households employing gentiles as servants. By 1867, Jews were granted full citizenship. Although anti-Semitism hardly disappeared, Vienna's Jews, who amounted to about 10 percent of the city's population by 1880, were leaders in the arts, science, medicine, publishing, and other fields. For talented Jews like Freud who were coming of age there, Vienna offered tremendous opportunities.

At his *Gymnasium*, or secondary school, as Freud proudly noted, "I was at the top of my class for seven years; I enjoyed special privileges there, and had scarcely ever to be examined in class." His father left it to him to decide what studies—and what career—he would pursue afterward. At that point, he had no interest in becoming a doctor. Influenced by an older schoolmate who later became a politician, he decided he wanted "to study law like him and engage in social activities." As Freud noted, such a career seemed like a reasonable aspiration at the time, since "every diligent Jewish schoolboy carried a ministerial portfolio in his satchel." But he was also fascinated by Charles Darwin's theories and, following a lecture by a popular professor on the natural world, he decided to study medicine instead.

———

When Freud enrolled at the University of Vienna in 1873, he suddenly was confronted by "appreciable disappointments," which were the product of pervasive prejudices. "Above all, I found that I was expected to feel myself inferior and an alien because I was a Jew," he recalled, adding that he "refused absolutely" to do so. "I have never been able to see why I should feel ashamed of my descent or, as people were beginning to say, of my 'race.'"

Freud was able to successfully continue his studies, but he believed those early brushes with anti-Semitism taught him a valuable lesson. "I was made familiar with the fate of being in the Opposition . . . The foundations were thus laid for a certain degree of independence of judgement," he wrote in *An Autobiographical Study*.

That independence included his refusal to deny his Jewish background. "My parents were Jews, and I have remained a Jew myself," he wrote. Yet he was neither religious nor observant. According to his sister Anna, "He grew up devoid of any belief in God. He had no need of it." She recalled that their father Jacob's motto was "to think morally, and to act ethically," but that none of her siblings received any religious instruction. Nonetheless, Jacob kept a family Bible and wrote Sigmund's name in it when he was born (he did not write the names of his subsequent children). Like Amalia, he was unabashedly partial to their talented first-born son.

Sigmund had little patience for those ultra-Orthodox Jews whose appearance and demeanor stood in such stark contrast to his own. In a letter to his Freiberg friend Emil Fluss, Freud described how "intolerable" he found the sight of one family on the train ride back to Vienna. The father was a "highly honorable old Jew," he wrote sarcastically, who was discussing religion with his "impudent, promising son." The boy, he concluded, "was of the kind of wood from which fate carves the swindler when the time is ripe: crafty, mendacious, encouraged by his dear relatives to think that he has talent, but without principles or a view of life." As Peter Gay pointed out, "A professional Jew-baiter could hardly have expressed it more forcefully."

It was not uncommon for successful secular Jews in Vienna, or Berlin for that matter, to resent their openly religious, visibly unas-similated brethren, most of whom came from more traditional Jewish enclaves in Eastern Europe. These secular Jews had devoted their en-ergies to fitting into Austrian and German society, and the latter part of the nineteenth century appeared to offer them the chance to do so more fully than ever. Arthur Schnitzler, the popular Austrian-Jewish playwright and novelist of that era, wrote: "In those days—the late blossoming period of liberalism—anti-Semitism existed, as it had al-ways done, as an emotion in the numerous hearts so inclined and an idea with great possibilities of development, but it did not play an important role politically or socially. The word hadn't even been in-vented."

But if the young Freud shared the condescension that many secular Jews felt toward the new arrivals from more "backward" regions, he was not at all ambivalent about the anti-Semitism of others. When he was twelve, his father told him about a disturbing incident. A gentile had knocked off his fur cap, sending it flying into the mud, and com-manded: "Jew, get off the pavement." Sigmund asked his father how he had reacted. "I stepped into the gutter and picked up my cap," he said. Shocked and disappointed, the younger Freud decided he would never allow himself to be humiliated like that.

As he matured, the young Freud recognized that, such anti-Semitism notwithstanding, he had every reason to aim high. Vienna offered the setting for him to pursue his goals, and his mother had instilled him with the necessary self-confidence to achieve them. "A man who has been the indisputable favorite of his mother keeps for life the feeling of a conqueror, that confidence of success that often induces real success," he wrote later.

In the summer of 1875, Freud visited his half brothers in Manchester, England. He had been studying British literature for years, obsessively trying to soak up the atmosphere of this foreign land that fired his imagination. In a letter two years earlier to his friend Eduard Silberstein, he wrote, only half-jokingly, that he might catch the "English disease." During his seven-week stay with his half brother Emmanuel and his family, who greeted him warmly, he became even more of an Anglophile.

Sigmund was struck by the "sober industriousness" of the English, along with "their sensitive feeling of justice" and much greater commitment to tolerance than he had experienced in Vienna, as exemplified by the fact that Prime Minister Benjamin Disraeli was a Jew. Some of that tolerance must have rubbed off on Emmanuel, who prevailed on him to soften his harsh view of their father's meek behavior when he was humiliated by the gentile who threw his cap in the mud.

Writing to Silberstein after his return to Vienna, Sigmund declared: "I would sooner live there than here, rain, fog, drunkenness and conservatism notwithstanding. Many peculiarities of the English character and country that other continentals might find intolerable agree very well with my own nature." He then added: "Who knows dear friend, but that after I have completed my studies a friendly wind might not blow me across to England and allow me to practice my hand there." It would take almost a full lifetime before that prophecy was fulfilled, but the seed was planted during that first visit.

A year later, Freud was chosen by one of his professors to travel to Trieste for a research project in the laboratory of the university's experimental marine biology station there. His assignment was to check on the claim of Polish scientist Simone de Syrski that he had solved the mystery of how eels reproduce by locating their gonads. Freud dissected more than four hundred eels before coming up with the evidence he was looking for: traces of the testes that indicated Syrski was right. It seemed fitting that one of the first achievements of the student who would later become famous for his theories about repressed sexual memories involved locating the elusive reproductive organs of eels.

Any young man visiting an Adriatic port city like Trieste in that era would have also noticed its other attractions—and Freud was no exception. Writing again to Silberstein, he mentioned the "Italian goddesses" he came across on his walks around town. But he kept his distance. "Since it is not permitted to dissect humans, I have in fact nothing to do with them," he wrote, attempting to make light of his bashfulness. The split between his private behavior and his daring future psychological theories was already apparent.

Back in Vienna, Freud ensconced himself in the laboratory of physiologist Ernst Brücke, where he "found rest and full satisfaction," as he put it, studying the nervous system. He admitted that he was "decidedly negligent" with his studies, which were interrupted for a year of obligatory military service, passing his medical exams for his doctorate only in 1881. He finally seemed set to embark on a career that would allow him to slowly climb the academic ladder. That is, until one afternoon in April 1882, when he returned home from the laboratory and met Martha Bernays, a twenty-one-year-old, slim, attractive visitor from northern Germany. It was an encounter that radically altered his life's trajectory.

———

Sigmund and Martha's meeting that day was not as much a product of serendipity as it might first appear. Although Martha was living with her widowed mother in Wandsbek, near Hamburg, the family had resided in Vienna earlier, and her older brother, Eli Bernays, was engaged to Sigmund's sister Anna. When Martha and her younger sister Minna returned to Vienna for a visit, they came to see the Freuds at their apartment. Since Sigmund was still living there, it was only natural that they should run into each other. By his own effusive accounts, Sigmund was drawn to Martha from the first moment he laid eyes on her, and he immediately set out to woo her. Two months later, they were engaged, on their way to a marriage that would produce six children and last for fifty-three years, until the end of his life.

In many ways, the two were an improbable match. Martha, who was five years younger than Sigmund, was born into a prominent Orthodox Jewish family. Her grandfather, Isaac Bernays, had been the chief rabbi of Hamburg, who vigorously opposed the Jewish reform movement. Both Martha's and Sigmund's fathers were merchants, but she grew up in a much more strictly observant household than he did. When Martha's father died in 1879, her mother was even more determined to maintain those rules. Sigmund had little patience for what he called Martha's "foolish superstitions" produced by her religious upbringing. For fear of antagonizing both her observant mother and brother, she initially kept their engagement a secret.

The most serious obstacle to their marriage, however, was their meager finances. As a widow, Martha's mother could not help them in any significant way, and Sigmund was not in a position to take on the responsibilities of a husband and, presumably, father. During his studies, Freud had relied on modest support from his father and the small grants and fees he collected for his publications. But he would not have had enough to live on if not for the occasional gifts disguised as "loans" from the physician Josef Breuer, his mentor, who treated Freud as his protégé and later was seen as his forerunner in what became known as the field of psychoanalysis. As a bachelor still living at home, Freud could make do with that irregular trickle of funding. As the head of a family, that would no longer be the case.

As much as he appreciated Freud's work in his laboratory, the physiologist Ernst Brücke had foreseen this problem earlier. Shortly before Sigmund met Martha, he had "corrected my father's improvidence by strongly advising me, in view of my bad financial situation, to abandon my theoretical career," Freud recalled. At first, he had ignored that advice. But once he met Martha, he reconsidered. He left his post in Brücke's laboratory and took a job as a junior physician in the General Hospital. He did not plan to remain there for long, but he needed to get the clinical experience that would allow him to open a private practice. This would offer him the prospect of earning a respectable living, which was what the couple needed before they could marry.

That day would not come until four years later. During their long separation, broken up only by extremely rare visits between Martha's home on the Baltic coast and Sigmund's home on the Danube, the couple wrote to each other almost daily. Sigmund penned more than nine hundred letters, offering insights into both their fast-blossoming relationship and his often-mercurial personality. In photos and drawings, Freud invariably appears as a stern, intensely serious figure, which is the image embedded in popular culture. In those missives, however, he comes across as an almost unbridled romantic, a young man carried away by the first truly passionate, still chaste relationship of his life. He addressed Martha as "My sweet Princess," "My beloved treasure," and "Fair mistress, sweet love," all part of a stream of his affectionate salutations.

They became engaged in Vienna on June 17, 1882, and the next day Martha was on her way back to Wandsbek. On June 19, Sigmund wrote a gushing letter expressing his conflicted feelings. "I knew it was only after you had gone that I would realize the full extent of my happiness and, alas! the degree of my loss as well . . . It must be true. Martha is mine, the sweet girl of whom everyone speaks with admiration, who despite all my resistance captivated my heart at our first meeting, the girl I feared to court and who came toward me with high-minded confidence, who strengthened my faith in my own value . . ."

As with his mother, Sigmund was seeking someone who would offer him unequivocal support for whatever endeavors he would pursue, which was a frequent refrain of his subsequent letters. "It is your doing that I have become a self-confident, courageous man," he wrote. He also left no doubt that he felt unabashedly possessive about Martha from the very beginning. "From now on you are but a guest in your family, like a jewel that I have pawned and that I am going to redeem as soon as I am rich."

In those early days of their engagement, he made an effort to sound conciliatory about their differences, particularly about religion. Referring to the generation of their parents and grandparents, he wrote: "Even if the form wherein the old Jews were happy no longer offers us any shelter, something of the core, of the essence of this meaningful and life-affirming Judaism will not be absent from our home."

Nonetheless, he also could be prickly, almost brutally so. At first, Martha was reluctant to write to him on the Sabbath—and, if she did, tried to hide what she was doing from her mother and brother. Sigmund reacted angrily to such concessions to their sensibilities. "If you can't be fond enough of me to renounce your family then you must lose me, wreck my life, and not get much yourself out of your family," he declared.

Despite such occasional outbursts, the couple's correspondence demonstrated their rapidly growing attachment to each other, how they both were anxiously waiting for that still distant day when they could cement their union, ending their separation. Sigmund made that point by quoting Shakespeare's *Twelfth Night*:

Journeys end in lovers meeting,
Every wise man's son doth know.

At the same time, he made no secret about his "old ways," especially when it came to the role he expected Martha to play in their marriage. He considered it "a completely unrealistic notion to send women into the struggle for existence in the same way as men." He would do everything to keep Martha out of that struggle and "into the quiet, undisturbed activity of my home." While conceding that women were acquiring new rights, he insisted that "the position of [a] woman cannot be other than what it is: to be an adored sweetheart in youth, and a beloved wife in maturity."

Martha willingly accepted that view, but she would rule the combined house and office with a sure hand, handling all the logistics and acting as its manager. And she knew how to maneuver to get what she wanted when the stakes were high enough. When Freud was able to quit his hospital job to set up his private practice in the spring of 1886, they could finally plan their wedding. This could have sparked a major conflict: Martha did not want to disappoint her mother, who was expecting an Orthodox ceremony, but she knew Sigmund dreaded such a prospect.

Proving herself to be a skilled diplomat, Martha pointed out that while Germany did not require religious weddings, Austria did. Thus, if they only had a civil ceremony in Wandsbek, their marriage would not be recognized as legal once they returned to Vienna. Sigmund reluctantly bowed to the inevitable, but Martha made sure that the Jewish wedding on September 14, 1886, at her mother's house was a low-key affair. It was held during the day, which eliminated the requirement of formal evening dress, and she limited the number of friends who could attend. Still, it was the religious ceremony that her family desperately wanted.

———

In his letters, Sigmund freely discussed his ambitions. As was so often the case, he could appear ambivalent at times. A year into their engagement, he affected a casual indifference to whether or not he would achieve a degree of fame. "I never was one of those people who can't bear the thought of being washed away by death before they scratched their names on the rock amidst the waves," he wrote. This was a classic case of protesting too much. When he wove in phrases like "what with all the work, chasing after money, position, and reputation, all of which hardly allows me to drop you an affectionate line," he was not signaling his irritation with that chase. In reality, he was saying one thing while meaning the opposite. In a candid moment, he wrote: "A man must get himself talked about."

As their marriage date drew closer, Freud wrote with visible pride about a conversation he had with Breuer, the physician who was like a godfather to him. "He told me he had discovered that hidden under the surface of timidity there lay in me an extremely daring and fearless human being," he reported. "I had always thought so, but never told anyone." And in an even more grandiose vein, he added: "I have often felt as though I had inherited all the defiance and all the passions with which our ancestors defended their Temple and could gladly sacrifice my life for one great moment in history."

But for a long time, Freud was far from certain where and how he could seek such a moment. In 1884, two years before their marriage, he wrote to Martha about one of his professors who had expounded on the difficulties of launching a career in Vienna and suggested that he could help Freud with contacts in Buenos Aires or Madrid, where it might be easier. Freud told him he was open to the idea of emigrating, but he wanted to try to make a go of it in Vienna first. "I have the capacity for work, and I am tied here by other things than the proximity of these beautiful buildings," he explained.

The more fundamental question was what Freud's specialty should be, how he could distinguish himself in the medical field. While he was still working at the General Hospital, he continued to be a voracious reader, and he was fascinated by Incan myths about the healing qualities of the coca leaf and subsequent accounts of European travelers in South America echoing those claims. In 1801, for instance, the German explorer Alexander von Humboldt described how Indian messengers in Peru survived on lime and coca, which suppressed their appetite while providing them with strength and endurance. But it was the suffering of Ernst von Fleischl-Marxow, a close colleague in the laboratory, that prompted Freud to experiment with cocaine directly. Soon, he convinced himself that he had not only found salvation for his friend but also a path to glory for himself.

Fleischl-Marxow had cut his thumb while working on a cadaver; instead of proving a minor annoyance, this accident led to a major infection, the amputation of the thumb, and his growing addiction to morphine. Seeing how the morphine was devastating him physically and emotionally, Freud offered to treat him with cocaine. Fleischl-Marxow was only too happy to try anything by then, and the initial results of this "cocaine therapy" looked almost miraculous. In reality, he was substituting one addictive substance for another. At that point, Freud did not recognize the dangers of what he described as the "magical drug" in *Über Coca* (On Cocaine), his first major scientific paper, which he hoped would help launch his career.

As part of his experimentation, Freud tried cocaine numerous times himself, reporting how quickly "one experiences a sudden exhilaration and feeling of lightness." He was so enthused by the results that he even sent small doses to Martha, urging her to try them. But Fleischl-Marxow's condition quickly deteriorated, turning him into a cocaine addict while not weaning him off morphine either. The combination of the two powerful drugs produced, as Freud described it after rushing to his apartment one evening, "delirium tremens with white snakes creeping over his skin." After years of agony, Fleischl-Marxow died at age forty-five in 1891, never freed of his addictions.

During the period when he was still pinning great hope on cocaine's potential as a wonder drug, Freud explored other avenues for healing as well. From October 1885 to February 1886, with the help of a modest travel grant, he studied and worked in Paris with the celebrity neurologist and pathologist Jean-Martin Charcot. The Frenchman's lectures at the Salpêtrière, a teaching hospital of the Sorbonne, and his examinations of patients with immediate commentary for the benefit of his acolytes, made a huge impression on Freud. On November 24, he wrote to Martha: "Charcot, who is one of the greatest physicians and a man whose common sense borders on genius, is simply wrecking all my aims and opinions. I sometimes come out of his lectures as from out of Notre Dame, with an entirely new idea about perfection."

Freud was particularly impressed by Charcot's explanations of hysteria in patients and his use of hypnosis to cure them. As with his early theories about cocaine, Freud was still on his quest for breakthrough treatments, and he was delighted when Charcot told him he would like him to translate some of his writings into German. Soon, he was also invited to dinner parties at his house. "I am now the only foreigner at Charcot's," he proudly reported to Martha, although he confessed nervousness about the adequacy of his French on such occasions. To steady himself, he reached for his drug of choice. In another letter, he fretted that "the bit of cocaine" he took may have made him too talkative.

Whether it was the cocaine or the stimulation of his surroundings, Freud sounded unusually emotional and playful in many of his letters from Paris. After meeting Charcot's daughter at one of his parties, he wrote to Martha that she was "small, rather buxom, and of an almost ridiculous resemblance to her great father, as a result so interesting that one doesn't ask oneself whether she is pretty or not. She is about twenty, very natural and amiable." In an almost teasing tone, he added: "Now just suppose I were not in love already and were something of an adventurer; it would be a strong temptation to court her, for nothing is more dangerous than a young girl bearing the features of a man whom one admires."

As much as Freud was excited by his entrée to Charcot's social circle, he had a hard time sorting out his feelings about Paris. As in the case of Vienna, he could sound completely contradictory notes. "What a magic city this Paris is!" he wrote, describing the plays he saw at the Comédie Française and other Parisian theaters—and marveling at the performances of Sarah Bernhardt. He also was fascinated by the collections of antiquities at the Louvre, especially the Greek and Roman statues. In a letter to Martha's sister Minna, whom he corresponded with frequently as well, he wrote that he was under "the full impact" of Paris. But he noted that the city was like "a vast overdressed Sphinx who gobbles up every foreigner unable to solve her riddles." As for Parisians, he viewed them as "a different species from ourselves; I feel they are all possessed of a thousand demons . . . I don't think they know the meaning of shame or fear." He concluded that "Paris is simply one long confused dream, and I shall be very glad to wake up."

His sojourn in the French capital had made him appreciate Vienna more than ever. And, despite his teasing talk of possible alternative romances, he was anxious to assure Martha that he could only envisage his future with her. Still writing from Paris, he reminded her of the first compliment he ever paid to her, saying "that roses and pearls fall from your lips as with the princess of a fairy tale." Which was why, he added, she was his "Little Princess." Both Sigmund and Martha were more than ready to start their life together.

———

In many ways, Vienna lived up to the young couple's expectations. Between 1887 and 1895, Martha gave birth to all six of their children. In 1891, they settled into Berggasse 19, which would be their home and

Sigmund's office until their departure for London in 1938. As Martin, the oldest son, recalled, "My mother ruled her household with great kindness and with an equally great firmness. She believed in punctuality in all things, something then unknown in leisurely Vienna." In 1896, Minna—whose fiancé, the Sanskrit scholar Ignaz Schönberg, had died from tuberculosis a decade earlier—moved in permanently with them, expanding the family further.

But in terms of his professional development, Sigmund often felt frustrated. Upon his return from Paris, he delivered papers and talks based on what he had learned from Charcot about treating patients with nervous diseases. An early presentation to the Society of Medicine "met with a bad reception," he noted. When he raised the subject of male hysteria, an older surgeon accused him of talking "nonsense," arguing that hysteria was by definition a woman's disease. "So how can a man be hysterical?" he demanded. While Freud won plaudits on other occasions, "the impression that the high authorities had rejected my innovations remained unshaken," he wrote.

Freud's "innovations," such as his early use of cocaine and experiments with electrotherapy, ultimately did not meet his own expectations either. Like Charcot, he was also fascinated by the possibilities of hypnosis, increasingly using "hypnotic suggestion" on his patients. In the summer of 1889, he visited the French city of Nancy, hoping to learn more from physicians there so that he could improve his technique. But it did not take long for him to begin to doubt the efficacy of hypnosis as well. "So I abandoned hypnotism, only retaining my practice of requiring the patient to lie upon a sofa while I sat behind him, seeing him, but not seen myself," he recalled.

In the last decade of the nineteenth century and the first years of the twentieth, Freud found a much clearer focus than before, discovering or introducing many of the concepts that came to define Freudian analysis. For years he had discussed cases of hysteria with Josef

Breuer, particularly the older physician's patient who was identified as "Anna O." Together, they published *Studies on Hysteria* in 1895. While Breuer had used hypnosis on his patient, it was his use of "the talking cure" that produced the breakthrough in her deeply troubled mental state. It wasn't until 1896 that Freud came up with a better term for that process: psychoanalysis. A year later, as he became increasingly convinced that repressed sexual memories were at the heart of most neuroses, he also first spelled out the idea of the Oedipus complex, which posited that young boys are sexually attracted to their mothers and view their fathers as rivals.

In retrospect, the work that most spectacularly catapulted Freud into the stratosphere of fame was *The Interpretation of Dreams*, which appeared in November 1899, although the publisher dated it 1900 so it would coincide with the dawn of the new century. But it was not the immediate sensation that Freud had hoped for. During the first six years on the market, it sold only 351 copies. Freud complained that it was "scarcely reviewed in the technical journals."

Freud's emphasis on repressed sexual memories and fantasies was hardly to everyone's liking—and it contributed to his split with Breuer after they coauthored their study of hysteria. More than a decade later, in 1907, the older physician wrote to a Swiss colleague that Freud's "immersion in the sexual in theory and practice is not to my taste." He also offered a more sweeping complaint that suggested how far the two men had drifted apart. "Freud is a man given to absolute and exclusive formulations," Breuer added. "This is a psychical need, which in my opinion, leads to excessive generalization."

For much of this period, Freud's closest friend, although mostly at a distance, was Wilhelm Fliess, an ear, nose, and throat specialist in Berlin. Fliess had met Freud in 1887, when he attended one of Freud's neurology lectures in Vienna. At that point, Freud was only beginning to explore the theories that would make him famous later, even if some of them were dismissed as eccentric at first. Meanwhile, Fliess promulgated his own theories, especially about sexuality, that earned him a reputation for even greater eccentricity—and would largely be discredited over time. He argued that the nose was the dominant organ that influenced human health and behavior, and that both men and women were subject to biorhythmic sexual cycles of twenty-three and twenty-eight days respectively. When they met in Vienna, Freud was delighted by Fliess's interest in his work, writing to him after his return to Berlin that he hoped they could continue their relationship since Fliess had left "a deep impression" on him.

In their extensive correspondence, Freud left no doubt that he was seeking a receptive audience for his ideas, someone who would applaud and stimulate his efforts. Fliess was only too happy to oblige, providing a steady stream of encouragement. "You are the only Other, the alter," Freud told him in 1894. He shared details about his personal life, including his worries about his heart condition and his relations with Martha. After the birth of their fifth child in 1893, he confided that Martha was able to take a break for a year since, as he put it, "We are now living in abstinence." Their sixth and last child, Anna, was born two years later.

The two men had no inhibitions discussing almost any idea that came to mind. In 1896, Freud told Fliess: "You have taught me that a bit of truth lurks behind every popular lunacy." But their relationship soured as Freud began to recognize that his "Other" was prone to bizarre theories that could not be reconciled with his more logical ones. Freud no longer saw Fliess as a worthy reviewer of his works and thoughts. In 1901, he bluntly told him: "You have reached the limits of your perspicacity."

All of which contributed to Freud's sense that he was alone and adrift. Describing the period after he broke with Breuer, he wrote: "I had no followers. I was completely isolated. In Vienna I was shunned;

abroad no notice was taken of me." He was somewhat overstating the case, but not by much.

———

Freud was acutely aware of his status as a Jew, as were so many of his contemporaries who similarly considered themselves both secular and assimilated. "It was not possible, especially not for a Jew in public life, to ignore the fact that he was a Jew," the popular writer Arthur Schnitzler pointed out. "Nobody else was doing so, not the Gentiles, and even less the Jews." But Schnitzler, who was six years younger than Freud, recalled that he "scarcely felt" any anti-Semitism during his school years, although that would change once he began his studies at the University of Vienna. Despite his subsequent literary success, "a certain separation of Gentiles and Jews into groups which were not kept strictly apart . . . could be felt always and everywhere."

This was the classical Viennese ambivalence, which incorporated so many of the contradictions of the city in that era. Amos Elon, the Vienna-born Israeli journalist and author, described the Austrian capital in the late nineteenth century as "a showpiece of intensive creativity brought about by cultural diversity." As for the specific issue of anti-Semitism, he explained, "At least until the early 1890s, when anti-Semitism of a particularly rabid form made its way through the streets and universities of Vienna, the position of Jews was also continually improving."

When he personally encountered anti-Semitism, Freud refused to be intimidated. While traveling by train in Germany in late 1883, he opened a window in his carriage to get a breath of air, triggering shouts for him to close it like all the others. "He's a dirty Jew!" one passenger chimed in, while another addressed him directly: "We Christians consider other people, you'd better think less of your precious self"—along with a string of other choice phrases. The passenger also announced that he would climb over the seats to teach him a lesson. As Freud wrote in his letter to Martha about the incident, "Even a year ago I would have been speechless with agitation, but now I am different; I was not in the least frightened of that mob." He challenged the especially belligerent passenger to face off with him. "I was quite prepared to kill him," Freud continued, "but he did not step up."

On a summer holiday on the outskirts of Vienna in 1900, two of Freud's sons—Martin and Oliver—were fishing from a rowboat on a lake when a group of men walking by peppered them with insults and threats. They called the boys "Israelites" and accused them of stealing fish, which, as Martin pointed out, was not the case since it was a popular fishing spot. They told their father what had happened, and that same afternoon the three of them rowed back across the lake. By then, a larger crowd had gathered, including women. As they moored the boat, the crowd shouted more anti-Semitic abuse. Cheered on by the women standing behind them, about ten men, armed with sticks and umbrellas, looked ready for a fight.

Freud jumped out of the boat, marching straight at the group. When Martin followed, Freud sharply ordered him to back off. Up until then, Martin recalled, "my mild-mannered father had never spoken to me in anything but kindly tones." Which is why his sharp tone was such a jolt for Martin, startling him more than the greeting party did. "In the meantime," Martin continued, "father, swinging his stick, charged the hostile crowd, which gave way before him and promptly dispersed, giving him free passage." As impressed as he was by this display of courage, Martin was struck even more by the fact that "there is no evidence that father was affected in the least." As far as he knew, his father never mentioned what happened that day to anyone else.

In part, Freud's instinct to take such an incident in stride may have been the product of his early upbringing: anti-Semitism had looked to be less prevalent and certainly less poisonous than it would soon thereafter. Particularly in Vienna, where so many Jews had flourished, many of them downplayed any evidence that the situation was taking a dangerous turn. According to Adolf Dessauer, a Jewish writer who was seven years older than Freud, Viennese anti-Semitism was merely "a passing fashion, a mood, a joke."

Yet there was nothing amusing about many of the trends that began to surface in the 1880s and then accelerated in the 1890s.

———

Among the Jews who gravitated to Vienna from other parts of the Austro-Hungarian Empire was Theodor Herzl, Freud's Budapest-born contemporary who moved to the capital in 1878 and enrolled in the University of Vienna, where he studied law. Herzl looked like the pro-totype of the assimilated Jew who was seeking to make a name for himself, first as a lawyer, then as a journalist and playwright. He had a gift for languages, reading in German, French, Italian, and English, but he particularly prized German culture. He pointed out that every "Viennese student was a Wagnerian, even before he heard a single bar of his music." At that point, there was nothing to indicate that Herzl would become the visionary founder of modern Zionism, the move-ment that propelled the creation of Israel long after his death at age forty-four in 1904.

During his student days, Herzl joined Albia, one of the fraternities espousing German nationalist views and promoting customs like du-eling. He was proud of the fact that, like a small number of Jews who were considered sufficiently German in their outlook, he was accepted into their ranks. Arthur Schnitzler recalled seeing Herzl "with his blue student's cap and black walking stick with the ivory handle and F.V.C. [the abbreviation for the Latin words that mean "To Flourish, To Live, To Grow] engraved on it, parading in step with his fraternity brothers."

But this was the period when the student fraternities turned increasingly anti-Semitic, and any remaining Jewish members were seen as an embarrassment; it was particularly embarrassing that some of those Jews were proving themselves to be better duelists than the gentiles they fought against. Herzl had fought a short duel and acquitted himself well, since both he and his opponent ended up with what were considered manly slashes on their faces. In 1882, the fraternities resolved that problem by passing what was called the Waidhofen Manifesto. Its language was as revealing as its content:

> Every son of a Jewish mother, every human being in whose veins flows Jewish blood, is from the day of his birth without honor and void of all the more refined emotions. He cannot differentiate between what is dirty and what is clean. He is ethically subhuman. Friendly intercourse with a Jew is therefore dishonorable; any association with him has to be avoided. It is impossible to insult a Jew; a Jew cannot therefore demand satisfaction for any suffered insult.

In other words, Jews were not only to be totally ostracized; fraternity members could not and should not accept challenges to duels from Jews.

At a memorial meeting for Richard Wagner, who died on February 13, 1883, a speaker from Albia extolled "Aryan" pan-Germanism and "Wagnerian anti-Semitism," which was a fully justified description of the composer's animus toward Jews. Although the speaker was expelled from the university, Herzl wrote to the fraternity: "I do not wish to retain my membership." Instead of accepting his resignation, his "brothers" formally struck him from the roster; they wanted to make clear that it was their decision to drive him out.

But such personal encounters with anti-Semitism in Vienna were not enough to make Herzl abandon his view that assimilation still provided the best path for Jews to improve their lot. It was only when he took up the job of Paris correspondent for the Viennese newspaper *Neue Freie Presse* that he changed his mind. The critical turning point was the 1894 arrest and trial, on trumped-up charges of high treason, of the Jewish French Army captain Alfred Dreyfus. The accompanying wave of anti-Semitism in France convinced him that Jews had to look for salvation in a Jewish state, prompting him to launch the Zionist movement.

Shortly after he returned to Vienna, Herzl lived for two years on the same street as Freud, at Berggasse 6, practically making them neighbors. The two never met, although Freud was certainly aware of Herzl's activities. In 1897, he saw Herzl's play *The New Ghetto*, which triggered one of his dreams, and the two men wrote to each other later. Unlike Herzl, however, Freud usually avoided politics.

But the world of politics, and of anti-Semitic vitriol, was difficult to keep at bay. Karl Kraus, the editor of *Die Fackel* (The Torch)—a Jew by birth who converted to Catholicism but then left that faith, too— proclaimed: "Psychoanalysis is the newest Jewish disease . . . They reach into our dreams as though they were our pockets." This was a preview of the charge, later a standard refrain of the Nazis, that Freud had invented a "Jewish science."

In the 1890s, though, the more serious threat to Vienna's Jews was the rapid rise of Karl Lueger, a talented municipal politician known as "Handsome Karl." When he entered politics in the 1870s, he was a Liberal and then a Democrat. Soon, he discovered the appeal of anti-Semitic rhetoric and, in 1891, founded the Christian Social Party. Portraying himself as the champion of ordinary people and a fierce defender of Austrian Catholicism, he declared: "These Jews, they are robbing us of everything we hold sacred! Fatherland! Nationality! And finally our property too!"

When his party won the municipal elections in 1895 and voted

Lueger in as mayor, Emperor Franz Josef refused to confirm their choice, since he viewed him as a dangerous firebrand. The one indication that the largely apolitical Freud was following these developments: he celebrated Franz Josef's effective veto by awarding "himself an extra ration of cigars that day."

But by 1897, when the City Council voted for Lueger a fourth time, the emperor gave in, and Lueger remained in office until his death in 1910. As mayor, he bolstered his popularity by overseeing the construction of new public buildings and the modernization of the city's infrastructure, including the introduction of the highly efficient tram system. George Clare, who was born into a Jewish family in Vienna in 1920 and escaped to Britain in 1938, conceded in his book *Last Waltz in Vienna* that Lueger "became the most beloved and also the most efficient Burgomaster Vienna ever had."

Among Vienna's Jews who grew up in Lueger's Vienna, there was a common tendency to downplay the significance of his anti-Semitism. The novelist Stefan Zweig wrote that "his administration of the city was blamelessly just and in fact a model of democracy, and the Jews, who had been terrified by the triumph of the anti-Semitic party, continued to enjoy respect and equal rights." Lueger still had dealings with Jews and was famously quoted as saying "*I* decide who is a Jew." The willingness of many Austrian Jews to shrug off open displays of anti-Semitism was epitomized by Victor Adler, the Jewish founder of the rival Social Democratic Workers' Party. Speaking to the Congress of International Socialist Parties in 1899, he asserted that Austria, while often prone to injustice, was "incapable of performing acts of oppression . . . we have despotism mellowed by indolence."

The notion that Austria would never resort to truly draconian policies was embedded in the psyche of Vienna's Jews of that generation—Freud's generation. His son Martin vividly recalled one incident that should have served as a warning. Martin was walking with his aunt

"Dolfi," Sigmund's youngest sister, Adolfine, when they passed "an ordinary kind of man, probably a Gentile, who as far as I knew took no notice of us." But Dolfi gripped Martin's arm "in terror," he wrote, and whispered: "Did you hear what that man said? He called me a dirty stinking Jewess and said it was time we were all killed."

Martin dismissed her alarm as a product of "a pathological phobia, or Dolfi's stupidity." He and his friends felt "perfectly happy and secure" in Vienna among gentiles, he added. "It seems strange that while none of us—professors, lawyers and people of education—had any idea of the tragedy which would destroy the children of the Jewish race, a lovable but rather silly old maid foresaw, or appeared to foresee, that future."

Dolfi would become one of the millions of victims of that tragedy, ending up in Theresienstadt where, on September 29, 1942, she died of starvation. Many prominent Jews perished at this "camp-ghetto" near Prague during the Holocaust, or were sent on to other camps such as Treblinka and Auschwitz.

"A CELT FROM WALES!"

DURING THE FIRST DECADE OF THE NEW CENTURY, FREUD RE-alized that his isolation was coming to an end. In 1897, his medical faculty colleagues had nominated him for a full professorship, or "Professor Extraordinarius." As Freud explained, the title was important as much for his practice as his academic standing, since it "elevates the physician in our society into a demigod for his patients." Final approval and the emperor's signature on the decree that granted Freud his wish did not come until 1902.

That was the same year that he launched his regular Wednesday evening meetings at Berggasse 19, attracting a small but slowly growing number of physicians, almost all of whom were Jewish at first. In 1908, they rebranded themselves as the Vienna Psychoanalytic Society. Freud also noted and relished other signals of his improved status. "I have obviously become reputable again, and my shyest admirers now greet me from a distance in the street," he wrote in one of his last letters to Fliess. Interest in psychoanalysis was spreading far beyond Vienna as well, offering Freud new possibilities for disseminating his ideas. He was on the way to becoming a man who was "talked about," as he had put it in his letter to Martha during their engagement.

At the same time as Freud grew increasingly confident that he was on the right path, a teenager from Linz, the capital of Upper Austria, arrived in Vienna, also hoping to find his path to success. But Adolf Hitler found nothing of the sort there. It is nearly impossible to exaggerate the magnitude of the ensuing consequences.

———

In *Mein Kampf*, Hitler blithely asserted that he found schoolwork to be "ridiculously easy," but he performed very poorly and abandoned his schooling altogether in 1905, when he was sixteen. His stern, authoritarian father had wanted him to follow his example and pursue his education longer in preparation for a career in the civil service, but he had died two years earlier. His doting mother had given birth to six children, of whom only Adolf and his younger sister Paula survived, but she had neither the will nor the ability to push her son in a direction that never interested him. Instead, as he told the neighborhood postmaster, his plan was "to become a great artist."

In Hitler's always fervid imagination, this transformation would take place in Vienna. On his first visit to that city in 1906 at age seventeen, he was mesmerized by what he saw. "For hours I could stand in front of the Opera, for hours I could gaze at the Parliament; the whole Ring Boulevard seemed to me like an enchantment out of *The Thousand-and-One-Nights*," he recalled in *Mein Kampf*, the autobiographical screed he wrote while serving his prison sentence for leading the fledgling Nazi Party's abortive Munich Beer Hall Putsch in November 1923. Convinced that, along with his painting, his talent for drawing had "developed amazingly," he found himself increasingly interested in architecture. He also went to the Opera to see Gustav Mahler conduct Richard Wagner's *Tristan and Isolde* and *The Flying Dutchman*; the fact that Mahler was Jewish did not dim his enthusiasm.

Upon his return to Linz, he announced to his mother and his one close friend, August Kubizek, that he had decided to attend the Vienna Academy of Fine Arts. As Kubizek wrote in his memoir of his friendship with the young Hitler: "Vienna was calling. That city had a thousand possibilities for an eager young man like Adolf, opportunities which might lead to the most sublime heights or to the most somber depths. A city magnificent and at the same time cruel, promising everything and denying everything—that was Vienna."

Hitler set off again for Vienna to take the entrance exams in September 1907, fully expecting to breeze through them and to enroll almost immediately. For the first step in that process, he submitted a collection of his drawings; they were deemed sufficient for him to qualify for the main examination.

On October 1 and 2, 113 candidates competed in two three-hour sessions, demonstrating their artistic abilities by producing drawings on specified subjects. Hitler's drawings were judged "unsatisfactory," which meant he was not among the twenty-eight candidates who won admission. The possibility of failure had not even crossed his mind earlier. "I was so confident that I would be successful that when I received my rejection, it struck me as a bolt from the blue," he wrote. In retrospect, this turn of events has figured in speculation that he may have blamed Jewish professors for his failure. But the reality was that not one of his examiners was Jewish.

The setback to Hitler's ambitions, combined with the death of his mother from breast cancer on December 21, 1907, changed his outlook entirely. In early 1908, he returned to Vienna, this time with only vague hopes of somehow still turning himself into an acclaimed artist while nourishing a growing sense of grievance against the cosmopolitan capital and almost everything it represented. His subsequent five years in Vienna was "the saddest period of my life," he wrote. In his friend Kubizek's words, he explored "the most somber depths" of the city rather than pursuing its many opportunities.

Hitler complained about his meager means, presumably the small inheritance he had brought with him from Linz, and called hunger his "faithful bodyguard." But other than producing postcard-size paintings of Vienna that one of his companions peddled and taking on a few odd jobs, he did little to improve his lot. He lived in men's hostels, rented rooms, and, in the particularly difficult autumn of 1909, at times bundled up for the night outside, anywhere he could.

Kubizek, who had gone on to study music in Vienna, shared lodgings with Hitler for part of that period. While his account is not always reliable, he probably reported accurately when he wrote that Hitler was in "a deep depression" during his early days back in Vienna. "I had the impression that Adolf had become unbalanced," Kubizek wrote. "He would fly into a temper at the slightest thing."

Among Hitler's early preoccupations were the city's red-light districts. He urged Kubizek to join him on a walk through "the sink of iniquity," growing angry at the prostitutes on display in the windows. "It seemed to me quite natural that Adolf should turn with disgust and repugnance from these and other sexual aberrations of the big city, that he refrained from masturbation which was commonly indulged in by youths," his friend recalled. He added that, whether out of fear of infection or general revulsion, Hitler maintained his "strict monk-like ascetism" throughout his stay in Vienna.

By Hitler's own account, his down-and-out years in the capital shaped his views on race, ethnicity, nationalism, and politics. Calling this period "the hardest school of my life," he explained that Vienna opened his eyes "to two menaces of which I had previously scarcely known the names, and whose terrible importance for the existence of the German people I certainly did not understand: Marxism and Jewry."

Vienna was the perfect laboratory for studying "the social question," as he put it. He decried "the dubious magic of the national melting pot," complaining that it was becoming "an un-German city" and a "linguistic babble." As a product of the Austrian hinterland who had learned no foreign languages and possessed few marketable skills, he was seething with resentment. "I was repelled by the conglomeration of races which the capital showed me, repelled by this whole mixture of Czechs, Poles, Hungarians, Ruthenians, Serbs, and Croats, and everywhere, the eternal mushroom of humanity—Jews and more Jews," he wrote. "To me the giant city seemed the embodiment of racial desecration."

While he deplored the "general Slavization of Austria," he was especially drawn to those who attacked the Jews as the source of all evil. He recalled how impressed he was by the pamphlets of Hans Goldzier, whose anti-Semitic rants he would echo later. Goldzier called Jews "a pest, degenerate, evil and noxious human beings." The pamphleteer was a minor figure who quickly disappeared from view, as Hitler noted somewhat sorrowfully in *Mein Kampf*. But the future dictator was also inspired by Mayor Karl Lueger, Vienna's most popular politician. "Today, more than ever, I regard this man as the greatest German of all time," Hitler wrote.

The young Hitler viewed Lueger as one of the men who taught him the value of anti-Semitism, seemingly oblivious to the fact that the mayor cynically exploited this issue but did not necessarily act on his inflammatory rhetoric. As Hitler saw it, such rhetoric was meant literally—and he took it all to heart. As a result of his experiences in Vienna, he explained, "I had ceased to be a weak-kneed cosmopolitan and become an anti-Semite." In his mind, this was proof of how much he had matured. "I had set foot in this town while still half a boy and I left it a man, grown quiet and grave," he wrote.

Just as Hitler ignored Lueger's efforts to balance his harsh anti-

Semitic oratory with more conciliatory actions, he paid scant attention to those who tried to balance their allegiance to Austria and Germany. In his mind, there was no room for Viennese ambivalence on that score. During the waning days of the Austro-Hungarian Empire, he especially admired Georg von Schönerer, the combative leader of the Pan-Germanic movement who was also a fervent Austrian anti-Semite.

On the opening page of *Mein Kampf*, Hitler spelled out the primary goal of that movement for the land of his birth: "German-Austria must return to the great German mother country . . . One blood demands one Reich." Long before Hitler had a shot at power, the Anschluss was already in his sights.

———

As Freud won increasing recognition for his novel treatment of his patients, his extensive writings and lectures, and his Wednesday evening gatherings at his home, he remained wedded to his daily rituals and routines. Getting up by seven, he was fastidious in his preparation for seeing his patients starting at eight. His son Martin claimed he was not at all vain, but "merely submitted without objection to the deeply entrenched medical tradition that a doctor should be well turned out, and so there was never a hair out of place on his head or on his chin." A daily visit to or by a barber ensured that result. "His clothing, rigidly conventional, was cut from the best materials and tailored to perfection," Martin added.

Much of his day was mapped out already, with lunch at one, followed by slight variations in the afternoon schedule depending on whether he was receiving more patients or visitors, writing or going out for his walks about town before or after a late supper, followed by an occasional game of cards, more reading, writing, or editing; he would then retire to bed at one in the morning. On Saturdays, he gave lectures at the university from five to seven, often followed by another card game with friends.

On Sundays, he visited his mother, Amalia, who had become a widow when his father, Jacob, died in 1896. Both parents instilled in him and his six siblings a strong belief in the importance of family. Anna, the second-born child, recalled how Sigmund came to their father at an early age with the Bible in hand. Referring to the fact that he was the oldest child and Alexander the youngest, with five sisters in between, he explained: "Our family is just like this book: the two strong covers are the boys and the pages in between are the five sisters."

Sigmund kept up his regular visits to his mother until her death in 1930 at the age of ninety-five. As his sister Anna noted, she was "mourned by her seven children, eighteen grandchildren and fourteen great-grandchildren."

Freud loved the set routines, along with the carefully planned lengthy summer vacations in Alpine settings like Berchtesgaden, the Bavarian resort later made infamous as Hitler's retreat, or Austrian spa towns like Bad Aussee and Bad Gastein. Martha attended to all the logistics of those sojourns, just as she did in Vienna. "She never overlooked a detail, exchanging her normal role of an ordinary, practical housewife for the cold and calculating organizing genius of a senior officer of the Prussian General Staff," Martin wrote.

Those holidays almost always included hunting for edible mushrooms (no one was worried about picking anything poisonous, Martin recalled, "because Father had taught us so much about fungi"), hiking, and swimming. Freud participated in all those activities, sticking with the breaststroke when he went swimming so that he could keep his coiffed beard out of the water. When the patriarch was busy writing, the children were often off on their own.

On separate trips, Freud pursued his interest in antiquities, visiting

Athens with his brother Alexander in 1904 and traveling extensively in Italy on several occasions. During his tour of Tuscany in 1896, he both marveled at its artistic treasures and confessed that he sometimes felt like the typical tourist suffering from sensory overload. "As soon as we got to Florence the city oppressed and overwhelmed us," he wrote. "The monuments lie along the street by the half dozen, the historical memories are so teeming that you can't keep them straight, the Florentines are making a hell of a fuss, shouting, cracking whips, trumpeting right on the street; in sum, it is unbearable."

Freud never made a secret of his many dislikes. When his sisters were young, his mother rented a piano so that they could take lessons. But, according to Anna, the oldest of the girls, "Sigmund was so disturbed by our scales and finger exercises that he threatened to leave home if we continued." As a result, the piano quickly disappeared and, once Sigmund married Martha and they had their own children, this mainstay of so many Viennese homes was similarly banned; none of their children ever took piano lessons. Freud also disliked bicycles, talking on the telephone, and certain foods like chicken and cauliflower.

As Martin recalled, his father complained frequently about Vienna. In 1900, the elder Freud wrote to Fliess: "I hate Vienna with a positively personal hatred and . . . I draw fresh strength whenever I remove my feet from the soil of this city which is my home." But Martin concluded that his father's sentiments on that score were neither "deep-seated or real." For all his protestations that he only enjoyed his outings in the mountains or the countryside, Freud was deeply attached to the capital. "My own feeling is that sometimes my father hated Vienna, and that sometimes he loved the old city, and that, in a general sense, he was devoted," Martin wrote. Many of the inhabitants of big cities like London or New York, he pointed out, developed a lifelong love-hate relationship with their surroundings—and his father was no exception.

On May 6, 1906, Freud turned fifty, and he had good reason to feel that he was leading a very productive and satisfying life. But, as always, he was prone to ruminate about his own mortality, speaking of himself as an old man and worrying who would carry on his teachings once he was gone. As he gathered more followers, treating the Wednesday evening regulars to black coffee, cakes, cigars, and cigarettes, along with his customary remarks to wind up each discussion, he was unsure if he would find a suitable candidate. His personal relations with his mentors and colleagues—Breuer, Fliess, and others—had often proceeded from mutual admiration to disillusionment. And while he was increasingly confident about his role as the founder of the new field of psychoanalysis, he remained uncertain about its future.

———

In those early days, Freud considered himself a "fisher of men," someone who was always on the lookout for those who would not only embrace psychoanalysis but also spread his gospel further. He was pleased by his regular group of adherents who gathered on Wednesdays at his apartment in Vienna, but he wanted to cast his lines elsewhere as well. At first almost by accident and then by design, he soon focused his attention and hopes on Zurich. This was a pond that appeared to be stocked with fish eager to bite.

Some of the most advanced work in psychology was taking place in the Burghölzli, the University of Zurich's psychiatric hospital led by Professor Eugen Bleuler, a famed psychiatrist who later introduced novel terms like schizophrenia and autism. Bleuler and, in particular, his young chief assistant Carl Gustav Jung took an early interest in Freud's work and methods. The son of a Swiss Protestant pastor, Jung had been tormented by troubling dreams growing up, which made him especially receptive to Freud's *The Interpretation of Dreams*. At Bleuler's request, he reported to the staff on the book and Freud's work on hysteria—and soon incorporated some of his theories into his own writing about dementia and other subjects.

In his foreword to his study *The Psychology of Dementia Praecox*, which was dated July 1906, Jung was effusive in his acknowledgment of Freud's influence. "Even a superficial glance at my work will show how much I am indebted to the brilliant discoveries of Freud," he wrote. While he expressed admiration of Freud's writings, he noted that this did not signal "unqualified submission to a dogma" or an inability to maintain "an independent judgment." In particular, he pointed out, his praise "does not mean that I attribute to the infantile sexual trauma the exclusive importance that Freud apparently does." But Jung categorized all such reservations "as the merest trifles compared with the psychological principles whose discovery is Freud's greatest merit."

Writing directly to Freud, Jung expressed similar enthusiasm for his work, while again indicating he was not in agreement on everything, not only about the role of early sexual development but also about the efficacy of the "therapeutic results" of psychoanalysis. But he left no doubt that he was siding with Freud against his many critics who were quick to dismiss his findings.

Freud was immensely grateful for Jung's support and insisted that he was not looking exclusively for praise. "I have always been aware of my fallibility," he wrote, adding on another occasion that he did not want to be "a cult object." But their initial exchanges indicated that both men were palpably excited by their rapidly blossoming relationship. Dismissing those whom he ironically called the "leading lights" of old-school psychiatry, Freud declared: "The future belongs to us and our views, and the younger men—everywhere most likely—side actively with us." Already, he was treating Jung as his partner.

In early 1907, Jung and his wife, Emma, accompanied by a young colleague from Zurich, traveled to Vienna to meet Freud for the first time. When he showed up at Berggasse 19 on Sunday, March 3, the two men talked for thirteen hours, not even interrupting their discussion of psychoanalysis during dinner with Martha and the children. Martin Freud, who was seventeen at the time, vividly recalled his impressions of the guest who eschewed normal "polite conversation" to continue addressing himself directly to his host while largely ignoring everyone else at the table. Jung "did all the talking and father with unconcealed delight did all the listening," he wrote.

Although Martin did not understand much of the exchange between his father and the visitor, Martin was impressed by "his vitality, his liveliness, his ability to project his personality" and "his commanding presence." Jung was only thirty-one then, two decades younger than Freud, and in so many ways his opposite in terms of appearance. "He was very tall and broad-shouldered, holding himself more like a soldier than a man of science and medicine," Martin continued. "His head was purely Teutonic with a strong chin, a small mustache, blue eyes and thin close-cropped hair."

In other words, Jung looked very much like the prototypical gentile—and a young, vibrant one at that. As Freud saw it, this was all to the good. He recognized early that he needed to avoid providing an excuse to those who wanted to write off psychoanalysis as a "Jewish science," developed and propagated only by Jews, not just in Vienna but elsewhere as well.

In a letter to Freud following his return to Switzerland, Jung declared that his visit to Vienna had improved his understanding of "your broadened conception of sexuality." In fact, the entire visit was "for me an event of the first importance." Freud responded just as effusively, writing that "you have inspired me with confidence for the future." Leaving no room for misunderstanding of the import of this assertion, he added: "I now realize that I am as replaceable as everyone else and that I could hope for no one better than yourself, as I have come to know you, to continue and complete my work." Freud was envisaging

Jung as his crown prince, a title that he had every reason to believe Jung would accept.

This did not mean that Freud was discouraging new Jewish followers—quite the contrary. He could do so with increased confidence precisely because a gentile would now be prominent in his movement. Two of his other visitors from Zurich that year, Max Eitingon and Karl Abraham, had worked with Bleuler and Jung, and Freud warmly welcomed them as well. Eitingon, who was born in Russia to a Jewish family, was still a medical student when he was in Zurich, while Abraham, a German Jew, was already an established psychiatrist. After settling back in Berlin, they would both play prominent roles in the development of not just the German but also the international psychoanalytic movement.

Abraham, the older of the two, had spent three years in Zurich. He was not nearly as enthusiastic about the prospect of elevating Jung to the de facto position of crown prince as Freud was—and he was far less in awe of his forceful personality. But Freud explained to Abraham why he felt that Jung, as a gentile, was particularly well suited for this role. "Our Aryan comrades are, after all, quite indispensable to us, otherwise, psychoanalysis would fall victim to anti-Semitism." And he particularly appreciated the fact that Jung, as the son of a pastor, could "find his way to me only against great inner resistance." The message was that Christians were less naturally inclined to accept psychoanalysis than Jews. As he put it in a later letter to Abraham, "We Jews have an easier time, having no mystical element."

Given the long tradition and multiple forms of Jewish mysticism, this was a highly disputable assertion. But Freud was referring to secular Jews like himself, who felt far removed from the "mystical element" at the core of Christianity.

Freud delivered a similar message to Sándor Ferenczi, who visited him from Budapest for the first time in early 1908 and soon became a close friend and colleague in the psychoanalytic movement. Although Ferenczi initially had been skeptical about Freud's dream theory, he quickly became an enthusiastic convert to his teachings. Freud was so taken by him during his first visit that he invited him to join his family on their vacation in Berchtesgaden that summer.

All of which meant that Freud's flock of disciples was growing. But like the weekly attendees at the Wednesday gatherings at his apartment and like Eitingon and Abraham, Ferenczi was Jewish. Freud didn't mind; in fact, he felt most comfortable with Jews who shared so many of his assumptions and experiences. But that made it all that more important, as he explained to Abraham, "not to neglect the Aryans, who are fundamentally alien to me."

For the moment, Freud believed that such problems could be overcome by the elevation of Jung to a leadership role. Given the looming clash between these two dominant personalities, this would later prove to be a major miscalculation. But while Freud's determination to enlist a gentile to protect his movement from the tide of anti-Semitism ultimately failed, it would prove a winning strategy when it came to saving himself and his family.

Freud had no inkling yet that he would need a rescue squad or that it would be comprised mostly of gentiles. By then, Jung's association with him had long ended, but another gentile, who received his introduction to Freud through Jung, would play the starring role.

Enter Ernest Jones.

———

In September 1907, a few months after his visit to Vienna, Jung attended the First International Congress of Psychiatry and Neurology in Amsterdam, where he made a discovery that he hastened to write about to Freud: "Now for a great surprise: among the English contingent there was a young man from London, Dr. Jones (a Celt from

Wales!) who knows your writings very well and does psychoanalytic work himself. He will probably visit you later. He is very intelligent and could do a lot of good."

This would prove to be a considerable understatement. Born in 1879 in Wales, Ernest Jones had already demonstrated that he was gifted, ambitious, possessed of a self-confidence that bordered on arrogance, and prone to land in seemingly compromising situations. When he was only sixteen, he enrolled at the University College of South Wales to study medicine. Noting that he was "emotionally precocious," he declared: "I had the pleasure of finding myself among equals instead of among children." Jones did not let the age gap or the height gap (he grew only to five feet, four inches) with most of the other students ever bother him.

At the end of his first year of studies in 1896, Jones and a classmate traveled to London for what he described as six weeks of "intensive coaching" at the University Tutorial College in Red Lion Square. It was his first exposure to the capital—or to any major city. He delighted in everything from "Cockney humor" to the faculty that included H. G. Wells, who taught biology before winning fame as a writer, and Paul Barbier, the French professor "straight out of the Second Empire, curly top-hat and all" and his daughter Marie, who Jones described as the belle of the college. "At the end of the six weeks, we felt like old Londoners," he declared.

After another two years in Cardiff, Jones returned to London for his clinical training at the University College Hospital. At age twenty-one, he became a licensed doctor, rapidly moving on to hospital stints in surgery, ophthalmology, gynecology, pediatrics, and neurology, which especially interested him. He scored high marks on his Bachelor of Medicine examination, winning a scholarship and two gold medals. He took those early academic and professional triumphs in stride, confessing later that they only fed his "omnipotence complex."

Writing about his early years, Jones also liked to boast about his other activities. "Nor was the opposite sex neglected all this time," he recalled. "When I have heard since from lonely and timid patients how hard it is in London to get to know anyone of the opposite sex, my own experiences assured me that their difficulty was a subjective one, since I cannot believe that London girls have become more coy in the course of the present century." In 1919, Joan Riviere, who underwent analysis with Jones and later also became a psychoanalyst and a translator of Freud, wrote in a letter that he was "irresistible to women, meeting them on their own ground."

While Jones looked full of promise, ready to embark on a successful medical career, he also could come across as a troublemaker. During his student days, he participated in the kind of pranks that led to brushes with the law. In May 1899, when British troops were leaving for the Boer War, he was in a rowdy crowd that attempted to storm a café, although he wasn't even sure what they were trying to accomplish. Nabbed by the police, he spent the night in jail. When a friend showed up at the station and pleaded for the release of what he called the "little fellow," claiming that he was very delicate, a policeman replied: "Yes, bloody delicate; it took three of us to hold him."

Jones bounced around a number of jobs in his early years as a physician. In early 1903, he became the resident medical officer at the Hospital for Children in Bethnal Green, a one-year appointment. But after he left his post without official permission, he was fired before his term was up. According to Jones, he had rushed to see his Welsh girlfriend when she had an appendectomy, and his "enemies" in the hospital were unforgiving and demanded his resignation. In fact, he had been absent without leave twice before. When he subsequently applied for other prestigious hospital jobs, he was turned down repeatedly. He finally did get stints as a clinical assistant at a couple of more modest hospitals, and augmented his income by tutoring students preparing for medical exams.

His other part-time jobs included oversight of what he called "mental defective schools" for the London County Council, and he furthered his studies by taking courses in public health. As part of his training, he worked in the Jewish quarter of London's East End. "It gave me much insight into foreign customs and modes of life," he wrote. It also made it easier for him later to relate to Freud's largely Jewish professional milieu.

According to Jones, his interest in psychiatry started in 1902, sparked by his Sunday visits to a friend who was a resident at an asylum near London. The two of them regularly discussed the afflictions of the patients there. In 1905, when Freud published his paper about Dora, the pseudonym for Ida Bauer, an eighteen-year-old suffering from what he diagnosed as hysteria when he treated her in 1900, Jones was intensely interested in the case and the methods Freud used to treat her. "I came away with a deep impression of there being a man in Vienna who actually listened with attention to every word his patients said to him," Jones recalled. "I was trying to do so myself but had never heard of anyone else doing it."

He was so intrigued by Freud's writings, most of which were still untranslated, and what he saw as his revolutionary approach that he worked with a tutor to improve his German. The more he read, the more he was impressed. "For Freud the most casual remarks of patients were really facts, data to be seriously examined and pondered over with the same intentness as that given by the geologist, the biologist, the chemist, to the data provided in their respective fields of work," he noted, pointing out that this provided a stark contrast with the attitude of most British physicians. "So here was a man who was seriously interested in investigating the mind."

Jones was rapidly concluding that he wanted to follow a similar path, but at the time he found himself enmeshed in a scandal that almost ended his career. In the course of conducting research on children and "the mechanism of speech" in early 1906, he wrote, "I underwent the most disagreeable experience of my life." After he conducted a speech test at a school for "mental defectives," he was accused by two girls of indecent behavior—specifically, that he had exposed himself to them. To his "amazement and horror," the girls' teacher appeared to believe their version of events.

The press played up the story, dwelling on the fact that Jones was already an accomplished physician with "a very considerable position." Two policemen then showed up with a warrant. In what Jones called a theatrical touch, the senior inspector declared: "Doctor, there are two ways out of this room, the door and the window; I hope you will choose the door." Before he was taken to a jail cell in the local police station where he spent the night, Jones was allowed to call his father, who lined up a top lawyer. Released on bail the next morning, Jones had to make his way through an assembled crowd. As he did so, he heard a worker saying, "He can cut his bloody throat, he can."

After four court hearings where the charges were repeated and repeatedly denied by Jones, the magistrate dismissed the case. In her biography of Jones, Brenda Maddox pointed out that he had good reason for doing so, since he knew "that no jury would convict on the evidence of mentally unreliable children." In his autobiography, Jones maintained that the girls must have been involved "in some sexual scene, and that I was being made the scapegoat for their sense of guilt."

The Lancet, the prestigious medical journal, offered its congratulations for "his complete exoneration from the infamous, and perfectly incredible, charges against him in connexion with his official visits at the schools for defective children." Yet neither his acquittal nor such expressions of support could fully dispel the shadow of doubt cast by the case.

———

Despite the damage to his reputation, Jones continued to enjoy considerable success in London social and intellectual circles. David Eder was a doctor, a Zionist, and a committed socialist who introduced Jones to the Fabian Society and its famous members, including George Bernard Shaw, Sidney Webb, and H. G. Wells, who was no longer teaching biology. Eder also introduced Jones to Louise Dorothea Kann, or "Loe" as everyone called her, a wealthy Dutch-Jewish woman who became Jones's partner for the next seven years. Jones noted that she was "as beautiful as she was rich," and maintained a network of intriguing international connections. Soon after they met in 1906, she enlisted Jones's help in entertaining a visiting delegation from the Duma, Russia's parliament. They made "a disappointingly unrevolutionary impression," he recalled.

For Jones, who was already thinking in Freudian terms, Kann was more than a lover: she was an object of fascination because of "her extraordinary qualities and even more extraordinary doings." As Jones put it, "Her peculiar kind of psychoneurotic constitution manifested itself mainly by developing various character traits in a much higher, and also finer, degree than is to be met with among the so-called normal." Because she suffered from renal problems, she took morphine twice daily. All of which contributed to her uncertainty about the future and probably to the fact that she appeared to be uninterested in marriage.

By the end of 1906, Jones began practicing psychoanalysis, taking as his first patient the sister of a colleague. The following year he not only attended the conference in Amsterdam where he first met Jung but then enrolled in a special postgraduate one-month course in psychiatry in Munich. As he noted proudly, his German had "got on far enough to make this possible." Another reason why he could do so was that Kann helped cover his expenses.

On his way back to England in November 1907, Jones went to Zurich to see Jung again and to visit the Burghölzli, where he worked. In a letter to Freud, Jung described his visitor as "an extremely gifted and active young man," who had spent five days there "chiefly to talk with me about your researches" since he was convinced of "the theoretical necessity of your views." Jung predicted that Jones would be "a staunch supporter of our cause," and reported that he had proposed the convening of "a congress of Freudian followers" in Innsbruck or Salzburg the following spring.

Freud was delighted by the news. "The congress in Salzburg in spring 1908 would make me very proud," he replied. Overruling Jung's preference for Innsbruck as the location, he had chosen Salzburg. As for the young man who had pitched the idea in the first place, Freud may have not immediately sensed his potential as a leader of his movement but he was very favorably disposed to him. "Your Englishman appeals to me because of his nationality," he asserted, disregarding Jones's Welsh origins. "I believe that once the English have become acquainted with our ideas they will never let them go." By contrast, he added, he had "less confidence" in the French.

While Jones was winning acceptance from both Jung and Freud, he also found himself enmeshed in another scandal at home in London in early 1908. At the West End Hospital for Nervous Diseases, he served as an assistant to Harry Campbell, who told him about a ten-year-old girl who had a "hysterical paralysis of the left arm," as Jones put it. Knowing of his interest in Freud, Campbell challenged him to find a sexual basis for the paralysis. After Jones met the girl, she told some of her friends that he had talked about sexual subjects with her—and word got out to the parents as well. In that era, this was considered shocking news. According to Jones, Campbell was "too weak, or frightened" to stand up for him, and he was asked to resign.

Jones concluded that this latest debacle meant that "all hope vanished" for him to keep his career on course in London. Hearing that the University of Toronto was planning to open a psychiatric clinic and was looking for a director, he applied for the job, "attracted by the opportunity of starting afresh in some other English-speaking country." But he had not entirely given up on London: he still hoped that he could return once memories of his problems there had faded.

Accepted for the Toronto position, Jones delayed his departure long enough to attend the Salzburg conference he had proposed and to undertake other travel on the continent. At the gathering in late April, Jones and Freud met for the first time. A bemused Jones noted that his already famed interlocutor introduced himself by saying "Freud, *Wien*," as if there could be any doubt that he was from Vienna. During this first talk, Freud asked Jones about the origin of his interest in psychoanalysis, and told him how Jung had described him as "very clever."

The next evening, Freud spoke to the participants about one of his particularly obsessive patients who was haunted by a memory from his military training that he could not get out of his mind. According to the patient who became known as "the rat man," he heard a captain describing a gruesome punishment for anyone who committed some alleged offense: tying the man down and placing, upside down, a container of hungry rats on his buttocks, which prompted them to gnaw their way into his anus. As Jones recalled, Freud's "intellectual powers" were on full display as he spoke about the case without notes for three hours. At that point, he suggested that he had been going on too long, but everyone pleaded for him to continue, which he did for another hour, ending at midnight. "I have never been so oblivious to the passage of time," Jones noted.

Accompanied by Abraham Brill, a Galician-born American psychiatrist whom he had first met in Zurich, Jones went on to Vienna in early May. Freud invited them to attend the regular Wednesday meeting of the Vienna Psychoanalytic Society at his apartment. Jung had belittled Freud's followers there, calling them a "degenerate and Bohemian crowd," and Jones later wrote his attitude off as a product of anti-Semitism, since all the regulars were Jews. But Jones was hardly in awe of the group either. "They were decidedly middle-class, and lacked the social manners and distinction I had been accustomed to in London," he wrote. "On the other hand, they were more cultivated and educated."

If Jones came away with mixed feelings about Vienna, Freud similarly expressed some puzzlement about him. Writing to Jung, he declared: "Jones is undoubtedly a very interesting and worthy man, but he gives me a feeling of, I was almost going to say racial strangeness." Somewhat enigmatically, he added, "He is a fanatic and doesn't eat enough . . . He almost reminds me of the lean and hungry Cassius." In another letter to Jung a couple of months later, Freud returned to the theme of his strangeness. "He is a Celt and consequently not quite accessible to us, the Teuton and the Mediterranean men."

Jones and Brill went on to Budapest, where Ferenczi showed them the sights, and then Brill returned to the United States while Jones traveled to Munich, exploring the castles, lakes, woods, and mountains of its surroundings. It was his way of relaxing before his journey across the Atlantic at the end of August. "I was bound for a New World, charged with new ideas," he wrote. Those ideas were still very much tied to Freud and Jung, and they would soon meet again in that New World.

———

Arriving in Toronto, Jones was highly appreciative of the opportunity for what he called "a fresh start in life." On September 28, he wrote to Freud: "Well, here I am landed in my new country which I like very much so far." With his usual energy, he quickly took on a variety of jobs and responsibilities, serving as the pathologist of the General Hospital, the director of the psychiatric clinic that was still in the planning stages, teaching, writing papers—and, above all, looking for ways to spread Freud's ideas both in Canada and the United States, which he visited frequently.

His initial admiration of his new home did not blind him to what he saw as its parochialism. Referring to the work of Professor Charles Clarke, "an excellent Canadian type"—who was his boss and chief advocate—Jones noted that his efforts to launch the new clinic and, thereby, elevate the teaching and practice of psychiatry faced formidable obstacles. "He had to contend with authorities whose only view of the insane was that they were a costly nuisance, and who would calmly hang a murderer however mad he was," he wrote.

As for the students he taught at the university, Jones expressed dismay at the "appalling illiteracy of their written papers" and at "how often they wrote in a fashion one would associate in England with the servant class." But he conceded his admiration for the "sturdy efforts" of many of the students who came from rural areas, working hard to master new disciplines and taking jobs as waiters or farmhands in the summers to pay their way.

Most significantly, Jones established a flourishing private psychoanalytic practice, with patients flocking to him from various parts of Canada, and even more from the United States. The young Welshman was much in demand. In December he was invited to Boston, where luminaries such as Morton Prince, the Harvard-trained neurologist and editor of the *Journal of Abnormal Psychology*, James Jackson Putnam of the Harvard Medical School and the Massachusetts General Hospital, and philosopher and psychologist William James, the brother of the novelist Henry James, frequently met to discuss new developments in their various disciplines.

Writing to Freud afterward, Jones reported that he was "exceedingly well received," and that, when it came to Freud's theories, "they were sympathetically inclined and very interested, especially in the sexual part." But he also cautioned that this interest was not widespread beyond Boston. He complained about the poor quality of many American neurologists and psychologists, who were "concerned mostly with making money." He added: "You see the problems here are peculiar to the Anglo-Saxon race, and one must know nicely the kinds of currents and prejudices in order to combat them most successively." Freud responded by praising him for "performing big work" by spreading his teachings, recognizing that Jones had already established himself as his de facto emissary to both Canada and the United States.

But Jones knew that he had to be careful about the way he discussed "the sexual part" of their cause. Fearing that he might be regarded as "a crank" and "tabooed as a sexual neurasthenic" if he wrote only papers about sexual subjects, he informed Freud: "Hence I shall dilute my sex articles with articles on other subjects alternately." He also had to be careful when it came to challenging local norms. For that reason, he always referred to Kann as his wife, although they were still unmarried. This became so much of a habit that he even referred to "my wife and I" in some of his letters to Freud, who knew better.

Soon after Jones had settled into his new home and role, Freud received an invitation from Clark University in Worcester, Massachusetts, which was celebrating its twentieth anniversary. The plan was for him to deliver five lectures on psychoanalysis, which was stirring increasing controversy and interest. Freud was hesitant at first to accept the invitation, but, when his hosts offered a more generous travel grant, he decided to make what would turn out to be his first and only trip to the United States in September 1909. Jung was invited as well, and Freud easily persuaded Ferenczi from Budapest to join them. The trio crossed the Atlantic together on the German luxury passenger liner *George Washington*, analyzing one another's dreams during their eight-day voyage from Bremen.

"Conference Brings Savants Together," proclaimed a headline in the *Worcester Telegram*. Speaking in German, Freud spelled out his theories and methods, including his ideas on the effects of sexual repression. G. Stanley Hall, Clark's president, who had invited them, awarded both Freud and Jung honorary degrees, which Freud gratefully called the "first official recognition of our endeavors." His lectures in Worcester "seemed like the realization of some incredible day-dream," he wrote in his autobiography. "Psychoanalysis was no longer a product of delusion; it had become a valuable part of reality."

In contrast to the resentment he often felt from the European medical establishment, he pointed out later, "over there I found myself received by the foremost men as an equal." He was particularly moved by his encounter with William James, who had come from Boston to see him. When they went on a walk together, the famed philosopher, who was seventy-seven at the time, abruptly stopped, handed Freud his bag, and explained that he was having an attack of angina pectoris and would catch up shortly. "He died of that disease a year later; and I have always wished that I might be as fearless as he was in the face of approaching death," Freud noted. It would prove to be a prophetic statement.

———

In a letter to Jung before their journey, Freud had told him that, at the cusp of launching his career, he had envisaged a two-month trial in Vienna and "if it did not prove satisfactory, I was planning to go to America and found an existence that I would subsequently have asked my fiancé in Hamburg to share." This seemed to indicate he was not predisposed to dislike the United States. Yet, when he finally visited that country, he developed a powerful aversion to it that would last for the rest of his life—despite the success of his lectures and all the accolades he received there.

As Jones recalled, Freud acknowledged the scale of the country's accomplishments while simultaneously conveying his opprobrium. "Yes, America is gigantic, but a gigantic mistake," he declared. This attitude would play a considerable role in his view of American leadership in the world later; it also meant that, when it came time to flee Vienna in 1938, he never considered the United States.

Freud did get to see more than just Clark University. After he, Jung, and Ferenczi had arrived in New York, Abraham Brill, who had left Austria-Hungary as a teenager, played host and guide, showing them around the city, with Jones coming down from Toronto to join them there. They also went to see Niagara Falls. After the ceremonies at Clark University, Harvard neurologist James Jackson Putnam hosted the group at his camp in the Adirondacks, putting up Freud, Jung, and Ferenczi in a log cabin called "Chatterbox."

Freud accumulated a litany of complaints during his trip. He was convinced that rich American food had aggravated his digestive system, and he was further irritated by the long trips he had to make at times to reach a toilet. Like many continental Europeans with a good grasp of British English, he found American pronunciation hard to follow, observing to Jung that the Americans didn't even seem to understand each other. During their stay at "Putnam's Shanty," as the camp was called, everyone called each other by their first names, which would have been unheard of in Austria, and the visitors were told to play board games. At Niagara Falls, a guide invited Freud to go in front of another group, saying, "Let the old fellow go first." Since he was only fifty-three then, this did not improve his mood.

Jones described Freud as "plainly disgruntled," although he viewed his complaints about the American diet as merely a pretext for his broader unease. "I imagine that the aversion had something to do with a feeling that commercial success dominated the values in the United States, and that scholarship, research, and profound reflection—all the things he stood for—were lightly esteemed," Jones wrote.

Upon his return home, Freud expressed his sense of relief in a letter to his daughter Mathilde. "I am very glad I am away from it [the United

States], and even more that I don't live there . . . But it was extremely interesting and probably highly significant for our cause. All in all one can call it a great success."

Staying on in Toronto, Jones worked hard as ever to continue that success. At a meeting in Washington in May 1910, he and Putnam became founding officers of the American Psychopathological Association. Its first president was Morton Prince, the editor of the *Journal of Abnormal Psychology*, which became the group's official publication. This offered further proof that Jones had cultivated the right people to advance "our cause." Freud left no doubt about his appreciation of his disciple's efforts, promptly writing to "express again my conviction that you are the most skillful, powerful and devote[d] helper, Psychoanalysis could have found in the New World."

In early 1911, Jones was again enmeshed in what he called "very serious personal trouble." A woman whom he described as "a severe hysteric" had accused him of having sex with her, denounced him to the president of the university, threatened legal action, and, as he put it in a letter to Putnam, "attempted to shoot me." He tried to calm his accuser and he admitted to "foolishly" paying her $500 to try to prevent another scandal—a staggering sum at the time, certainly provided by Kann. Encouraged by "some doctors with doubtful views," the woman persisted in her accusations, he reported. But Sir Alexander Falconer, the university president, refused to believe her and she was soon dispatched to a sanitorium.

It was another narrow escape for Jones. Nonetheless, Freud maintained his faith in him, treating the episode as further confirmation of his concept of "transference," whereby a patient redirects her feelings for someone else toward her therapist. In his early days when he was still experimenting with hypnosis, Freud had been embarrassed by a patient who had eagerly embraced him while undergoing treatment. Much later, he explained to Jung: "To be slandered and scorched by the love with which we operate—such are the perils of our trade, which we are certainly not going to abandon on their account."

But this latest incident did not help Jones's standing with Professor Charles Clarke, his main patron in Toronto, who had become the Dean of the Faculty of Medicine at the university. Earlier, Clarke had begun to waver in his support for the Welshman he had brought over. When he heard the rumors that Jones and Kann were not married as he had assumed, he confronted Jones, who admitted the truth. There were plenty of other rumors about Jones and his alleged advocacy of sexual licentiousness, with the implication that this reflected the broader agenda of psychoanalysis.

Those kinds of setbacks took their toll on Jones—and even more so on Kann, who had never been happy in Toronto. The morphine she took for her "almost constant pain" was making her life miserable, Jones reported to Freud, and she worried about Jones's reputation "although she does not believe in my work." Whether Kann knew of it or not, Jones was not helping things by conducting an affair with her young maid at the same time. Finally, Jones and Kann made the decision to leave for Vienna; the plan was for Kann to undergo treatment with Freud before their return to London.

Freud expressed regret that Jones was leaving North America when there was still so much left to do on that continent, but he took the decision gracefully. "You have, as it were, conquered America in no more than two years," he wrote. And he was happy to hear that Jones was planning to return to England, "as I expect you will do the same for your mother country."

That he would. In 1913, he founded the London Psychoanalytical Society, and he assumed an increasingly prominent role in the international movement. While undergoing therapy with Freud, Kann left Jones for another man—an American poet with the name, ironically, of Herbert Jones, whose father was also undergoing treatment with

Freud. In the meantime, the Welsh Jones resumed the affair he had started in Toronto with Kann's maid. He also underwent psychoanalysis himself, traveling to Budapest so that Ferenczi could be his analyst. He probably felt too involved with Freud in so many other ways to ask him to assume that role, especially since he was still treating Kann. But Freud offered Ferenczi his advice: "Be strict and tender with him."

Despite all the tensions inherent in their interwoven professional and personal connections, Freud and Jones had developed into a team. They would stick together until the end of Freud's life—and even beyond, when Jones authored the first major biography of his mentor.

4.

"A LONG POLAR NIGHT"

SETTLING BACK INTO HIS VIENNA ROUTINE IN OCTOBER 1909 after his trip to the United States, Freud, as Jones wrote, "was in a position where he could look forward to a career of recognition and fame on which he had never counted in his lifetime." Although he still might face "misunderstanding, criticism, opposition and even abuse . . . he was at the height of his powers and eager to employ them to the full."

Freud continued to attract new followers, including ones who would become lifelong associates. At the Weimar psychoanalytic congress in 1911, he met the Russian-German writer Lou Andreas-Salomé. She was born in St. Petersburg, studied at the University of Zurich, and then settled in Germany. Only five years younger than Freud, she was still a glamorous presence at the conference, which she attended as the companion of the Swedish psychoanalyst Poul Bjerre. Strikingly beautiful in her youth, she had taken up with such famous figures as the philosopher Friedrich Nietzsche and the poet Rainer Maria Rilke, who also became the subjects of her books. The fact that she was married to Friedrich Carl Andreas, an Orientalist at the University of Göttingen, did not prevent her from attracting an impressive procession of lovers.

Intrigued by Freud, she diligently studied his works after the Weimar conference and soon wrote to him about her desire to study psychoanalysis for a few months in Vienna. During her stay there in the fall of 1912, she attended the Wednesday evening meetings in Freud's apartment and completely won him over. He called her "a female of dangerous intelligence," and he valued her as a colleague and friend, "a muse," as he once put it, with no amorous component of their relationship. "Her interests are really of a purely intellectual nature," Freud added. "She is a very considerable woman." According to Jones, "Freud greatly admired her lofty and serene character as something far above his own, and she had a full appreciation of Freud's achievements."

Those were to be Freud's "last happy years," Jones concluded, cut short by the outbreak of hostilities, first between Austria and Serbia after the assassination in Sarajevo of Archduke Franz Ferdinand, heir to the Habsburg throne, on June 28, 1914, and then by the conflagration that engulfed all the major European powers. "The First World War ended for us, as for so many, a period of freedom, prosperity and security," Martin Freud recalled. It had been "a golden age," now gone forever.

But none of that meant that the immediate years before the war were easy for his father or his movement. At the March 1910 Second Congress of the International Psychoanalytical Association in Nuremberg, Freud had had to persuade his resentful colleagues from Vienna that he made the right call by backing Jung's election to the presidency of the group. "Most of you are Jews, and therefore you are incompetent to win friends for the new teaching," he bluntly told them. "Jews must be content with the modest role of preparing the ground." A few months later, he cautioned Ferenczi in Budapest not to overlook Jung's contributions to the cause. "I am more convinced than ever that he is the man of the future," he wrote.

To assuage the bruised feelings of his Vienna colleagues, Freud handed over the formal role of leader of the Wednesday group who gathered at his apartment to Alfred Adler, one of the most visible malcontents. In a letter to Jones, Freud claimed this was producing a salutary result. "All are full of fresh hope and promise to work," he declared. "I am retiring to the backgrounds, as behaves an elderly gentleman [no more compliments pray!]." It was a tongue-in-cheek way of saying that he had rearranged the lineup while still orchestrating every move.

But those maneuvers did not quell the chronic discontent in his Vienna circle or mollify some of the others who remained upset that they were relegated to secondary roles in the broader movement. On June 19, 1910, he wrote to Jung: "You know how jealous they all are—here and elsewhere—over your privileged position with me (it is the same with Ferenczi; I mean, his closeness to me is equally begrudged), and I think I am justified in feeling that what people say against you as a result is being said against me."

Freud quickly came to regret choosing Adler to lead the Vienna group, since he proved to be a testy personality with few saving graces that could help calm tensions there. "With Adler, it is getting really bad," Freud reported to Jung in December. He was just as disturbed by Adler's theories, which downplayed the role of sexuality and the subconscious in favor of more emphasis on biology, predicting that they would damage psychoanalysis. In a subsequent letter to Jung, Freud wrote: "Recently he expressed the opinion that the motivation even for coitus was not exclusively sexual, but also included the individual's desire to *seem* masculine to himself." That kind of reasoning, he continued, would make it impossible to understand the feelings of neurotics.

By June 1911, the break was almost complete. "I have got rid of Adler at last," he boasted to Jung. Adler left the Wednesday evening gatherings, taking a few supporters with him. It was no accident that this first major split in the psychoanalytic movement was triggered by Freud's uncompromising insistence on the primary role of sexuality in determining human behavior, which had also contributed to his earlier break with Breuer.

Freud's emphasis on sex made him an easy target for personal attacks. Moses Allen Starr, an American neurologist who had worked briefly with him in Vienna early in his career, denounced his theories to his colleagues at a meeting of the Neurological Section of the Academy of Medicine in New York on April 4, 1912. According to *The New York Times*, Starr criticized his notion that the "psychological life of human beings is based on the sex drive," and segued into a portrayal of Freud as a product of his allegedly sordid surroundings. "Vienna is not a particularly moral city," he declared. "Freud was not a man who lived on a particularly high moral plane. He was not self-repressed. He was not an ascetic . . . his scientific theory is largely the result of his environment and of the peculiar life he led."

Freud always considered such attacks on his character, which would surface with some regularity, as wildly off the mark. They were unfair, as he wrote in a letter to James Putnam in Boston, because "I consider myself a very moral human being." He explained that he was speaking in terms of social not sexual morality, and he prided himself on never acting or doing anything "mean or malicious," never making others suffer or taking advantage of them.

But Freud had very strong feelings about what he saw as America's or any other society's hypocritical and outdated puritanism. "Sexual morality as defined by society, in its most extreme form that of America, strikes me as very contemptible," he declared. "I stand for an infinitely freer sexual life, although I myself have made very little use of such freedom. Only so far as I considered myself entitled to." The last part of that statement summed up the contrast between his radical theories and his conservative way of life. But it was his teachings, not his lifestyle, that generated the most serious conflicts within his movement.

———

From the very beginning of their relationship, Jung had indicated to Freud that he, too, harbored misgivings concerning his theories about human sexuality. Yet both men were eager to downplay their differences and praised each other's accomplishments. The extent to which Freud felt comfortable confiding in his Swiss crown prince was apparent in his letters, which had a tendency to digress from their official business to personal subjects. They also contained more than a touch of irreverence about the steady stream of patients coming to see Freud, drawn by his growing fame. Returning from one of his Italian journeys, he wrote on October 1, 1910: "Today I resumed my practice and saw my first batch of nuts again. I must now transmit the nervous energy gained during my holiday into money to fill my depleted purse."

But even in those early days there was an undercurrent of tension in the Freud–Jung relationship. Acutely conscious of Freud's earlier close ties to Wilhelm Fliess, the Berlin ear, nose, and throat specialist, and the abrupt end of that friendship, Jung assured Freud that "nothing Fliess-like is going to happen." In the same letter from March 11, 1909, he added: "Except for moments of infatuation my affection is lasting and reliable." Since Freud knew of Jung's reputation as a womanizer, he would have understood that allusion.

Despite his efforts to convince Freud of his loyalty, Jung could be slow in responding to his letters, leaving the impression that he often had more pressing priorities. Shortly before Jung was to preside over the meetings of the International Psychoanalytical Association in

Nuremberg from March 30 to 31, 1910, he returned to the United States to deal with what he described as a "severe conflict of duties." The mother of his patient Joseph Medill McCormick, heir to the wealthy family that controlled the *Chicago Tribune*, reported that he had suffered an alcoholic breakdown and urgently needed Jung's help. "Now don't get cross with me for my pranks!" Jung wrote Freud from Paris on March 9. "You will already have heard from my wife that I am on my way to America." His effort to make light of this last-minute journey, which would allow him to take care of McCormick and a "few other things besides," revealed his nervousness about Freud's reaction. He informed him that his wife, Emma, was helping with the preparations for Nuremberg, and that he would stay only a week in America and return in time for the proceedings there.

A couple of other prominent members of the Zurich group had already declined the invitation to attend, and Freud fretted that Jung might not make it either. "What will happen if the Zurichers desert me?" he asked. But Emma kept in touch with him about the program and assured him that her husband would be back as promised. In fact, Jung arrived in Nuremberg by train at 5 a.m. on the first day of the conference, allowing him to fulfill all his duties. As a relieved Freud wrote to Jones, who was still in Toronto, the event was a "success," living up to his expectations.

Freud had never completely opened up to Jung, despite their growing cooperation. During their trip to the United States, they had discussed some of their dreams and a few "delicate" personal matters, according to Jung. But Freud balked at Jung's offer to analyze him more fully. "My dear boy, I cannot risk my authority," he told the younger man. As Jung wrote to Freud a couple of months later, "It is a hard lot to be compelled to work side by side with the creator."

Freud was much less reticent in his conversations with Emma, whom he had first met when the Jungs had visited him in Vienna. He was quite taken with her, and he admired how protective she was of her husband, despite his affairs with other women. He told her that his children were his "only true joy," and, somewhat perplexingly, that his marriage to Martha was "amortized." By doing so, he may have been signaling that much of the original passion was gone, or this may have been his way of suggesting to Emma that the problems in her marriage were far from exceptional.

Emma, in turn, sensed that, despite the mutual admiration between her husband and Freud, there were already problems in their relationship. With what she described as "brazen candor," she asked Freud why he seemed to be in such a hurry to anoint her husband as his successor. She pointed out that Freud was still a vigorous man who should be enjoying his "well-earned fame and success." While she was clearly delighted to see her husband as the crown prince, she saw no reason why Freud should be stepping back at that point. She intuitively understood that the founder could come to resent his presumptive heir, even if he had invited him to assume that role. And Freud understood—and appreciated—her efforts to defuse any nascent tensions between him and Jung, calling her a "solver of riddles."

———

Both men were intensely interested in primitive societies and mythology, and Freud's "partiality for the pre-historic," as he put it, helped explain his fascination with archeology and the art objects that he collected all his life. It also explained why he wrote *Totem and Taboo* during this period, a collection of essays on subjects like the incest taboo, animism, and magic—all of which he felt established connections between the thinking of earlier peoples and modern neurotics, once again highlighting the primary role of human sexuality.

Although they had common interests, the two men had differing backgrounds when it came to such issues. In 1902, at the University of Basel, Jung had written his dissertation titled "On the Psychology and Pathology of So-Called Occult Phenomena." Once he started his collaboration with Freud, he left no doubt that this was not a passing preoccupation. "Occultism is another field we shall have to conquer," he asserted. He also mentioned his fascination with astrology, "which seems indispensable for a proper understanding of mythology."

Freud tried to be understanding at first. "I am aware that you are driven by innermost inclination to the study of the occult," he wrote to Jung on May 12, 1911. "I cannot argue with that, it is always right to go where your impulses lead." He cautioned him, though, that he would be accused of mysticism. In Freud's mind, mysticism was a pejorative term often connoting irrational Christian or other religious beliefs.

Jones, who was initially impressed by Jung, later offered a verdict on him that reflected the opinion that Freud developed as their relationship deteriorated. In private conversations, Jones wrote, "Jung had revealed himself to me as a man with deep mystical tendencies that prevented a clear vision of a scientific attitude in general or a psychoanalytic one in particular; the superstructure was brilliant and talented, but the foundation was insecure." Or, as he put it more simply, Jung had a "confused mind."

The foundation for everyone, as Freud saw it, was always sexuality; this meant embracing his concept of the libido, the sex drive, as the primary determinant of human behavior and neuroses. Jung was far from fully convinced on that score, although he initially tried to placate Freud by saying, for instance, that the occult could be understood "with the aid of the libido theory." But in his lectures and writings, Jung talked increasingly about external factors other than sexuality and placed less emphasis on subconscious repression. In effect, he was laying the groundwork for launching his brand of analytic psychology as an alternative to Freudian psychoanalysis.

Along with the frequent perceived slights that both men detected from the other, those more substantive emerging conflicts were soon reflected in their correspondence. Freud changed the way he addressed Jung, using the more formal *"Lieber Herr Doktor"* (Dear Doctor) instead of his previous *"Lieber Freund"* (Dear Friend). To other colleagues, he complained openly about Jung's "regressive" tendencies. To Jung, he sounded positively peevish, writing, for example, on December 22, 1912: "In regard to your allegation that since I misuse psychoanalysis to keep my students in a state of infantile dependency I myself am responsible for their infantile behavior . . ." Freud wrote to Jones that Jung "seems all out of his wits, he is behaving quite crazy."

Although Freud tried to delay a formal break, the relationship was doomed. By the end of 1913, he was complaining to Karl Abraham in Berlin that he was "infuriated" with Jung and accused him of "emotional stupidity." On April 20, 1914, Jung resigned as president of the International Psychoanalytical Association. By the summer, Freud exclaimed to Abraham again: "So we are rid of them at last, the brutal holy Jung and his pious parrots." Soon, his attacks on the erstwhile crown prince grew even more vitriolic. He accused Jung of "lies, brutality and anti-Semitic condescension toward me."

To this day, scholars debate whether or not Jung qualified as an anti-Semite, despite his early collaboration with Freud. Asked directly by Freud when they first met whether he was an anti-Semite, Jung replied: "No, no! Anti-Semitism is out of the question." But Jung was sympathetic to far-right political movements. On a visit to Berlin in 1937, he watched Hitler and Mussolini review the troops on parade, impressed by the flamboyant Italian dictator who, as he put it, "had a certain style, a certain format of an original man with good taste in certain matters."

Jung's attitude toward Hitler was more ambivalent, but it still left him open to accusations that he was a Nazi sympathizer—a charge he vehemently denied. On a trip to the United States in 1936, he tried to preempt his critics by emphasizing his "neutral Swiss" outlook. "I despise politics wholeheartedly: thus I am neither a Bolshevik, nor a National Socialist, nor an anti-Semite," he declared. Nonetheless, the cloud of suspicion that lingered over him about his purported anti-Semitism and his views about the Nazis could hardly have coexisted with a continuation of his ties with Freud and his mostly Jewish colleagues.

All of which meant that, ironically, it was fortunate that Jung and Freud parted ways long before the rise of Hitler, allowing Jones to emerge as the most prominent gentile in the psychoanalytic movement. Although he had almost no contact with Jews until he embarked on his medical career, the Welshman was proud that he was accepted by both Freud and his Jewish adherents. "They would almost forget my Gentile extraction, and would freely share with me their characteristic jokes, anecdotes, points of view, and outlook," he recalled. "I knew their characteristics with an intimacy that must have fallen to the lot of few Gentiles."

But Jones freely admitted that this did not make him an expert on Judaism since he was acquainted only with non-religious Jews. "It has never been my fortune to know a Jew possessing any religious belief, let alone an orthodox one," he wrote. Observant Jews did not enlist in Freud's psychoanalytic army.

———

The Freud–Jung split was big news for the small community of specialists in several countries, but largely unnoticed by the general public. A far larger conflict was about to engulf almost everyone in Europe, however, and then pull in the United States as well. It was not surprising that the spark for World War I, the assassination of Archduke Franz Ferdinand and his wife, Sophie, by a Bosnian Serb nationalist, took place in the Balkans, the most troubled part of the weakening Austro-

Hungarian Empire. But in the Habsburg capital, Freud—along with so many of his compatriots—initially failed to comprehend the scale of the tragedy that was rapidly unfolding during the summer of 1914.

This was a result of Freud's reluctance to admit that his surroundings, and all the associated assumptions about the world he had grown up in, were seriously imperiled. According to his son Martin, the entire family accepted the Habsburg monarchy: "We Freud children were all stout loyalists, delighted to hear, or to see, all we could of the Imperial Court." He recalled how excited they were whenever they caught sight of a *Hofwagen*, a court coach. "We could tell with precision the extent of the passenger's importance by the color of the high wheels and the angle at which the magnificently liveried coachman held his whip."

Martha, his mother, who had spent the first eight years of her life in Hamburg, never lost her North German accent. Nor, as Martin pointed out, did she lose "her feelings of patriotic devotion to the Imperial German family." Since Austria-Hungary was Germany's ally, there was no problem reconciling Sigmund's and Martha's loyalties. While he was growing up, Sigmund had followed Prussia's wars that led to the unification of Germany and its victory over France in 1871. His sister Anna remembered how Sigmund, a young teenager at the time, hung large maps in his room, sticking pins in them to show the movement of the rival armies. "Every evening I could listen to the conversation between father and son on the state of the war," she noted.

After the assassination in Sarajevo, Freud failed to recognize how quickly events were spiraling out of control. On July 23, Austria, with the backing of Germany's Kaiser Wilhelm II, issued an ultimatum to Serbia, including demands for the suppression of "subversive" elements that "constitute a standing menace to the peace of the Monarchy," knowing that the Serbian government would reject them. Yet, on July 26, Freud wrote to his German colleague Abraham expressing his support of this action. "Perhaps for the first time in thirty years

I feel myself an Austrian, and would like just once more to give this unpromising empire a chance." He optimistically added: "Should the war remain localized to the Balkans it won't be too bad."

On July 28, Austria declared war on Serbia. The next day, Freud asserted to his brother Alexander: "I believe that no great power will bring about a general war." If proven wrong in that prediction, he wrote to Abraham in Berlin on August 2, he would still support their side "with all my heart, if I did not know that England is on the wrong side." Two days later, German troops invaded Belgium and then moved on to France, where they battled French and British troops. The Central Powers, Germany and Austria-Hungary, were soon joined by Turkey and Bulgaria, facing off in a widening war against the Triple Entente of Britain, France, and Russia. Italy proclaimed itself neutral at the start of the war, but declared war on Austria-Hungary in 1915. This was the "general war" that Freud had claimed would be avoided.

Nonetheless, he was buoyed by the initial military successes of Germany and Austria, rekindling the sense that there was unity in the German-speaking world. In September, he traveled to Hamburg to see his daughter Sophie, who had given birth to his first grandson. In a letter to Abraham, he explained that he had visited the city before but for the first time it did not feel "as though I were in a foreign city."

Freud was inclined to believe the early optimistic predictions of victory by the Austrian and German authorities, although he wasn't eager to see his sons enlist. But Martin, the eldest, had served a few months in the Imperial Horse Artillery in 1910–1911, until he broke a leg in a skiing accident, and he quickly volunteered to return to duty when the war started. His old regiment took him back as a junior officer. His father congratulated him, while admonishing him to care for his health. "Frankly, so far as you are concerned, I am more afraid of epidemics, whose acquaintance can be made very easily just now, than of enemy bullets," he wrote. "It is not cowardice to protect oneself as far as possible from epidemics."

As the fighting intensified, Freud began worrying more about the bullets, too. On December 20, 1914, in another letter, he urged Martin not to take unnecessary risks. "I still think you regard the war as a kind of sporting excursion," he wrote, adding that he and Martha would be spending a "sad and quiet" Christmas. Martin noted that his father's letters were "severely practical," lacking in any expressions of sentiment. Still, they conveyed his concern. So did the fact that the only time he spoke to Martin by phone, the instrument he loathed, was when Martin was passing through Vienna during the war but had no time to see his parents.

Freud's worries about Martin were accentuated by his knowledge that his son still clung to romantic notions of warfare. Martin's wartime experiences, which differed dramatically from those of millions of other soldiers bogged down in murderous trench warfare, did little to change his outlook. "The truth is I was then enjoying the happiest time of my life," he wrote. During the Austrian victories in early 1915, Martin rode on patrol on a "magnificent chestnut," seemingly fulfilling a dream from early childhood. In that dream, "I saw myself mounted on a magnificent war charger riding into a freed city to be welcomed with flowers and kisses from the liberated maidens, all very beautiful," he recalled in his autobiography. "The reality, as it turned out, was even more colorful and the girls more lovely: and I was indeed completely happy." He fought on both the Russian and Italian fronts, winning seven medals for bravery.

The dream could not last forever, and Martin was shot in the thigh in 1918. Shortly before hostilities ceased later that year, he was captured by the British in Italy and ended up in an Italian prisoner-of-war camp for officers. He described himself as "one of the victims of the downfall of an ancient empire," and he was not released until August

1919. Like his father, he was disappointed by the war's outcome and his spirits had finally sagged, but he could not complain about his conditions in captivity. He pointed out that he returned to Vienna "somewhat plump as the result of a diet of spaghetti and risotto."

Freud's other two sons also served, enlisting a bit later than Martin, and they were lucky enough to emerge unscathed. Oliver, the second son, was an engineer assigned to a railway regiment, while Ernst, the youngest son, spent two years on the Italian front before he came down with tuberculosis and a duodenal ulcer, leading to his discharge right before the war ended. Compared to so many other families, the Freuds were extraordinarily lucky.

———

The war not only split Europe but also the psychoanalytic movement, quite unevenly. With the exception of Jones, who was in London, Freud's other top lieutenants were based in cities like Berlin and Budapest, which meant that they, like Freud, were on the side of the Central Powers. The International Psychoanalytical Association was to hold a congress in September 1914 in Dresden, but the war scuttled those plans; several of those who would have participated were called up to serve as army physicians. It wasn't until September 1918 that another congress was held, this time in Budapest, but it included only participants from the Central Powers and neutral Holland, which made it less than truly international.

Although direct mail was suspended between the two sides, Jones and Freud managed to keep up their correspondence via friends in neutral countries like Switzerland, Holland, Sweden, and, initially, Italy. From the beginning of the conflict, their letters signaled their differing perspectives on the war. On August 3, 1914, Jones wrote: "We are prejudiced against Germany . . . Austria is unpopular for getting everyone into trouble, but her attitude toward the Slav people is fairly well understood. No one doubts here, however, that Germany and Austria will be badly defeated, the odds are too much against them."

At that point, Freud was confidently expecting victory for his side, and, as Jones noted, he proclaimed: "All my libido is given to Austro-Hungary." His usual Anglophile tendencies were suddenly suppressed. To Abraham, he complained about the "incredible arrogance" of the British, and that Jones's predictions about the war showed him to be a "real Anglo"—which was clearly not meant as a compliment.

Yet both Freud and Jones were intent on not allowing the war to destroy their personal and professional ties. On October 3, 1914, Freud reported that he had returned from a visit to Abraham in Berlin. "We cannot bring ourselves to regard you as an enemy!" he told Jones. The Welshman welcomed that reassurance. "I am pleased to hear that our circle has decided not to regard me as an enemy," he replied. "I also have no difficulty in separating personal friendship from national rivalry."

A strong undercurrent of tension remained, however. On October 22, 1914, Freud warned Jones about the perils of believing British propaganda. "Regardless of what you read in the newspapers, do not forget that lies are rampant now," he wrote. "We are not suffering from any restrictions, any epidemics and are in very good spirits." Jones replied that he was able to read the German papers, which helped him understand that the British accounts were often "greatly exaggerated." Alluding to the disinformation on the other side, he added: "In return I ask you to believe that the Bank of England had not been destroyed by bombs, that Egypt and India have not revolted, and that our coasts have not been bombarded by the German Fleet!"

Neither man was swayed by the occasional barbed comments of the other. But it did not take Freud too long to begin reexamining his own view of the war, recognizing that its consequences would be devastating for both sides. On November 25, 1914, he wrote to Lou

Andreas-Salomé, that "humanity will get over this war, too, but I know for certain that I and my contemporaries will see the world cheerful no more. It is too vile." And, he realized, everyone had been wildly overoptimistic about its duration. "It is a long polar night," he wrote to Abraham, "and one must wait until the sun rises again."

In his 1915 essays entitled "Thoughts for the Times on War and Death," Freud expressed his profound disillusionment with the escalating brutality of the war. "Not only is it more bloody and more destructive than any war of other days, because of the enormously increased perfection of weapons of attack and defense; it is at least as cruel, as embittered, as implacable as any that has preceded it," he wrote. The conflict ignored all notions of international law such as the distinction between civilians and combatants or the "prerogatives of the wounded and the medical service," he added. "It tramples in blind fury on all that comes in its way, as though there was no future and no peace among men after it is over."

He decried the "almost incredible phenomenon" of "civilized nations" turning against each other "with hate and loathing." As he noted, "We had expected the great world-dominating nations of white race upon whom the leadership of the world had fallen . . . to succeed in discovering another way of settling misunderstandings and conflicts of interest." Instead, the war was cutting "all the common bonds between the contending peoples, and threatens to leave a legacy of embitterment that will make any renewal of those bonds impossible for a long time to come."

Judged in isolation, such statements look remarkably prophetic, suggesting that Freud was already foreseeing the long-term consequences of the conflict—not in any detail, but at least in broad outline. They also suggest that he was focused on the destructive forces unleashed around him, absorbed in trying to understand the fighting raging across the continent. But that was true only up to a point.

Freud could not ignore the cascade of cataclysmic events, especially since they swept up his sons and almost everyone else around him. But, as he told Abraham in 1918, most of all he wanted to keep his head down and focus on psychoanalysis. The Wednesday evening sessions in his apartment were briefly suspended at the beginning of the war, but resumed during the first winter, held every three weeks with a much smaller group of participants. Between 1915 and 1917, Freud delivered three series of introductory lectures on psychoanalysis at the University of Vienna, drawing large audiences. He also continued writing regularly, exploring the variations of neuroses and penning works like "Mourning and Melancholia" that also reflected his mood. As he explained to Ferenczi, "I am working morosely, yet steadily."

In 1917, he was disappointed when, contrary to rumors, he failed to win the Nobel Prize—a recognition that he had been longing for. But Freud was not about to let anything weaken his commitment to his lifelong preoccupations. Jones marveled at his ability to remain single-minded in his interests, despite the daily headlines about the latest news from the battlefields. "He would glance through the newspaper, toss it aside with the condemnation 'scheusslich' (horrible) and go on with his work," his Welsh disciple wrote.

That self-discipline allowed Freud to continue to be highly productive no matter what was happening around him. But it also indicated why he could be blindsided by events later on, when the "legacy of embitterment" that he had predicted bore its poisoned fruit.

———

Jones admired Freud's ability to tune out much of the war news and focus on his usual work, but he felt incapable of following his example. "I either lacked the necessary strength of mind or else had too much of a social conscience to devote my attention entirely to it, which in the circumstances would doubtless have been the most useful thing to do." He found the war too distracting, he explained, and he eagerly followed the daily reports from the front and read up on military strategy and history.

Jones was thirty-five when the war started, and "free and unattached," as he put it, since he and Kann had split in 1913. While torn about how best to use his skills, he felt compelled to volunteer for military service. "'England hath need of thee' exercised a potent spell," he noted. Because he suffered from rheumatoid arthritis and the medical board was "apparently unimpressed with my physique," Jones recalled, he was rejected twice on medical grounds. In addition, as he wrote to Freud, "The War Office decided I was of more use to the Army at my present work than doing hospital duty in France."

This proved to be very much the case. Jones's practice was flourishing, most of it with "officers suffering from some form of war neurosis." In that era, post-traumatic stress disorder (PTSD) was an unknown concept, and even the notion of neurosis was looked upon with suspicion, with the military usually writing off anyone with symptoms such as depression and phobias as a malingerer—or at most, the victim of a brain concussion. As a result, Jones had to constantly battle with army medical boards to get enough time with his patients to put them through his lengthy psychoanalytic treatment.

"The situations were often extremely pathetic," Jones wrote. After treating a military intelligence officer "who was paralyzed with depression and a crushing sense of inferiority," he felt he was making good progress. But before he could complete the treatment, the officer was reassigned and offered no follow-up. After a couple of months, his body was found crushed on the railroad tracks; he had lain down in front of an express train. Jones stressed that this was the only time he knew of when one of his former patients committed suicide. But as he laconically put it in a letter to Freud, "The shock cases in the war are highly interesting."

Freud fretted about the lost opportunities during the war, writing that the "flowering time of our science has been violently disrupted." But Jones was convinced that the war was also presenting new challenges that could bolster their cause. "If there is ever to be any salvation of the world from these nightmares it will surely be psycho-analysis that will point the way," he wrote to Freud on December 15, 1914. Or, as W.H.R. Rivers, another British psychiatrist who also worked with army officers during the war, put it: "Fate would seem to have presented us at the present time with an unexemplified opportunity to test the truth of Freud's theory of the unconscious, in so far as it is concerned with the production of the mental and functional nervous disorders."

For all his talk about how distracted he was, Jones maintained his usual hectic pace, still managing to write some scientific papers and seeing patients from early morning till evening. While the London Psychoanalytical Society that he had founded in 1913 was largely inactive in this period, some of the members met informally on occasion.

Like Freud—who had analyzed Gustav Mahler in 1910, helping the famed composer overcome his potency problems with his wife, Alma, who was nineteen years younger than him—Jones also had his brushes with celebrities from other fields. The one who intrigued him the most: the writer D. H. Lawrence and his German wife, Frieda. "They were both impelled by mischievous demons to goad each other to frenzy," Jones recalled. "When this culminated in a sadistic orgy there was again peace for a time, but it was not always so."

Jones was impressed by the way Lawrence "dominated every company with his eager assertive manner, his vital—all too vital—personality, and his penetrating intelligence." But when the writer talked about moving to the United States to form a utopian community and urged Jones to join him, the Welshman dismissed his ideas as "decidedly hare-brained." As a psychologist, he concluded that Lawrence was a person with an "obvious lack of balance." He could have also pointed out that Lawrence's novels—especially *Sons and Lovers*—were ideally suited for Freudian analysis.

Jones's letters to Freud about his activities lifted the spirits of his mentor in Vienna. "I can only applaud your resolve to guard the flag of psychoanalysis," Freud wrote to him. He was also pleased when Jones reported in February 1917 that he had married Morfydd Owen. "She is Welsh, young (twenty-three), very pretty, intelligent, and musical," he wrote. In fact, Owen was a musical prodigy who was already winning praise as a pianist, singer, and composer; in 1918, she became an associate professor at the Royal Academy of Music. According to Freud, Jones had assured him he was a "reformed character." The clear implication: he was settling down into a domestic routine that was less likely to produce scandals in the future.

But the bride was prone to depression and the marriage was troubled from the start. In his autobiography, Jones was circumspect in his description of her. "Singularly mature, and with unerring integrity of soul in all that concerned her art, Morfydd's mental evolution had not proceeded evenly in all directions," he wrote. While the couple was on holiday in South Wales in August 1918, she became very ill, and a local doctor performed an emergency operation on what appeared to be an abscessed appendix. Jones summoned all the medical help he could, but she died on September 7. Whatever the difficulties in their short marriage, Jones was genuinely bereft. "It is a staggering blow to me, and although I am trying to start work again I am quite overwhelmed inside," he wrote to Freud.

If anything, this tragedy brought the two men even closer together, despite the war that was keeping them apart. "I had hoped that you had found lasting happiness," Freud replied. "I am terribly sorry that it has turned out differently, for the years of separation have done little to change my feelings for you."

———

After the two sides signed the armistice on November 11, 1918, to end World War I, Jones assured Freud that he was trying to recover from his loss. Welcoming the fact that they could now communicate directly again, without sending their letters through third countries, he wrote on December 7: "You see I can look forward in life, although I have been through hell itself these last months." He noted that he had just read Freud's paper "on grief and melancholy," which was particularly apt and made "a great impression" on him.

His melancholy mood also came through in his subsequent letters. "Tomorrow, New Year's Day, I shall be 40, and life's greatest happiness is past, forever," he wrote on December 31. "But do not fear that I shall lose heart for the work. That I find worth doing." For his part, Freud found himself in the rare position of admitting that, unlike Jones, he had erred in his earlier estimations of the conflict that had just ended. "I concede all your predictions about the war and its consequences have come true," he wrote.

Jones delivered on his promise not to lose heart for his work. He was busy setting up a new International Psychoanalytic Press in London, along with a bookshop to sell its books and other publications. He was convinced of the need to translate more of Freud's works and those of other German-speakers into English, allowing them to reach a broader audience in Britain and the United States.

To help him in those endeavors, Jones was eager to employ a bilingual secretary. A member of Freud's inner circle suggested Katharina (Kitty) Jokl, who, like Freud, grew up in a Moravian Jewish family that moved to Vienna. She went to the same school as Freud's daughters, then earned a doctorate at the University of Zurich; she worked at the Austrian consulate in Geneva and a hotel in Zurich. In May 1919, when Jones wrote to offer her the job in London, she was twenty-seven, single, and a virgin. She vacillated at first, but Jones followed up by traveling to Switzerland that summer. When they met in Zurich, it took only three days for Jones to propose—and Jokl immediately accepted. Her worldly suitor had employed the full power of his romantic charms. "Did I live before I knew you?" she asked in a letter after he left for Vienna.

Their subsequent marriage was long and produced four children. Jones referred to Kitty as "my secretarial wife." There was nothing demeaning in this appellation: it was his way of recognizing how important a role she played in his professional and personal life.

Finally, both of those parts of Jones's life were in sync, positioning him to make good on his promise to devote all his energies to Freud's movement. In 1919, he revived what was initially called the London Psychoanalytical Society under a new name, the British Psychoanalytical Society, and, in 1920, he was elected president of the International Psychoanalytical Association, the position once held by Jung. The group's congress in The Hague that year attracted sixty-two members and fifty-seven guests from both the victorious and defeated powers, giving the affair a reunion-like feel, with Freud elaborating on his theories about dreams. Jones also founded the *International Journal of Psychoanalysis* that year, which he edited until 1939.

"Both in Germany and the countries of Western Europe the war had actually stimulated interest in psycho-analysis," Freud noted, again recognizing that reality later than Jones had. He credited Jones for taking full advantage of those more receptive conditions, producing a new beginning for their movement.

Jones, in turn, credited Freud with his personal new beginning. "To me it is clear that I owe my career, my livelihood, my position, and my capacity of happiness in marriage—in short, everything—to you and the work you have done," he declared. Whatever contributions he himself had made to their movement, Jones added, would not "redress" the debt he felt he owed Freud. There was no hyperbole in those expressions of gratitude: they were utterly sincere.

———

In the wake of World War I and the peace terms spelled out in the Treaty of Versailles signed on June 28, 1919, the Austro-Hungarian Empire vanished from the map of Europe. Vienna was no longer the imperial capital for fifty million people of numerous nationalities; the new Austrian state had a population of 6.5 million people and a fraction of its previous territory. The losses of the Austro-Hungarian armed forces were estimated at about 1.2 million, with hundreds of thousands still missing and presumed dead—all this in service of a losing cause.

H. V. Kaltenborn, an American journalist who would soon become a famous radio commentator, reported on the stark conditions in the city, which was dependent on American food aid for its starving children and general population. Hyperinflation took off even more quickly than it did in Germany, wiping out people's savings, and morale could not have been lower. "Vienna appeared to me the saddest city in Europe, perhaps because it had been once the gayest," he wrote.

Dorothy Thompson, another rising American media star, was living in Vienna at the time. Earlier, she had associated Vienna with "Strauss waltzes, Spanish Baroque, damask interiors . . . a sumptuous court," she recalled, but now she found herself in a "city of dread," full of refugees, returning soldiers, and "gentlefolk, starving gracefully in Biedermeier salons."

As he walked with his wife along the Danube one evening, Kaltenborn heard shouting. Learning that a man had jumped into the water, he asked: "Can't we try to save him?" Someone responded in a soft voice: "Oh, no, he jumped in deliberately. If a man wants to take his life these days he is entitled to have his way." As Kaltenborn grimly concluded, "That was the philosophy of postwar Vienna."

Freud and his family were not exempt from the economic consequences of the conflict. Martin recalled that when he returned to the city after he was released from the Italian POW camp in August 1919, he discovered that inflation had wiped out all his military pay that he had been saving during the war. His thousands of kronen, the Austrian currency at the time, "were not enough to pay for the re-soling of one pair of civilian shoes," he wrote. His father, too, had lost his savings, he pointed out.

However, Freud was in a position, as Martin put it, "to restore his finances." Martin could provide him with legal and other practical advice, but it was Jones who proved to be his real savior. Tapping his connections on both sides of the Atlantic, he sent Freud British and American patients who eagerly sought his treatment. They paid in hard currency, two guineas or ten dollars an hour, for his services—a princely sum in that impoverished era. Since the sessions were all in English, Freud took more language lessons to improve his skills.

Jones also valued his patients from abroad. As his and Freud's income grew, he opened up accounts for both of them, along with one for the International Psychoanalytic Press, with a private banking firm based in Amsterdam. This shielded them from some of the taxes they would have had to pay at home. Freud was particularly concerned that he could put aside enough money that would not be subject to inheritance taxes once he was gone.

Gradually, as Martin put it, "the reconstruction of the Austrian rump allowed people to awaken from a nightmare of disorder and dissolution and to begin at least an adequate if not a secure way of life." In Freud's case, it would prove to be more than adequate.

But the overall situation in Europe remained extremely precarious. In his autobiography, Jones claimed to know from the very beginning where the greatest danger lay. "I never wavered in my conviction that Germany would rise again, reassemble her forces, and attack us once more in the hope of catching us in a state of complacent unpreparedness," he wrote. "So it proved. For us the Great War was finally over; for the Germans the first round had been fought."

It is hard to judge whether this was an accurate portrayal of his views at the time or an embellishment with the benefit of hindsight. But if he really concluded as much at the end of World War I, he was prescient indeed.

5.

"VESTAL"

AT THE DAWN OF THE INTERWAR ERA, ONLY ONE MEMBER OF Sigmund Freud's inner circle, Ernest Jones, was clearly positioned to be a part of his future rescue squad. To be sure, neither Jones nor anyone else at that point had any inkling that a rescue operation would be needed. No one could envisage the magnitude of the threat looming over him and all the Jews of Europe, and this remained the case for most of the 1920s and even beyond. Yet in Freud's case, that decade also saw the emergence of almost all the key figures who would later join forces with Jones to save Freud. In effect, they were taking up their advance positions for the roles they would play in that drama.

The newcomers who were about to step onstage included William Bullitt, an American journalist and diplomat; Marie Bonaparte, Napoleon's great-grandniece; and Max Schur, the Viennese doctor who would take charge of Freud's care for the last decade of his life. And then there was the emergence and blossoming of Freud's youngest child, Anna, who would soon occupy a central role in his personal and professional life.

By the summer of 1914, Anna—unlike her five older siblings—was still living with her parents and her aunt Minna at Berggasse 19 in Vienna. She was eighteen and preparing for a career as a teacher. After taking the teacher's examination in June, she embarked on a journey to visit the Freud relatives in Manchester, visiting England for the first time. In many ways, she was retracing the footsteps of her father when he made his first trip to England at age nineteen—and he was happy to see her doing so.

But Freud was also worried about Anna's journey. Although she sailed from Hamburg to England in mid-July, a period when tensions were rapidly escalating between Austria-Hungary and Serbia following the assassination of Archduke Franz Ferdinand, it wasn't the prospect of a war that worried her father. After all, he failed to recognize the signs that a major conflagration was about to erupt, with the possibility that she would be trapped on the opposing side. What really worried him was her possible vulnerability, as an innocent young woman, to the overtures of a man almost exactly twice her age who was eager to serve as her host: Ernest Jones.

When Anna arrived in Southampton, Jones greeted her with a large bouquet of flowers and served as her guide around England. As she wrote in a tribute to Jones in 1979, more than two decades after his death, he showed her the "beauties of England which he loved," took her on a "never forgotten trip in a boat going up the river Thames," and "took every opportunity" to correct and improve her English. Anna still vividly recalled how she was "flattered and impressed" by all the attention Jones lavished on her, "though not without a lurking suspicion that his interest was directed more to my father than to myself."

Her suspicions were heightened because she was forewarned that Jones, whose relationship with Loe Kann had ended earlier, might try to make her his new conquest. In fact, Kann, who had undergone treatment with Freud in Vienna, had kept up with London gossip and informed him of Jones's intentions. Freud's subsequent letter to Anna bristled with the predictable admonitions of a protective father:

"I know from the most reliable sources that Doctor Jones has serious intentions of wooing you. It is the first time in your young life, and I have no thought of granting you the freedom of choice your two sisters enjoyed. For it has so happened that you have lived more intimately with us than they, and I would like to believe that you would find it more difficult to make such a decision for life without our—in this case my—consent. Our wish is that you should not marry or become engaged while you are so young and inexperienced."

Freud wrote to Jones with a similar message, although couching it in expressions of gratitude "for your kindness with my little daughter." Pointing out that Jones did not know her well, he described her as the "most gifted and accomplished of my children" who was eager to learn about the world. He then bluntly declared: "She does not claim to be treated as a woman, being still far away from sexual longings and rather refusing man." In case there was any remaining doubt about the import of his words, Freud mentioned an "outspoken understanding between me and her" that she would not even consider marriage for at least two or three more years. "I don't think she will break the treaty," he declared.

If some women found Jones to be irresistible, that was hardly the case for Anna. It wasn't simply her father's warnings that punctured any hopes that Jones may have had for romance: the young visitor was always courteous and grateful for his company and help, but she never responded emotionally to him. Freud soon realized that he had no reason to worry about such a possibility. For his part, Jones assured Freud that he respected his concerns—although he couldn't resist inserting a barbed commentary: "She has a beautiful character and will surely be a remarkable woman later on, provided that her sexual repression does not injure her," he wrote. "She is of course tremendously bound to you, and it is one of those rare cases where the actual father corresponds to the father-imago."

While Anna never harbored any romantic notions about Jones, he wrote to her much later, in 1953, to correct the record about his feelings. According to Jones, her father had been convinced that his interest in her that summer was more practical than romantic, since he believed the Welshman just wanted a quick replacement for his former partner Loe Kann. "He seems to have forgotten the existence of the sexual instinct, for I had found you (and still do) most attractive," he wrote. As someone who had settled into a long and apparently happy marriage, he hastened to add: "In any case, I have always loved you, and in quite an honest fashion."

When World War I started, Anna was still in England but eager to rejoin her parents in Vienna—as eager as they were to have her back. Jones wrote to Freud that, if needed, he could "certainly get her as far as the Austrian frontier, for there are several ways of doing this." Later, he conceded he had foolishly overestimated his capabilities. However, the Austrian ambassador in London took her under his wing, traveling with her back to Vienna via Gibraltar and Genoa, a circuitous journey that took ten days. On August 26, Freud wrote an exultant note to his son Martin about her return. "She is very well and behaved bravely," he reported.

While Jones had not accompanied Anna for any part of her journey, he had helped make some of the preliminary arrangements. In October, Freud declared to Jones in a letter: "I have not yet had the opportunity in these miserable times that impoverish us in ideal as in material goods, to thank you for the adroit and expedient way of sending my little daughter back to me, and for all the friendship behind it." Whatever tensions there were earlier between the two men about Jones's supposed designs on Anna had dissipated by that point.

———

As often happens with a youngest child, Anna especially delighted her father. After her birth on December 3, 1895, Freud wrote to Fliess, his chief correspondent at the time, to inform him of the new addition to the family. "She arrived today at 3:15 during my consulting hours, and seems to be a nice, complete little woman." From then on, he called her "Annerl," a diminutive that can be translated as "little Anna."

During her earliest years, Freud often mentioned her in his letters, revealing how much he enjoyed her rapidly blossoming personality. He called her "delightfully cheeky" and "positively beautified by naughtiness." In another letter, he wrote that Anna had recently complained that Mathilde, her oldest sister, had eaten all the apples. Her proposed solution: slit open Mathilde's belly. This was inspired by the fairy tale about the wolf who gobbles up six of seven little billy goats who were left alone by their mother; when the mother goat returns, she learns from the youngest of the lot, the billy goat who hid, what happened, and she saves the others by slitting open the wolf's belly. "She is turning into a charming child," Freud concluded. His mood was further lifted by the fact that Anna's arrival coincided with an uptick in demand for his services. "We like to think that the baby has brought a doubling of my practice," he wrote to Fliess.

While Anna shared many of her siblings' warm memories of mushroom hunting with her father and other family outings, she also vividly recalled times when she was left behind by the others—missing a circus, for example, because she had a cold. Or, on another occasion, when her five siblings went out on a boat without her "either because the boat was full or I was 'too little,'" she declared. But in that instance, Freud, who had observed their departure, made a special point of praising her for taking it well. "That made me so happy that nothing else mattered," she said.

Anna shared a bedroom with her sister Sophie, the fifth child, who was two years older than her, and the two girls competed for their parents' attention. By most accounts, their mother, Martha, who ran the household and commanded the children with stern authority, clearly favored Sophie. As Anna recalled, her sister was very sick at age seven or eight, suffering from a high temperature. "I want my mummy, no not your mummy, I want my mummy," she kept repeating in her delirium.

The fact that everyone, including her father, considered Sophie to be the most attractive of the sisters only heightened Anna's sense that she lived in her shadow, encouraging her tendency to daydream and create her own fantasy world. In school, she had few friends but regularly displayed her imagination and intellect. For an assignment where the students were supposed to describe where they lived, Anna wrote that her room had "three walls"; the fourth wall, she asserted, was Sophie.

Once the two girls were older, Freud urged them to be more understanding of each other, specifically encouraging Anna to be "generous" with Sophie. He pointed out that "love and hate are not very different." But Anna stepped up her battle for his love, writing daily to him whenever he was away. She also explicitly predicted that, since Mathilde, the oldest sister, was already married and Sophie would likely follow suit, she was the "one who is soon to be your only daughter." On the eve of Sophie's wedding in January 1913, Anna confessed that, although "it is not nice to say it," she was relieved that her sister would be starting a new life elsewhere, since that would end the quarrels between them. She liked and admired Sophie, she insisted, but the separation would be good for them.

Even after Sophie married the photographer Max Halberstadt, who would soon take the most famous portraits of his father-in-law, and moved to his hometown of Hamburg in 1913, she continued to be seen as the most glamorous of the Freud children. When Sophie gave birth a year later to Freud's first grandson, Ernst, at the beginning of World War I, the proud grandfather traveled to Hamburg to see him. Writing to Karl Abraham in Berlin, he exulted about the "charming little fellow, who manages to laugh so engagingly whenever one pays attention to him," adding that "he is a decent, civilized being, which is doubly valuable in these times of unleashed bestiality." Sophie gave birth to another son, Heinz, better known as Heinele, in late 1918.

Then tragedy struck—twice. Sophie, who was only twenty-six, died on January 25, 1920, a victim of the Spanish flu epidemic sweeping across the continent. In a letter to Ferenczi in Budapest, Freud tried to sound philosophical, but his despair was readily apparent. "The death, painful as it is, does not affect my attitude toward life," he wrote. "For years I was prepared for the loss of our sons; now it is our daughter; as a confirmed unbeliever I have no one to accuse and realize that there is no place where I could lodge a complaint."

Freud grew all the more attached to Heinele when he spent several months in Vienna at age four, charming all the members of his extended family who cared for him. Freud described him as the "wittiest child of that age" in a letter to Ferenczi. But the boy was also sickly, as the worried grandfather added, "skinny and frail, nothing but eyes, hair and bones." Despite all the efforts to save him, he died of miliary tuberculosis in June of that year. "I am taking this loss so badly, I believe that I have never experienced anything harder," Freud admitted. Coupled with the loss of Sophie, this meant that "everything had lost its value."

Anna also was shaken and depressed by the loss of her sister and nephew, yet those tragedies meant that she was bound more closely to Freud than ever. Mathilde, the other surviving sister, still lived with her husband in Vienna, but she had been the first one to move out of her parents' house. Martin had returned from the war and started his own family in Vienna, while the two other brothers moved to

Berlin. Oliver found work as a civil engineer. Ernst was a successful architect and interior designer, later incorporating psychoanalytic consulting rooms into houses for clients who were part of his father's movement.

Anna decided early that she would become a schoolteacher, despite the fact that she was often bored at school. At the same time, she was intensely interested in learning from her father. Perched on a small library ladder, she would listen to the discussions at the Wednesday evening meetings of the Vienna Psychoanalytic Society. When she was about fourteen, she was walking with Freud through an elegant part of town near the Prater, a large public park. "You see these houses with their lovely facades?" he asked. "Things are not necessarily so lovely behind the facades. And so it is with human beings too."

Like her father, she wanted to become proficient in foreign languages. She studied English and French at school, and made use of her vacations in Italy to learn basic Italian; later, she also joined Freud for private lessons with an English tutor. Eager to travel, she was disappointed when she was told that she was too young to accompany her father on his visit to the United States in 1909 for his lectures on psychoanalysis at Clark University. She was an avid reader of the novels of Karl May, the hugely popular German writer who invented adventure stories about the American Wild West. She was equally interested in Rudyard Kipling's tales of India.

After her return from England, Anna spent two years as a student teacher in a Vienna elementary school, and then continued as a regular teacher until 1920. A former pupil later described the impression she made. "One day we children were electrified: a young, slender woman, dark-haired and with interesting eyes, was introduced to us and immediately took over the direction of the class . . . She was such a marvelous and simple figure that I loved her deeply at that time."

And Anna appeared to love teaching. "In those days, of course, we were all more formal with one another, but I recall the fun we had, much fun," she told the famed American child psychiatrist and author Robert Coles decades later. "I had yet to study dreams, but I loved listening to the children tell of their dreams—what they wanted to be when they grew up, and how they wanted to live; their daydreams." She was fascinated when the children closed their eyes and described what images they were seeing. The five years she spent teaching were critically important to her development, she continued. "They offered me a chance to get to know normal children, before I started seeing children who were in trouble for one reason or another."

While teaching, she already began exploring the kinds of subjects that preoccupied her father. Thanks to him, she was able to accompany the young psychiatrists Heinz Hartmann and Paul Schilder on their rounds at the Psychiatric Clinic of the Vienna General Hospital. Those experiences were "highly instructive," she recalled. "We all listened spellbound to the revelations made by the patients, their dreams, delusions, fantastic systems, which the analytically knowledgeable among us fitted into a scheme."

Most significantly, her father became her analyst in 1918 and she would remain in analysis with him for three years. As Coles pointed out in his 1992 biography of Anna, "Such an arrangement—between a psychoanalyst parent and a child of whatever age—is now unthinkable." But he also pointed out that those were the earliest days of psychoanalysis, when many of the procedures and rules were still not set or understood. Nor were the requirements for fledgling psychoanalysts spelled out. They obtained most of their training from whoever was analyzing them. "We were trained by our personal analysts," Anna said. In her case, it was her father.

During her analysis, Anna wrote poetry, something that she often did as a child but not with the same revelatory intensity. A sample stanza:

Only when my mind was churned more deeply,
When I was struggling with wild, dark forces,
Did I, alone in my need, feel with fear
That each poet sings but his own sorrow.

Although Freud would caution others later about serving as psychoanalysts of their own children, he believed that his treatment of Anna had been successful. It certainly accelerated the intermingling of their personal and professional ties. Freud not only discussed his ideas and writings with her, he also brought her along on some of his working trips—notably, to The Hague for the International Psychoanalytical Congress in 1920. In 1922, she wrote a paper on "Beating Fantasies and Daydreams," delivering it as a lecture to the Vienna Psychanalytic Society; this met the requirement for her elevation from observer to full member of that Wednesday evening group. She also began seeing patients herself, launching her career as a child psychoanalyst.

Whatever regrets Anna may have felt about leaving her teaching job for psychoanalysis were overshadowed by her absorption in the movement her father had launched. "Back then in Vienna we were all so excited—full of energy," she recalled. "It was as if a whole new continent was being explored, and we were the explorers, and we now had a chance to change things—to come back from that continent, you could say, with what we had learned, and offer it to the world, to people who hadn't been there."

Freud was delighted to see his youngest child "blooming and in good spirits," as he informed Max Eitingon in Berlin. "I only wish she would soon find some reason to exchange her attachment to her old father for some more lasting one." Yet Freud was less than convincing on that score. In 1921, when Anna had departed on a trip to see Eitingon in Berlin and her sister Sophie's children in Hamburg, Freud admitted how conflicted his own feelings were about Anna's future. "If she really should go away, I should feel as deprived as I do now, and as I should do if I had to give up smoking!" he wrote. In other words, he was as addicted to Anna as he was to his cigars. And she was every bit as attached to him as he was to her.

―――

By early 1923, father and daughter were drawn even more closely together by another development: his deteriorating health. Freud had long worried about the strength of his heart, but the real problem was in his jaw, the direct result of those cigars he refused to give up. When he consulted Marcus Hajek, a physician he had known for a long time, about a growth he had detected on his right jaw and palate, Hajek blamed the growth on his smoking and told him to come to his clinic to have it removed. It would be a "very slight operation," Hajek told him, although coupling that bit of reassurance with the statement: "No one can expect to live forever." Freud may have suspected that he was not getting the full story, but, after some hesitation, reported to the clinic on April 20 without telling Martha or Anna.

Mother and daughter were caught by surprise when they received a message from the clinic asking them to bring a few necessities over since Freud would be spending the night there. According to Jones's biography of him, the regular rooms in the clinic were all filled at the time, which meant relegating Freud to an improvised bed in a tiny room that he had to share with another patient, whom he described as a dwarf. When Martha and Anna rushed over, they were confronted by the sight of Freud sitting on a kitchen chair in the outpatient department "with blood all over his clothes." As Jones laconically put it, "The operation had not gone as had been expected."

After Martha and Anna were sent home at lunchtime when visitors were not permitted, Freud once again started bleeding profusely. Unable to speak, he rang for help but the bell was not working. The dwarf ran for assistance and the bleeding was stanched. "Perhaps his action saved Freud's life," Jones concluded. Learning what happened, Anna insisted on spending the night at her father's bedside, watching over him as he struggled through the pain. The following day he was allowed to go home, but this was only the first of a long series of operations, thirty-three in all, that he would endure throughout the rest of his life. Hajek and Felix Deutsch, Freud's personal doctor at the time, learned that the excised growth was malignant, but they did not share that information with the patient or his family.

Freud was eager to believe that he was doing better than he really was, despite the fact that he had already been informed of the need for more surgery after the summer holidays. In a letter to Andreas-Salomé on May 10, he claimed the immediate post-operation prognosis was good, but added in a darker vein: "You realize that this means no more than a slight lessening of the suspense that is bound to hover over the years to come."

The suspense followed Freud and Anna to Rome, where the two escaped to seek a bit of relief. As Anna recalled, they threw coins in the Trevi Fountain, "hoping to return, which because of his impending operation, was a very uncertain matter." During that trip, she assumed two of the key roles that she would take on for the rest of her father's life—as his closest companion and, effectively, personal nurse. When he had another bleeding episode, she dealt with it very adeptly. Writing from the Italian capital to Andreas-Salomé, Freud declared: "I realize here for the first time what good company my little daughter is."

As a result of the subsequent operations on his jaw, he had to start wearing an always uncomfortable prosthesis, which was extremely tricky—and at times painful—to insert or take out. In the household, only Anna mastered the art of doing so, and she also regularly cleaned the device, which Freud referred to as the "Monster." Neither Martha nor Minna attempted to take on those difficult vital tasks.

Anna's increasingly prominent role in almost all aspects Freud's life triggered mixed feelings in both of the older women who shared the same quarters, and led to a reconfiguration of the relationships at home. Ever since Minna had moved in with her sister and brother-in-law in 1896, she had occupied a special place in Freud's life, which was apparent to anyone who spent any amount of time at Berggasse 19. Now Anna was encroaching into what had once been mostly her aunt's domain.

Paula Fichtl was a latecomer to that household when she was hired as a chambermaid in 1929; she was twenty-seven then, and she would remain as the Freuds' housekeeper, first in Vienna and later in London, until Anna's death in 1982. In interviews with German journalist Detlef Berthelsen, who promised not to publish anything she said as long as Anna was still alive, Fichtl offered insightful glimpses into the relationships among the three women in the Freud household.

The new chambermaid's first impressions of the arrangements at Berggasse 19 were that "all is so serious, so strict," and she worried that she would not fit in. She observed that Martha was a "very quiet woman, a real housewife" who kept close tabs on everything. By contrast, Minna spoke loudly, appeared resolute and "quite possessive"—presumably of Freud, with whom she talked at length about his work, books, and other intellectual matters. "There was no book that she had not read, even foreign ones," Paula declared. All of which was in contrast to Martha, who focused largely on the practical aspects of running their complex household, which also included her husband's and Anna's consulting rooms and offices, and she usually stayed out of any discussions about psychoanalysis.

Throughout their marriage, Martha and Sigmund shared two wooden beds that were pushed together to make a double bed. Nonetheless, Fichtl described their marriage as "quiet, peaceful, but not necessarily happy." The fact that she arrived when the couple was in their later years undoubtedly colored her perceptions; she of course had no direct knowledge of their early years when their mutual affection was much more evident. Nor was she privy to—or made any mention of—speculation that Minna and Freud may have been more than just intellectual companions during their earlier days as well.

Long after Freud's death, his former colleague turned embittered rival Carl Jung claimed that Minna had confided in him that she and her brother-in-law had been having an affair, and she felt guilty about it. But even Frank McLynn, who penned a major biography of Jung, concedes that the "idea of an affair between Freud and Minna Bernays strains credulity to snapping point, which is not to say that the story might not still be true."

Freud did travel with Minna, including to Italy and other destinations, on several occasions, and she would often accompany him on walks around Vienna. Martha regularly joined him on family vacations, but often skipped his other journeys. Nonetheless, most Freud biographers dismiss the notion that he had an affair with Minna at any point. Max Eastman, a prominent American leftist editor who visited Freud in 1926, insisted that anyone who believed that his revolutionary views about the human mind translated into a radical lifestyle was sorely mistaken. In his personal life, "Freud was a prude and a puritan, a fanatical monogamist, not sexy by nature, and so 'chaste' in speech and conduct that he 'would have been out of place in the usual club room,'" Eastman wrote.

Even if his behavior looked impeccable, Freud triggered jealousy at home. Fichtl was struck by the fact that both sisters responded to "Frau Professor Freud," the normal appellation for the wife of a professor. As the chambermaid pointedly noted, the "real Frau Professor" was not pleased by this conflating of their roles, although there is no indication Martha ever raised such subjects. Minna was much more likely to show her feelings. At one point, Fichtl complained to Anna that her aunt "is always so angry with me, as if I cannot do anything right." Anna told her not to worry, explaining that Minna was "jealous" because Freud always treated the young chambermaid so nicely.

Such feelings had been brewing for a long time. In December 1925, Anna had delivered a report to the Vienna Psychoanalytic Society on "Jealousy and the Desire for Masculinity." It is hardly a stretch to conclude that the subject was inspired in part by her domestic observations. As Anna became Freud's primary companion on his walks around Vienna and trips elsewhere, while also serving as his chief domestic intellectual interlocutor, Minna inevitably felt demoted. Freud still played tarok, his favorite card game, with her, and they still discussed books and ideas. But while Freud continued to show respect for her intelligence and judgment, the pecking order had changed.

Martha also could fall victim to the expanded competition for Freud's attention. When Anna learned that her father was planning a two-week stay at the Tegel sanatorium in Berlin in 1929, she already had a full calendar of patient appointments for that period, which left an opening for Martha. In a letter to Andreas-Salomé, with whom she had developed almost as close a friendship as her father had, Anna admitted: "At first Mama wanted to go in my place, but I did not want that at all." In other words, she was determined to guard her place next to her father—even from her mother. Anna rearranged her schedule to make it possible for her to join him on that trip, leaving Martha behind.

———

Aside from attracting a steady stream of children to her consulting room at Berggasse 19, Anna took on additional roles in the psychoanalytic movement. When some of Freud's acolytes launched a training institute in Vienna in 1924, Anna became its secretary. She was especially eager to offer psychoanalytic training to teachers of young children, which meant that she participated in almost all of the institute's main activities. In the wake of Freud's first operations, she acted as his envoy to the annual gatherings of International Psychoanalytical Association, and she took the official title of secretary there as well. At its congress in Bad Homburg, near Frankfurt, in 1925, she read her father's paper "Some Psychical Consequences of the Anatomical Distinction Between the Sexes."

Freud was delighted when Abraham wrote to him afterward: "The news that Miss Anna would read a paper of yours evoked spontaneous applause at the beginning of the Congress which I wish you could have heard for yourself. Her extremely clear way of speaking did full justice to its contents."

Such reactions left Freud feeling confident that he could entrust his daughter with more such missions, since he was increasingly reluctant or unable to travel. When he was awarded the Goethe Prize by the city of Frankfurt in 1930, he wrote to the organizers expressing his gratitude, while explaining that his health would not allow him to attend the celebration there and Anna would go instead. "The audience will lose nothing by my absence," he said. "My daughter is certainly more pleasant to the eye than I am." Afterward, he reported to Jones on how she had represented him there, concluding with the remark: "Her importance to me can hardly be increased."

In 1927, Anna assembled the lectures she delivered at the training institute for publication as her first book, *Introduction to the Technique of Child Analysis*. This proved to be one of the opening salvos in a long-running dispute with Melanie Klein, an older Viennese-born rival in the same field who was highly critical of Anna's techniques and theories. Klein argued that the Oedipus complex appeared in children at a younger age than Anna believed it did, and she dismissively treated Anna as a latecomer to child psychoanalysis. Anna, in turn, disparaged Klein's propensity to see every act of a young child in symbolic terms, arguing that "harmless explanations" were sometimes just as likely.

While Anna was still primarily known as Freud's daughter, she was already emerging as an authority in her own right. The fact that she was now the focal point for debates, as her father was in the broader field of psychoanalysis for all age groups, underscored just how fast her reputation was growing.

In late 1925, when she was still in the early stages of assuming her larger role, Anna sounded ambivalent about her accumulating responsibilities. In a letter to Andreas-Salomé, she wrote: "I feel like I carry a double load now, and it is especially so because I am required to do a man's tasks in the Vienna society, in its training program, in negotiations, in complicated situations, even in making money (for the moment)."

Her mentions of a "man's tasks" underscored her tacit acceptance of the social norms of her era, even if her own professional role amounted to a de facto refutation of them. While she professed herself pleased "to be acquiring a degree of independence in the eyes of other people (not before Papa)," she claimed that she would still prefer "to give and to serve than to acquire and to demand."

Those protestations underscored how much she wanted to continue to serve her father; as she saw it, all other considerations were secondary. She admitted to Eitingon that she sometimes felt jealous of the young women who came to her father for treatment. And she was decidedly uninterested in potential suitors. After one of them, Hans Lampl—who had attended school with her brother Martin, then studied medicine at the University of Vienna and attended Freud's lectures there—visited her in January 1924, she wrote to Andreas-Salomé that she could be friendly with him "but I am not suitable for marriage."

Marie Bonaparte, who began analysis with Freud in 1925, quickly concluded that Anna was a "vestal"—a virgin fixated on her father. As his daughter's analyst, Freud knew this already, and he alluded to his worries on that score to some of his correspondents. In a letter to Andreas-Salomé in late 1927, he praised Anna as "splendid and intellectually independent," but pointed out that she had "no sexual life." Once he was gone, he wondered, "What will she do without her father?"

For Anna, the main reward for all her dedication to her father was that, in the words of the housekeeper Paula Fichtl, she became the "legitimate crown princess." As Freud's cancer and successive operations frequently confined him for long periods to what he only half-jokingly called "house arrest," she played that role to perfection. If that included providing personal care that must have been trying on many an occasion, especially after the latest surgery, Anna had no qualms on that account. Everything she did kept her close to her father and his work. "One cannot ask for the raisins without the surrounding bun," she explained. "I understand that."

———

Despite her father's worries, Anna was not condemned to loneliness once he was gone. In 1925, a new person appeared with whom she maintained, as she put it, a long "precious relationship"—first in Vienna and then London. Since that person was a woman, marriage was not an option. Nonetheless, the two of them became, for all practical purposes, a couple. Freud and most others in their circle remained convinced that Anna had no sexual life, but the question has always lingered whether this relationship may have disproved that assumption.

Dorothy Burlingham was four years older than Anna, American, and, certainly by the standards of Vienna in the 1920s, tremendously wealthy. She was the granddaughter of Charles Tiffany, the renowned jeweler who founded Tiffany & Co., and the youngest child of his son Louis Comfort Tiffany, the equally renowned designer of a broad range of stained-glass creations.

Dorothy was estranged from her husband Robert Burlingham, a gifted surgeon who battled manic depression, eventually lost his private practice, and later committed suicide. All of which left her worried about her own mental health, as well as that of her four young children, especially her oldest son's. Learning about Anna's work with children and intrigued by the possibility of undergoing psychoanalysis herself, she decided to take them to Europe without even informing Robert at first. It was a break—not just with him but with her life in the United States—that would last a lifetime, although Robert did visit them in Europe. Despite her initial expectations that she would stay in Europe for no more than a year, she became a permanent expat. It was also a break that positioned Dorothy to play a supporting role for Anna and the rest of Freud's rescue squad in 1938.

After a brief stint in Geneva, Dorothy reached out to Anna, requesting that she take on Bob, her oldest son, who was suffering from a psychosomatic disorder, as a patient. When Anna agreed to do so, Dorothy and the children moved to Vienna. Anna also lined up Theodor Reik, Freud's colleague and friend, as an analyst for Dorothy. Reik devoted six hours a week to her. Soon, Anna found herself busy with the whole family, analyzing and helping with the education of the other children as well. As her friend Eva Rosenfeld put it, "Dorothy and her children came as strangers and Anna's mind and heart became their home."

Dorothy and Anna took long walks in the Vienna Woods and other places on the outskirts of the city, discussing the children and the other interests they had in common. Those outings, which sometimes included Sigmund Freud, were made easier by the fact that Dorothy owned a Model T Ford, a rare luxury at the time in the Austrian capital. Freud wryly observed that Anna was making good money treating "naughty American children." He described their mother—whom he later took over as a patient, replacing Reik as her analyst—as "quite congenial," while also diagnosing her condition as "hysterical or obsessive neurosis, with fear."

In 1927, Anna and Dorothy vacationed in Italy, the first of many trips they would take together. As Anna explained to her father, they had quickly developed the "most agreeable and most unalloyed comradeship." Dorothy also endeared herself to the older Freud in 1928 by presenting him with the gift of a chow, who quickly became his *grosser Liebling* (big darling), according to Fichtl. This was despite the fact that his wife, Martha, never shared his and Anna's delight in their pets. Anna already had a dog, an Alsatian named Wolf, who had joined the household about three years earlier.

Initially, however, Anna was far more conflicted emotionally about Dorothy than she let on to her father. Writing to Eitingon in Berlin about her sessions with the children, she confessed that she had "thoughts which go along with my work but do not have a proper place in it." By way of explanation, she added: "I think sometimes that I want not only to make them healthy but also, at the same time, to have them, or at least to have something of them, for myself." While claiming that she only wanted this "temporarily," she then declared: "Toward the mother of the children it is not very different with me." This was followed by an even more direct admission that she was "very much ashamed of all these things, especially in front of Papa, and therefore I tell him nothing about it."

According to Robert Coles, who knew Anna when she was much older, her "complex" relationship with Dorothy was hard to understand without the chance to talk with both women. "I don't think, however, that it takes a psychiatric wizard to figure out that Anna Freud found it much easier and more appealing to get close emotionally to women than to men," he wrote, "and that her initially professional relationship with Mrs. Burlingham and her children became familial in nature—in a way that today would be certain to raise eyebrows among admission committees at psychoanalytic institutes."

On the familial nature of their ties, Freud was in complete agreement, showing no signs of any reservations about it. "Our symbiosis with an American family (husbandless), whose children my daughter is bringing up analytically with a firm hand, is growing continually stronger," he wrote in a letter in January 1929. That symbiosis was further facilitated by the fact that Anna's "American friend," as she was widely known, moved around that time into an apartment in Berggasse 19, just two floors above the mezzanine level where the Freuds lived and worked in two adjacent apartments. Dorothy carried out extensive renovations, allowing her to live comfortably there with her children and maids. She also installed a direct phone line between her bedroom and Anna's bedroom downstairs.

Dorothy was still deeply troubled, even intermittently considering whether she should try to return to Robert in the United States. She was prone to "black moods while reliving childhood sorrows in analysis," her grandson and biographer Michael Burlingham wrote. Freud tried to bolster her self-confidence so that she could free herself of such thoughts. At the same time, Dorothy's and Anna's lives were woven increasingly tighter together. In 1930, they purchased a small farm less than an hour's drive from Berggasse, fixing up and furnishing the cottage called Hochroterd (High Red Earth), which was situated on the side of a hill. As Freud noted with approval, this served as a perfect spot for weekend getaways.

Dorothy's sessions with Freud were transformed into training analysis, which was the first step in her preparation for her career as a child psychoanalyst and educator, following in Anna's footsteps. The fact that Dorothy had to raise four children of her own meant that she came to psychoanalysis "the hard way," as Anna put it. But the challenges she faced as a mother meant that she never criticized "the mothers of her patients for complaining about or even breaking down under the inevitable strain." In 1932, Dorothy wrote a paper entitled "Child Analysis and the Mother," which set her up to become an associate member of the Vienna Psychoanalytic Society. Two years later, she began to treat patients.

The personal and professional lives of Anna and Dorothy now intersected everywhere. Dorothy had two older sisters who were twins, and, in a letter to Anna much later, she ruminated on the propensity of people who have such twin siblings to invent a twin, someone who "represents an ideal of himself, his super-ego." The two of them were in just such a relationship, an "ideal friendship," she concluded. Anna was only too happy to agree.

———

Starting in late 1926, Anna, Dorothy, and a friend named Eva Rosenfeld made plans to launch a small school where they could create the kind of ambience they felt was most conducive to fostering the analytic approach they favored. The idea was to enroll Dorothy's and Eva's children, along with other children who boarded with Eva, and a few from other families, some of whose parents were also analysts or foreigners who had come to Vienna for treatment. Many of the pupils were in analysis themselves—in most cases, with Anna.

Eva Rosenfeld offered the backyard of her home in Vienna's Hietzing district as the location for the new school, which opened in 1927. Dorothy funded the construction of the two-story Norwegian timber building, which was just large enough to accommodate the fifteen or so pupils who, on average, were enrolled there. Aside from continuing with her analysis of several of the children, Anna taught English, and part-time teachers were hired for such subjects as Latin and math. But the two key recruits for the school proved to be two young men who later became famous as child psychoanalysts in their own right.

Rosenfeld was responsible for bringing in Peter Blos, who served as the school's director and biology teacher. Rosenfeld had lived earlier in Karlsruhe, where Blos grew up. He, in turn, recruited a former schoolmate from the same German city, Erik Homburger, who later went by the name of Erik Erikson, to teach art (his specialty), history, and German literature. All the teachers were encouraged to explore a broad range of subjects with their pupils, and Erikson picked unusual ones for the time such as Native American and Viking culture, with relevant writing and drawing assignments. Dorothy's children, Rosenfeld noted, benefitted especially from the emphasis on art due to their "superior interest . . . in drawing, painting and all things visual," all of which was Erikson's domain. Soon, he also started analysis with Anna, which proved to be the first step in his career in that field.

According to Peter Heller, the son of a chocolate manufacturer who was one of the pupils and later wrote about the school and its methods: "Anna Freud impressed me right away as a beautiful and interesting grown-up, commanding respect . . . She was not one of those silly grown-ups, but natural in her ways, and one felt almost free in her presence without being encouraged or provoked to be naughty." Anna understood how the young boy could be attracted to her, but Heller also noted: "The impression of puritanical distance remains; as well as the suspicion that she who had insight into other people had little insight into their relationship to her, or was not quite capable of guiding such a relationship." She exuded a "spinsterish holiness," he added, and "was not really friendly to sexuality."

Many of her fellow members of the Vienna Psychoanalytic Society shared that impression. At one meeting, Eduard Hitschmann, who had joined the group in its early days and watched Anna take an increasingly prominent role later, took advantage of the absence of both father and daughter to draw the contrast between them. Pointing to Anna's empty chair, he quipped: "There Freud sat and taught us the *drives*, and now Anna sits there and teaches us the *defenses*."

While the three women who had founded the school—Anna, Dorothy, and Eva—were generally pleased with the work of Blos and Erikson at first, Anna came to the conclusion that they were too free-wheeling in their ways. "All they know is compulsion or liberation from compulsion," she complained to Eva in 1929. "And the latter results in chaos." Dorothy claimed that her children may not have been well served by the school either, since it failed to prepare them for the more rigid educational practices employed elsewhere. Heller detected, at least in retrospect, "a tinge of hostility to masculine ways and to men" inherent in such criticism.

The school closed in 1932, the same year that Eva moved to Berlin and some of the American families with children there had returned to the United States. The disagreements over Blos's and Erikson's methods may have contributed to that outcome, but the two of them considered the experiment to be largely a success. Anna had mixed feelings, but remained on good terms with Erikson, who continued to progress in his psychoanalytic training with her. At times, he was bothered by her habit of knitting during their sessions, but she disarmed him one day by handing him a blue knitted sweater for his first son. (Observing Anna's knitting and sewing, Freud liked to tease her: "If the day comes when there is no more psychoanalysis, you can be a seamstress in Tel Aviv.")

Erikson described this period in Vienna as one of "great hope and promise and experimentation . . . We were just beginning to learn how to *do* psychoanalysis." He always felt grateful to Anna and others in her father's circle "who took me in and opened a life's work for me." He felt that he was participating in something that was akin to the "Paulinian days of Christianity."

Erikson stayed on in Vienna long enough to take some courses at the university and to be elected to the Vienna Psychoanalytic Institute in 1933. That was also the year that Hitler came to power in Germany, prompting Erikson to move with his family to the United States. When he told Anna about their decision, "she was not pleased," he recalled, since this signaled a further loss for their tight-knit community. "It didn't take a political genius, though, to figure out what was going to happen in Austria, and the rest of Europe."

But Anna—and, most of all, her father—had no intention of following suit. As Erikson put it, Freud's age and illness made him want to believe that such a drastic step was not necessary. "He'd seen so much happen in his life—I guess he figured: Hitler, too, will pass," making it safe for him to stay on in Vienna. "And if he wouldn't think of leaving, she wouldn't either."

6.

"A MAN OF THE WORLD"

As William Bullitt explained to his longtime friend and fellow Philadelphian George Biddle, he first decided to seek help after he nearly fell off a horse. He was a highly experienced rider, yet his foot had slipped out of the stirrup, almost sending him flying. "Can you even imagine me falling off a horse?" he asked Biddle. "Then it dawned on me that I had wanted to fall off my horse. Frightening." After offering that bit of speculation about his subconscious motivation, he added: "Fortunately, I've read a great deal about psychoanalysis . . . And I knew, George, there was only one man for me to go to see: Freud."

According to Biddle, Bullitt also told him about his first meeting with Freud in 1925, when he showed up unannounced at Berggasse 19. Informed that Freud was not feeling well and not accepting new patients, he introduced himself and sent up his card. Freud had evidently heard him from upstairs and came down to greet him, explaining that he knew of him and would be happy to make an exception and take him on if he was interested in a longer-term association. In fact, this was the beginning of a relationship that would last until Freud's death—and would include Bullitt playing a critical role as one of his rescuers.

The two men—the already renowned psychiatrist and the soon-to-be high-ranking American diplomat—were brought together not just by psychoanalysis but also by their shared hatred of President Woodrow Wilson and the Treaty of Versailles. In Bullitt's case, this was a product of his thwarted youthful ambition to play a major role in shaping the peace; in Freud's case, it was the result of his conviction that the American president, due to his arrogance and ignorance, had lost control of a process that disregarded his earlier lofty rhetoric about a just postwar order, allowing the vengeful victors to unduly punish the losers, especially Austria.

Bullitt was one of only three people granted the privilege of addressing Freud just by his surname, dispensing with the usual "Herr Doktor" or "Herr Professor" titles before it. (The other two were the British writer H. G. Wells and the French cabaret singer and actress Yvette Guilbert, a family friend.) The bond between them proved remarkably strong, even though Bullitt was thirty-five years younger than Freud. As happened with the other members of the future rescue squad, those bonds would be put to the ultimate stress test in 1938.

———

Bullitt is mostly remembered today for his diplomatic roles in the 1930s. When President Franklin D. Roosevelt formally recognized the Soviet Union in 1933, he appointed Bullitt as his first ambassador in Moscow. His next assignment, as ambassador to France, coincided with Hitler's early conquests, including the Anschluss, the incorporation of Austria into the Third Reich—the event that put Freud in immediate danger. In both postings, Bullitt found himself at the center of the upheavals triggered by the rise of two totalitarian powers.

Bullitt seemed ideally suited for the challenges of those jobs. As

George Kennan, who worked under him as a young embassy staffer in Moscow before achieving even greater prominence as a diplomat and historian, wrote, Bullitt "was charming, brilliant, well-educated, imaginative, a man of the world capable of holding his own intellectually with anyone."

Kennan saw Bullitt "as a member of that remarkable group of young Americans . . . for whom the First World War was the great electrifying experience of life. They were a striking generation, full of talent and exuberance." Its ranks included, among others, literary stars Ernest Hemingway and F. Scott Fitzgerald, composer and songwriter Cole Porter, and the American Communist propagandist John Reed, all of whom crossed paths with Bullitt.

In retrospect, however, Kennan also detected other, less appealing qualities in the boss he admired, concluding that "he bore within himself, I always thought, the seeds of his own misfortune." At one of his first meetings with Bullitt on their way to Moscow to open the new embassy there, Kennan gained an "impression of quick sensitivity, of great egocentricity and pride, and of a certain dangerous freedom—the freedom of a man, who as he himself confessed to me on that occasion, had never subordinated his life to the needs of any other human being."

Putting it in today's terms, Bullitt grew up enveloped in all the trappings of privilege—with the kind of natural sense of entitlement that was inculcated from birth in the upper classes of that era. Born in 1891, he was raised by parents who were pillars of Old Philadelphia, the historic center of the city that was home to wealthy families like his whose roots extended back before the American Revolution.

On his father's side, he was a descendent of Joseph Boulet, a French Huguenot who arrived in Maryland in 1637 and changed his name to Bullitt. His progeny and relatives by marriage included some of the most famous families in American history. When Bullitt unsuccessfully ran for mayor of Philadelphia in 1943, *Time* magazine wrote: "His family tree is ornamented by the father of George Washington, the sister of Patrick Henry, Pocahontas herself." His father, William Christian Bullitt Senior, was a lawyer who made his fortune in railroads and coal, managing the lucrative deliveries of Pennsylvania coal to the United States and other navies along with transatlantic shipping companies.

His mother, Louisa Gross Horwitz, was a descendant of European Jews who converted in the New World. Joseph Horwitz, the first of them to cross the Atlantic, arrived in about 1710, joined the Episcopal Church, and became a doctor. Other ancestors distinguished themselves as medical practitioners, professors, and writers. Louisa made sure her two sons received the proper upbringing, speaking French with William and his brother and encouraging him to master German as well. She took William along on her summer excursions to Europe, which included visits to his grandmother in Paris and an aunt in Rome, and familiarized him with European history from an early age.

Bullitt's ambitions were in evidence early. "I'm going to be a lawyer and Governor and Secretary of State and President," he declared. He would fall short of those goals, but in so many other ways he was a high-flyer. At De Lancey, a private school in Philadelphia, he impressed his classmates with his seemingly endless energy. "Bill Bullitt has the time to study, play, go out for baseball, and write romantic verses," the school magazine noted. "How does he do it?" He also was not easily cowed. When a teacher accused him of cheating in his German class, Bullitt called him a "damned liar"—and his father's subsequent protest to the school led to the teacher's dismissal.

At Yale, where he enrolled in 1908, Bullitt did not push himself to take the most difficult courses, preferring to glide through beginning and intermediate German classes, while also gliding through his English classes, offering regular displays of his wit and sophistication. But he was no slacker. He was captain of the debating team; a member of the editorial board of the *News*; a founder, along with Cole Porter who was a year ahead of him, of the satirical Mince Pie Club; and the president of the Yale Dramatic Association. All of which prompted his peers to vote him the most brilliant member of their class.

Bullitt's often-dazzling public persona on campus did not prevent him from suffering some kind of collapse at the end of his junior year, marked by acute intestinal pain and problems with his hearing and eyesight. At the University of Pennsylvania Hospital in Philadelphia, the doctors who examined him were perplexed by his symptoms yet alarmed enough to conclude that he might not survive more than a few months. Taking a year off from Yale, he spent time in California and Europe, underwent an appendectomy back in Philadelphia, and, disregarding instructions to stick with a bland diet of spinach and milk, opted for lobster and champagne instead. Feeling better, he returned to graduate from Yale with honors in 1913.

Bullitt took a psychology class at Yale taught by Roswell Angier, who had joined the faculty in 1906. Before then, Angier had studied in Freiburg and Berlin, working as an assistant in the physiology laboratory of the University of Berlin. Based on his experiences there, he introduced his students to the ideas of Freudian psychoanalysis. Bullitt was so intrigued that he briefly considered making psychology his primary field of study and work. It's unclear whether he was already trying to figure out whether his own somewhat mysterious ailments were partly psychosomatic, but this amounted to the first step in his journey that would lead him later to Freud in Vienna.

Bullitt enrolled at Harvard Law School to make good on his childhood prediction to become a lawyer. But he was restless there, experienced more digestive problems, and was often enraged by the way some of the professors ridiculed first-year students like him to test their intellectual mettle. After his father died in March 1914, Bullitt dropped out and set his sights on a new career path, one that would lead him to journalism and diplomacy.

———

Bullitt helped his mother rebound from the loss of her husband by accompanying her on a trip to Russia and Germany in the fateful summer of 1914. When Austria-Hungary declared war on Serbia on July 28, which signaled the start of World War I, they were in Moscow. From the National Hotel where they were staying, they heard a crowd shouting and singing "God Save the Tsar," the imperial anthem. The momentous nature of those events excited the young American visitor. "I was naïve enough to make up my mind . . . that I was going to stop the war," Bullitt later recalled.

While they realized it was time to get out of Russia, Bullitt and his mother were in no rush to leave Europe. From their room in Berlin's Adlon Hotel, they watched German troops marching on the day war was declared. Moving on to London, Bullitt, who had the foresight to come to Europe armed with a letter from *The New York Times* expressing interest in his reports, tried but failed to obtain accreditation as a war correspondent. He also dashed over to Paris to recover the family jewels of his grandmother, who had recently died.

Upon Bullitt's return to Philadelphia, his family connections helped him land an entry level reporting job at *The Public Ledger*, the city's top newspaper. He wrote lively stories about everything from murders and gambling raids to the suicide of a young man who could not afford the pair of dress shoes that he needed to accompany his girlfriend to the Easter promenade. He also started writing about the war for the editorial page, which earned him quick promotions.

In late 1915, Bullitt was the only representative of a Philadelphia newspaper to be invited to cover a quixotic peace mission to Europe organized by the automobile magnate Henry Ford. Although Bullitt had recently harbored his own grandiose visions of peacemaking, his syndicated reports from the *Oscar II*, a Swedish ship chartered by

Ford, were filled with acerbic descriptions that delighted the readers of his nationally syndicated pieces. "The *Oscar* pitched amazingly, and when the pilgrims who are to stop the war assembled for afternoon service . . . they did not look capable of stopping anything larger than a battle between pet Pomeranians," he wrote.

While expressing genuine admiration of Ford's good intentions, even comparing him to Christ, he also mercilessly mocked him and his followers for believing that they could "bring the boys out of the trenches" with fuzzy declarations, no concrete proposals, and no knowledge of European history. "Mr. Ford was the tenderest of the tender and the vaguest of the vague; a charming child," he wrote. The Ford expedition proved to be a fiasco, but it was a godsend for Bullitt, who had transformed himself into the *Public Ledger*'s star writer.

Bullitt's personal life also looked increasingly promising. In March 1916, he married Ernesta Drinker, seemingly the perfect match for him. Her family had deep Quaker roots in William Penn's colony, and her father was the president of Lehigh University. Although she never finished college, she studied at the Sorbonne and Radcliffe, and her striking beauty attracted a stream of suitors. According to her younger sister Catherine, she turned down fifty marriage proposals before she stopped counting. "Whichever way my sister turned her head on that long neck there was enchantment," Catherine wrote. "I have seen men catch their breath, looking at Ernesta."

The new bride was captivated by Bullitt's energy and eagerness for adventure. Their honeymoon consisted of a trip to Germany and Austria-Hungary, which doubled as an opportunity for Bullitt to report on the war from the perspective of the Central Powers. The United States had not yet entered the war, and he was determined to put his German language skills and contacts to good use. Ernesta also planned on reporting, keeping a travel diary that was later published, and she looked into the role of women in the wartime workforce, despite the initial efforts by her German hosts to occupy her with shopping.

Ernesta's diary entries provided not only a valuable record of their trip but also proof that she was a lively writer with a wry sense of humor. Before the United States entered the war in 1917, many Americans were not convinced that either side had a monopoly on virtue—and blame for the initiation of the conflict was far from a simple matter. Bullitt felt considerable sympathy for the Germans, which was something else he had in common with Freud even before they met. The couple arrived "laden with the milk of human kindness," Ernesta wrote on May 14, 1916. "We—particularly Billy—were ready to understand Germany. Billy said he could see their point of view perfectly."

But Billy, as Ernesta called him, quickly lost "some of his broad-mindedness." A military inspector on the train ignored the letters Bullitt had brought along from a German diplomat vouching for them and rifled through everything in their luggage. He confiscated books, writing paper, calling cards—and even pencils. "Billy bore those losses with fortitude, but when his eleven tubes of hair tonic were placed among the other things, his manhood was undone," she recorded, chiding her husband for his vanity about his wavy brown hair, much of which he would lose at a relatively early age.

More seriously, she noted that Bullitt was developing an increasingly critical view of his hosts and their conduct in the war. "Billy says the Germans are the most moral people in the world when it comes to dealing with Germans, and the most immoral in their dealings with the rest of the world," she wrote. Nonetheless, he was enjoying the trip immensely, interviewing top officials and industrialists, and even talking the German military into allowing him to visit the Eastern front, a trip that he called a great success. "He went up in an aeroplane over the Russian lines and got shot at and had all sorts of a good time," Ernesta noted.

To get the perspective of Germany's Austro-Hungarian partners, Bullitt visited Vienna and Budapest. While he did not meet Freud then, he was soaking up everything he could about the world he inhabited. Bullitt's contemporary Walter Lippmann, an editor at *The New Republic* who later became a famed columnist, hailed him as the "sharpest of the American correspondents."

Bullitt's bosses at *The Public Ledger* certainly noticed: in November 1916, they tapped him to head their Washington bureau. The big story then was the increasingly likely prospect that the United States would enter the war, and he was well prepared to handle it. As 1917 dawned, everything appeared to be going his way—that is, until March 21, when Ernesta gave birth to a boy who did not survive. Two days later, Bullitt wrote to Lippmann, with whom he had become friendly, that the loss of their son "wrecked her emotionally." Avoiding any commentary about his own mental state, he reported: "I buried him today."

———

Even before Bullitt moved to Washington, he demonstrated his eagerness to be more than an observer of politics and foreign affairs: he wanted to be a player, someone who was involved directly in policy decisions. Upon his return from his trip to Germany and Austria-Hungary, he wrote to Frank L. Polk, a top official at the State Department, on October 20, 1916: "I have a lot of information I cannot publish . . . which might interest you." As that note indicates, he was not just willing but also eager to share his off-the-record information from his travels in Europe with the Wilson Administration.

Almost as soon as he settled in Washington, he established a close relationship with Edward M. House, Wilson's closest advisor, whom he interviewed in February 1917. Colonel House, as the Texan was known although he had never served in the military, was impressed by Bullitt's articles on European affairs and was only too happy to receive his reports, particularly on internal German politics. In one of them, Bullitt predicted that the failure of Germany's latest offensive would allow German liberals to take power later and they would be willing to chart a new course "if they can be convinced of the bona fides of American liberalism." He was already operating on the assumption that the United States would be entering the war soon and then would help shape the peace terms.

In early April, when the United States entered the war, Bullitt briefly met Wilson. He took the opportunity to praise the president lavishly for his speech to a joint session of Congress. "You've made yourself the leader of everyone in the world who wants real peace," Bullitt told him. His enthusiasm was genuine, an indication of his belief at the time that Wilson was truly America's gift to the world—something that would make his subsequent disillusionment all the more intense.

Only twenty-six then, Bullitt was still of draft age but, as he wrote to House on July 5, "The unhappy results of an appendicitis operation make it impossible for me to do military service." The purpose of his letter was to convince House to line up a job for him as a presidential assistant. That did not come through, but House arranged for him to be appointed an assistant secretary of state in December. His transition from journalism to diplomacy was now complete.

Bullitt immediately turned much of his attention to Russia, the country he had first visited with his mother. Led by Vladimir Lenin, the Bolsheviks had seized power in November 1917, vowing to make good on their promise to end Russian participation in the war. On March 3, 1918, they signed the Treaty of Brest-Litovsk, a separate peace with the Central Powers, which not only dictated the dismemberment of the Russian empire but also outraged the Western powers who were still fighting. The question for the Wilson Administration was how they should assess—and what they should do about—the Bolsheviks and the civil war that their revolution had sparked all across Russia.

Wilson made his famous speech to Congress on January 8, 1918, spelling out the Fourteen Points that he envisaged as the basis for a peace treaty once the war ended. The sixth point included the "evacuation of all Russian territory and such a settlement of all questions affecting Russia as will secure the best and freest cooperation of the other nations of the world." While the thirteenth point called for the creation of an independent Poland, which meant that Moscow would not retain control of all of its former empire, Wilson cautioned the allies that their treatment of Russia "will be the acid test of their good will."

Despite such conciliatory language, Washington was deeply divided when it came to Russia. In November 1917, Secretary of State Robert Lansing wrote a memorandum spelling out his dark view of developments there. "The Russian 'Terror' will far surpass in brutality and destruction of life and property the Terror of the French Revolution," he wrote. Calling the country a "seething caldron of anarchy and violence," he concluded: "I can conceive of no more frightful calamity for a people than that which seems to be about to fall upon Russia."

Lansing's sense of foreboding would prove to be fully justified, but many Americans, especially young leftists, saw things differently. They hailed the revolutionaries as heroes who would liberate Russia, and later all humanity, from capitalist oppression. The most prominent proponent of that view was John Reed, a journalist for the left-wing publication *The Masses*, who had reported on American labor unrest, the Mexican Revolution, and the war in Europe. Along with his wife and fellow leftist writer, Louise Bryant, he set out to cover the Russian Revolution, sending back enthusiastic reports that were the basis for his enormously popular book *Ten Days That Shook the World*. He became an active participant in the events he covered, hobnobbing with Lenin, Leon Trotsky, and other Bolshevik leaders while working directly for them.

Bullitt avidly followed Reed's adventures, and he shared his conviction that the United States would make a huge mistake by siding against the Bolsheviks in the civil war. Writing to House on February 3, 1918, he urged the recognition of the new Bolshevik regime and later passed on a memorandum on the Russian situation that he had solicited from Reed.

But Bullitt realized that Reed could be accused of sedition because of his support for communism and fervent opposition to American participation in the war. As a result, he sought to put some distance between himself and Reed. "I wish I could see Russia with as simple an eye as Reed," he said, pointing out that the "welter of conflicting reports" about the Bolsheviks prevented him from reaching clear-cut conclusions about the nature of the new rulers. Bullitt proposed the designation of a task force composed of "men of deep wisdom and liberality" to sort out those issues.

———

Since the fall of 1917, a group of 150 scholars had been participating in an effort known as the Inquiry, gathering information and writing confidential reports in preparation for the peace negotiations after the war. On December 4, 1918, President Wilson sailed for France on the USS *George Washington*, with twenty-three members of the Inquiry among his party of 113 people, along with White House aides and negotiators. As a twenty-seven-year-old staffer of the American Commission to Negotiate Peace, Bullitt could have been expected to work quietly in the background during the voyage—but that was hardly the case.

Four days into the Atlantic crossing, he took advantage of the fact that he was seated next to Wilson in the ship's theater before the screening of a film. Never bashful, he appealed to the president to gather his delegation and "explain to them the spirit in which he was approaching the conference and so far as possible the policies he intended to pursue." He pointed out that there was widespread skepticism and ignorance "concerning his intentions," which could have a "fatal effect" on their performance at the peace talks in Paris, particularly in dealing with the British and French. In short, they needed clarity about their mission.

Although Bullitt recalled that Wilson was surprised to hear this blunt assessment from him, the president responded remarkably well. The following day, Wilson summoned the commission staffers and briefed them in detail. He explained why he felt that "if this peace is not made on the highest principles of justice, it will be swept away by the peoples of the world in less than a generation," and argued that Germany should not be shackled by "open-ended bills for the cost of the whole war." He also elaborated on his vision for a League of Nations whose primary goal would be to prevent future conflicts. The key question that Wilson wanted the Americans to keep asking themselves about every proposed solution, he insisted, was, "Is it just?"

For Bullitt, this was a deeply satisfying moment. Wilson had not only thanked him for his suggestion but acted on it—and then performed beautifully for the most part. "I have never seen the President in a franker and more engaging mood," he recalled. "He was overflowing with warmth and good nature."

On February 18, 1919, Secretary of State Lansing dispatched Bullitt to Russia "for the benefit of the American Commissioners plenipotentiary to negotiate peace." After consultations with Prime Minister David Lloyd George's secretary, Bullitt was convinced that he had the backing of both Washington and London to broker a deal with the Bolsheviks. In Moscow, he met with Lenin, who appeared to accept most of the terms Lloyd George had insisted on, provided that the Western powers quickly finalized them. The ebullient young American emissary expected to be hailed for engineering a major diplomatic breakthrough.

———

As soon as Bullitt returned to Paris on March 25, he discovered otherwise. Word began to leak out about his negotiations, and *The Times* of London denounced the "idea of a shameful deal with the Bolshevists." In Parliament, Lloyd George claimed ignorance of the Bullitt mission. Despite Bullitt's urgent entreaties, Wilson never agreed to see him, and soon fell ill.

Bullitt was suddenly disowned, nearly toxic. The fact that he had gone to Russia with the backing of both the U.S. and British governments was conveniently ignored. Reacting to Lloyd George's refusal to acknowledge that he was fully informed of his mission, Bullitt declared: "It was a most egregious case of misleading the public, perhaps the boldest that I have ever known." But Bullitt's greatest sense of disappointment was with Wilson. His initial admiration of the American president gave way to a sense of personal betrayal. Lenin's deadline for the acceptance of the peace terms with his government came and went without any action.

Aside from the failure of his Russia mission, Bullitt was dismayed by the draft peace terms that would soon become the Treaty of Versailles. The punitive measures against Germany and the way that the Austro-Hungarian Empire was to be carved up, he warned, were a recipe for continuing conflict. "This isn't a treaty of peace, I can see at least eleven wars in it," he declared.

On May 17, he resigned from the American delegation, seemingly ending his meteoric diplomatic career. In a letter to Wilson, he declared that he "was one of the millions who trusted confidently and implicitly in your leadership" to accomplish a "permanent peace." Instead, "our Government has consented now to deliver the suffering peoples of the world to new oppression, subjugation, and dismemberments—a new century of war." And Russia "has not even been understood."

Bullitt's disillusionment was so complete that he vowed to oppose ratification of the treaty by the United States or its participation in the League of Nations, Wilson's pet project that was supposed to offset all the failures of the peace process. Called to testify before the U.S. Senate Committee on Foreign Relations on September 12, 1919, Bullitt wounded Wilson's case by revealing that even Secretary of State Lansing considered "many parts of the treaty thoroughly bad," including the plans for the League. Wilson was infuriated by his testimony.

The entire episode would also explain why Bullitt would later seize the opportunity to team up with Freud to produce a fervent indictment of Wilson's performance.

———

It wasn't Bullitt's politics that led him to Freud in the first place but personal problems. Returning from Paris, he moved to New York where he took a job with the Paramount-Famous-Lasky Corporation, which would later change its name to Paramount Pictures, editing scripts for silent films. His marriage to Ernesta Drinker fell apart in 1921, although their divorce did not come through until 1923. The fact that they had lost a child was certainly a factor, but there were other sexual sources of tension.

Bullitt published a novel, *It's Not Done*, in 1926, where the main character is John Corsey, his unmistakable alter ego who is a newspaper editor in a town resembling Philadelphia. Corsey marries a beautiful society woman, much like Ernesta, who insists on separate bedrooms and keeps him out of her bed as much as possible. "Only peasants sleep in the same bed," she insists. Listening to his woes, his doctor, who is also his closest friend, can't understand why he doesn't leave her. "I hate frigid, virtuous females like hell," the doctor tells him. "A lot more men are killed by their wives' virtues than by their wives' adulteries."

Corsey claims he still loves his wife, but he is torn between her and an earlier flame, a sensuous French sculptress who is shockingly liberated by the standards of the times. The doctor offers his impromptu analysis with its heavily Freudian overtones. "You'll never let yourself feel right about anything short of marriage with a girl your mother approves of," he says. "And you'll want her to be a virgin nymphomaniac. Unfortunately they don't exist."

The inspiration for the French sculptress character was Louise Bryant, the widow of John Reed; he had died in Moscow in 1920, apparently of influenza or typhus. In 1921, Bryant pitched Reed's book *Ten Days That Shook the World* to Bullitt, hoping Paramount would take it on. That did not happen, but he took an immediate interest in the woman who had shared so many experiences with Reed and written her own book, *Six Red Months in Russia*.

Bullitt's near hero worship of Reed may have been one reason he was drawn to Bryant; another was the fact that she represented such a sharp contrast to Ernesta. Twice married already, she was known for her radical politics and lifestyle, including an unconcealed affair with the playwright Eugene O'Neill. Reed's death made her even more inclined to let loose. "The only way to endure is to become utterly reckless and live each day as if no dawn would come," she wrote to a friend, the painter Andrew Dasburg. Since Bullitt's marriage was in tatters, he understood that sentiment.

By then, Bryant was a successful reporter for the Hearst chain of publications, continuing to write about the Bolsheviks and traveling around Europe for other stories. According to Mary Dearborn, one of Bryant's biographers, Bullitt "followed her around Europe like a puppy" while waiting to finalize his divorce. When she started working for the International News Service in Constantinople, he rented a historic villa on the Bosporus for them.

Bullitt was intent on marrying Bryant. She put him off at first, but when she became pregnant in 1923, she agreed and gave up her International News Service job. They were married on December 5, and their daughter, Anne, was born on February 24, 1924. Bullitt, who had suffered the loss of a child with Ernesta, was delighted. So was Bryant, who a friend described as enthralled by the "ecstasy of motherhood."

Bryant had led Bullitt to believe that she was only twenty-nine when they married; in reality, she was thirty-eight, six years older than him and conscious that this might be her final chance to experience that "ecstasy." Many of her friends assumed that, despite her radical politics, she also welcomed the chance to be pampered by her wealthy new husband. For a while, they settled in Paris, the home to so many American expats, including Hemingway and Fitzgerald. Bullitt played tennis and went to the racetrack with Hemingway, who nonetheless mentioned him in a letter to Fitzgerald as a "big Jew from Yale and fellow novel writer"—harking back to Bullitt's distant Jewish roots on his mother's side and ignoring his Episcopalian upbringing.

Bullitt did achieve momentary fame with *It's Not Done* shortly after Fitzgerald's *The Great Gatsby* hit the market; he dedicated it to Louise, who had encouraged him to complete it. Initially, Bullitt's sales—which totaled 150,000 in several printings—eclipsed Fitzgerald's, whose first printing was 20,000 copies. Bullitt's book was a deliberate affront to the pretenses of American high society, ridiculing them while titillating its readers. ("Lord, what a night!" the French sculptress declares to her lover on a torpid evening. "Nasty as a hot body you've been too long in bed with.")

Bullitt's second marriage soon ended. Bryant left no doubt that John Reed had been the biggest love of her life—and that her current life, with the comforts provided by Bullitt's wealth, felt like a letdown after all her previous adventures. Among the expats in Paris, alcohol flowed freely, and soon she was drinking much more than just socially. Charmion von Wiegand, an American painter who was the daughter of another famous Hearst correspondent, recalled visiting the Bullitt home in Paris and hearing Bryant say: "I live a useless life."

In 1925 when Bullitt first met Freud, he was seeking help for his marriage—and for his deepening despair, which by some accounts included suicidal thoughts. Kitty Cannell, a friend of Louise, claimed that he had problems with impotence. "Anyone who read his novel would know that—the burden of it is that his first wife made him impotent."

Perhaps, but about this same time he had an affair with Eleanor "Cissy" Patterson, the granddaughter of the owner of the *Chicago Tribune* who would become a major publisher and editor in her own right. Writing to a friend, she somewhat sheepishly called herself an "old fool" for falling in love with Bullitt on the Riviera, despite the fact that she was ten years older than he was. But she defiantly declared: "I didn't suppose this world held anyone as fascinating—just for *me*—as that man."

By 1928, when their marriage was near the breaking point, Louise took up with Gwen Le Gallienne, an English sculptress. In the proceedings that led to their divorce in 1930, Bullitt cited this lesbian affair, along with Louise's heavy drinking, as reasons for the breakup— and he was awarded sole custody of their daughter, Anne. Louise was also suffering from Dercum's disease, a rare disorder that produces numerous painful growths of fatty tissue known as lipomas; she died at age fifty in 1936.

Bullitt often claimed that his original motivation for meeting Freud was to get help for Louise—and he did try to talk her into agreeing to treatment, without success. She occasionally accompanied him to Vienna, but Freud treated him, not her, despite Bullitt's obfuscation on which of them was the patient. According to the writer Vincent Sheean, another friend of Louise, she returned to Vienna's Imperial Hotel one evening to find that Bullitt had stacked up all the furniture in their room at the door, trying to block her from entering. "An embarrassing scene, among many," Sheehan noted. There were several other times, Louise maintained, that she could see that he was "really ill and in despair."

Freud was able to help Bullitt regain his emotional footing, but he could not save his marriage.

———

On May 4, 1930, Freud traveled to Berlin for a new prosthesis. Bullitt visited him there and was struck by how depressed he felt. "Somberly he said that he had not long to live and that his death would be unimportant to him or to anyone else, because he had written everything he wished to write and his mind was emptied," the American reported.

Freud asked Bullitt what he was working on, and he replied that his current project was a book on the Treaty of Versailles, which would contain "studies of Clemenceau, Orlando, Lloyd George, Lenin and Woodrow Wilson—all of whom I happened to know personally." To his astonishment, "Freud's eyes brightened," as he recalled, and he declared that he would like to collaborate with him in writing the chapter about Wilson.

Bullitt was initially amused by the suggestion, considering it "delightful but bizarre." He had envisaged a book aimed at an audience of foreign policy experts. If Freud would write about Wilson, he believed, the potential audience would be huge. "Every educated man would wish to read it," Bullitt concluded. And it would be a colossal mistake to "bury Freud on Wilson in a chapter of my book" since "the part would be greater than the whole." In short, such a book would need to focus entirely on Wilson—that is, if Freud was serious about his offer.

Freud assured Bullitt that he was completely serious. He pointed out that he had been interested in the American president ever since he learned that Wilson was born in 1856, the same year he was. Freud rarely ignored such seeming coincidences. Moreover, he liked the idea of writing a study of a contemporary public figure, whose life and work could be examined closely. Bullitt could gather up the records and the testimonies of people who had worked with Wilson, which he would share with Freud, who would provide much of the analysis. That would allow them to produce a psychoanalytic biography.

Nearly a decade earlier, Freud had refused to comment on a book about Wilson by one of the president's embittered former publicists, insisting that "psychoanalysis should never be used as a weapon in literary and political polemics." He pointed out that his own "deep-going antipathy" toward Wilson was all the more reason to avoid indulging in such an exercise. When he and Bullitt cooked up the idea of producing their own book, he cast all such reservations aside.

In 1919, John Maynard Keynes, a British delegate to the Paris Peace Conference, had written a short book, *The Economic Consequences of the Peace*, that echoed Bullitt's accusations that Wilson had abandoned his principles by agreeing to the harsh terms of the Treaty of Versailles. In that study, the famed economist also practically invited Freud to analyze Wilson's performance, suggesting that any conventional political analysis would prove to be inadequate. "In the language of medical psychology, to suggest to the President that the Treaty was an abandonment of his professions was to touch on the raw a Freudian complex," Keynes wrote. "It was a subject intolerable to discuss, and every subconscious instinct plotted to defeat its further exploration."

The project proceeded fitfully, although Bullitt worked with his usual energy collecting documents and testimonies that he shared with Freud. By 1932, they had a full manuscript. But at that point Freud added wording that Bullitt disagreed with, including his theories on such subjects as Christianity's views of bisexuality, and their work stalled. In the meantime, Bullitt returned to politics and diplomacy, culminating in his appointment as U.S. ambassador to Moscow.

Only years later would Bullitt and Freud work on resolving their differences, but then again put off publishing their book because of its highly critical portrayal of Edith Wilson, the president's second wife and widow, who was still alive. In the end, *Thomas Woodrow Wilson: A Psychological Study* was published right before Bullitt's death in 1967, nearly three decades after Freud had died in London.

Wilson is portrayed as a man who is firmly convinced of his divine purpose, someone who "in his unconscious was God and Christ." He believed that only "noble intentions" mattered, which meant that he "lacked motive to reduce his ignorance by learning facts." Citing the prime minister of France Georges Clemenceau's mocking comment that Wilson considered himself to be "another Jesus Christ come upon the earth to reform men," the authors—in this passage's case, most likely Freud—wrote: "Clemenceau probably knew nothing about psychoanalysis, but Wilson's unconscious identification of himself with the Savior had become so obvious that it compelled even those who had never studied the deeper psychic strata to recognize its existence."

Wilson's capitulation, in particular, to Clemenceau's punitive peace terms showed how the American leader "had adopted the weapons of femininity," the authors continued. "His offer was the gesture of a woman who says: 'I submit utterly to your wishes, now be kind to me.'" Wilson further displayed his weak character, they added, by the way he treated Edith, his second wife, as a "mother substitute."

When the book was finally published, even some of Wilson's critics were upset by the authors' use of psychoanalysis as a political weapon, precisely what Freud had warned against earlier. The authors' reputations were hardly enhanced by the book, which received mostly dismissive reviews, and it was nothing like the bestseller that Bullitt had predicted. Many readers found it puzzling that Freud agreed to participate in the project in the first place.

Part of the explanation can be found in Freud's visceral dislike of the United States—not just of Wilson—which dated back to his only visit to the United States in 1909. Max Eastman, the editor of *The Masses* who visited him in Vienna in 1926, wanted to know why he held such strong views on the subject. Despite his admiration of Freud and his achievements, Eastman was annoyed by Freud's "European superiority complex" and "snooty attitude toward American culture," which was immediately apparent.

"What makes you hate America so?" the visitor asked.

"Hate America?" Freud replied. "I don't hate America, I regret it." Laughing, he added: "I regret that Columbus ever discovered it."

Warming to his theme, he continued in an increasingly jocular mood, but he was using humor as a way to take the sting out of his observations not to offend his guest. "America is a bad experiment conducted by Providence," he said. "At least, I think it must have been Providence. I at least should hate to be held responsible."

Eastman, as he pointed out, was not a touchy nationalist, and he laughed along with him, and, by his own admission "rather egged him on." When he asked Freud what he objected to, his host pointed to "the prudery, the hypocrisy" and claimed that Americans demonstrated "no independent thinking." He urged his visitor to write a book with the title *The Miscarriage of American Civilization,* which would "tell the truth about the whole awful catastrophe . . . [and] make you immortal."

For Bullitt, the book about Wilson was a way of settling personal scores; for Freud, it was that and more, a way of settling his scores against both the politician and his country. But, ironically enough, it provided Freud with a close connection with a prominent American diplomat who would be in a position to help him in his moment of greatest peril.

"NO PRUDISHNESS WHATSOEVER"

MARIE BONAPARTE HAD EVERYTHING GOING FOR HER: ONE OF the most famous family names in European history (she was Napoleon's great-grandniece); a royal title by virtue of marriage; inherited wealth; and a procession of lovers, including, most famously, Aristide Briand, who served eleven terms as France's prime minister and won, along with the foreign minister of Germany Gustav Stresemann, the Nobel Peace Prize in 1926. After Freud first began treating her for "frigidity" in 1925, she also quickly became an accomplished psychoanalyst in her own right, a prolific author in her new field, and a member of the great master's inner circle, one of his most devoted disciples and future saviors.

Yet, as Ernest Jones pointed out, everything that positioned her as a member of Europe's high society could have served as a huge impediment to her pursuit of a serious career. If she had simply lived up to the expectations of her era, she would have been content to confine herself to the role of a celebrity royal hostess, surrounded only by the rich and famous, never challenging herself professionally and intellectually.

"Marie Bonaparte embarked on a scientific career with as severe social handicaps as the familiar starving poet in an attic; that they were of an opposite form is irrelevant for their effects," Jones asserted. "One would have to search far in history to find someone who has succeeded in such circumstances." Even more remarkably, he continued, "she succeeded not by deserting one world for another, but by shining in both. It was a triumph of sheer personality." In other words, Marie was both at home among the stars of the haut monde and among the men and women of Freud's new science.

Most significantly, she was very much at home with Freud, and Freud with her. The speed of her transformation from patient to trusted confidante is evident in their earliest conversations, correspondence, and recollections. Bonaparte recalled her feelings after her first meeting with Freud at Berggasse 19: "The impression he made on me surpasses everything I expected. First his great kindness, combined with so much power. One feels in him 'sympathy' with all humanity, which he has been able to understand and of which one is only an imperceptible fragment."

Within a very short time, Freud had formed a similarly positive impression of her. "Look, I've known you for only three weeks and I'm telling you more than to other people after two years," he declared.

By the time of his seventieth birthday festivities on May 6, 1926, Freud was sharing his feelings with her about a wide range of subjects, including his family's reactions to the flood of public tributes to him on that occasion. "My wife, who is fundamentally quite ambitious, has been very satisfied by it all," he reported in a letter dated May 10. "Anna, on the other hand, shares my feeling that it is embarrassing to be exposed to praise." Nonetheless, his own sense of satisfaction, while tempered, was evident. "The world has acquired a certain respect for my work," he concluded. "But so far analysis has been accepted only by analysts."

In the most revealing passage of his letter, Freud, a Jewish atheist, opened up to Bonaparte, a gentile, about the accolades he received from Jewish organizations. "The Jewish societies in Vienna and the University in Jerusalem (of which I am a trustee), in short the Jews altogether, have celebrated me as a national hero, although my service to the Jewish cause is confined to the single point that I have never denied my Jewishness," he wrote.

All of which testified to the intimacy between them, something that would last until the end of Freud's life. From 1929 until his death in 1939, he kept a diary of sorts, just terse notes about the main events in his life. Apart from family members, the most frequently mentioned person there was Bonaparte, "my Princess," as he affectionately called her.

———

To outsiders, Marie's life was glamorous from the start. Her great-grandfather Lucien Bonaparte was Napoleon's brother, who played a key role in the coup of 18 Brumaire (November 9, 1799). Lucien was a philanderer and appeared to pass on the philandering habit to his son Pierre, Marie's grandfather. Even by the loose standards of the time, Pierre was notorious for bedding his servants and peasant girls. More significantly, he could boast none of the political accomplishments of his cousin Napoleon III, who became emperor of France in 1852. This may have accounted for his frequently erratic—and risky—behavior. In 1870, when his cousin's Second Empire was beginning to crumble, he denounced the republicans pushing for a new more liberal order—and shot and killed a republican journalist who had come to challenge him to a duel. He was acquitted of the crime, but his wife and children, including Marie's father, Roland, fell on hard times.

Marie was born in 1882, a year after her grandfather died in the company of one of his servants who also had been his mistress. By then, the family's fortunes had improved thanks to the shrewd maneuvers of her grandmother, who was the daughter of an uneducated worker but a "truly phallic woman," as Marie described her later. The grandmother parlayed the family's fame and arranged the marriage of her son Roland to Marie-Félix Blanc, the daughter of a gambler whose winnings and business acumen catapulted him from obscurity to vast wealth, including ownership of the Monte Carlo casino. All of which meant that Marie was born to riches—but also to early tragedy. Shortly after giving birth to Marie, her mother collapsed and died of an embolism.

Marie was raised by her father, whom she constantly tried to please, and her grandmother, who insisted on an austere existence despite the family's newfound wealth, and by various servants. She soon became aware of what had happened to her mother, and of the unsubstantiated but disturbing rumors that the death of the rich heiress may not have been an accident, the result instead of a plot by her father to seize her wealth. As Marie recalled later, "The conflict, between my ardent love for my adored father, and the dazzling horror that these imaginary crimes inspired in me, already lacerated the depths of my young heart."

Marie became convinced that she, too, might die early, since she was like the "dreamy and poetic mother with her musical soul"—which was the image she had formed of her mother. At age four, Marie had a mild form of tuberculosis. While lying sick in bed, she overheard one of the adults say, "It is just like her poor mother." Subsequently, both her grandmother and father tried to shield her from illness by keeping her away from children her age, which meant she developed almost no friendships outside the household. This overly protective upbringing was also the result of her grandmother's suspicions that outsiders might somehow seek to profit from the family's wealth.

As a Bonaparte, Marie was no stranger to tales of violence, and she soon became fascinated by the news of the anarchists and bomb throwers of her era. Among her childhood fixations: Jack the Ripper, who she described as a "supermurderer and a superanarchist." As an older woman, she would also champion the cause of Caryl Chessman, an American convicted kidnapper, rapist, and robber who died in San Quentin's gas chamber in 1960.

Roland, her father, was intent on providing her with a good education, including English and German lessons from a very early age, but his goal—like his mother's—was to prepare her for a marriage that would translate into more wealth and prestige. He had little interest in her intellectual development and he was emotionally distant, largely oblivious to Marie's efforts to win his approval. His daughter wanted to be part of his life, and she bitterly recalled how dismayed she was when, on a rare Parisian snowy day, he rejected her appeal to join him on a sleigh ride. She did get to go to the inauguration of the Eiffel Tower and the International Exposition of 1889, but not to the reception at her house on that occasion that she desperately wanted to attend.

Thomas Edison was on the guest list and she was eager to see his talking machine, otherwise known as the phonograph. In honor of the famed American, the party also included what were billed as American Indians—although, in all likelihood, they were no more genuine than their costumes. For a young girl with a vivid imagination, nothing could have been more exciting. Yet her father categorically rejected her plea to be allowed to come downstairs briefly to the reception. "Oh Papa, cruel Papa!" she wrote to him later. She protested that she was not an "ordinary woman," adding pointedly: "I am the true daughter of your brain. I am interested in science as you are."

Long after her father's death in 1924, Marie found a batch of letters she had written to him in 1893, when he was visiting the United States. He had noted the date of his receipt of the letters on the envelopes, but then never opened them. The messages of his lonely ten-year-old daughter back in Paris were evidently not of interest to him.

In today's terms, Marie was largely homeschooled. She was taught by adults while living among adults. The two dominant figures in her life continued to make very few concessions to her feelings. When she was about eight, her grandmother reprimanded her for flinching at the sound of cannon shots during the regatta in Dieppe. "How dare you?" she declared. "A Bonaparte mustn't be afraid of cannon." From an early age, her father would lecture her sternly on the need to save money, although the family had more than enough to live a comfortable, upper class existence thanks to the wealth he had inherited from his wife.

———

Marie's main outlet for her emotions was writing: she described the process of dipping her pen in ink and then moving it across paper as a "physical pleasure for me." She filled up notebooks as a child and started what she called a "monthly magazine" in her teens—all of which was only a prelude to her prolific output later. She also discovered the opera and theater, entranced but puzzled by the Comédie Française's production of *Oedipus Rex*, which she viewed several times in 1896. Coincidentally, Freud first used the term "psychoanalysis" in print that same year, although he had not yet developed his theory of the Oedipus complex.

As she matured, Marie was told in no uncertain terms that she could not expect the same treatment as her peers. She was tutored by excellent teachers who taught at the Lycée Racine, a high school for girls, and they assured her that she was every bit as good a student as the best ones in their classrooms. But when it came time for her to register for the baccalaureate, the final exam that qualifies pupils for the university, her grandmother informed her that she would not be allowed to take it. The ostensible reason: in a republican era, the Bonaparte name was a major liability and the examiners could fail her merely because of who she was. According to her grandmother, she was sparing her "needless humiliation and disappointment."

Marie immediately understood that this was an excuse to justify a decision her grandmother and father had made from the start: she would be allowed to study, but only up to a point. She did not deny that her name, social status, and wealth could have worked against her, but the real reason was the "curse" of her sex. "Because if I were a boy, you wouldn't have stopped me from taking the baccalauréat, in spite of my name, as Papa once did, and after all he didn't fail!" she declared.

Marie felt that she suffered from that "curse" for a long time. As she wrote much later, "In the culture created by men, women do not have the position, the freedom, the happiness that they ought to; I feel myself one of the oppressed."

Like most teenage girls, Marie also embarked on her first flirtations—but, in her case, one of them quickly reinforced the notion that she was particularly vulnerable to exploitation. The man who soon demonstrated that peril was Antoine Leandri, her father's second secretary. Marie later recalled how naïve she was to believe that his overtures were inspired by passion. He was the "Corsican secretary, black hair, blue eyes, pointed beard—I was sixteen, he was thirty-eight. I was ugly. He was handsome," she wrote, clearly heightening the contrast in anger at what transpired next.

Leandri was married and his wife was part of their entourage, but Marie still believed him when he exclaimed: "The virgin drives me wild!" He, in turn, instructed her to send him a lock of her hair along with a note affirming her love for him. She eagerly obliged, writing "from Marie who loves him passionately and will never forget him." All of which provided Leandri with the ammunition he needed to blackmail her father. Although she had not slept with him, the revelation of their "affair" would have torpedoed Marie's chances for a high society marriage. To Marie's and the family's dismay, Leandri did not let up on his threats until he was finally paid off to the tune of 100,000 francs in cash. Marie was not bothered by the sum, but the entire experience served as a rude awakening and reinforced many of her insecurities. When suitors came to call, she found herself "nauseated by all this greed, especially when it pretends to be love."

Her distant father was hardly a source of reassurance. While anxiously trying to marry her off, she recalled how he once coldly told her: "If I saw you in a brothel, you are certainly not the one I would pick." Nonetheless, when her father hosted a ball for her shortly before she turned seventeen and she was appropriately decked out for the occasion, she realized that she was far from an ugly duckling. "I am beautiful for the first time," she noted. But, after the death of her grandmother in 1905, her father became even more withdrawn and dour—and, at the same time, visibly nervous whenever Marie left the house. She did not attend a ball at someone else's house until she was nearly twenty-five.

———

In the summer of 1907, Marie's father hosted a lunch for King George I of the Hellenes, who was the son of King Christian IX of Denmark. As with so much of European royalty, the family line crossed national frontiers, and King George's second son, Prince George of Greece and Denmark, was raised in both countries. The monarch suggested to his delighted host that he would welcome a match between this son and Marie. Despite her initial misgivings, Marie found her suitor to be a "handsome giant," tall, slim, blond, and someone who "above all seems so kind, so kind." The prince further strengthened his case by declaring that he wished to keep their assets separate, thereby relieving Marie and her father of any worries that he was hoping to profit from her wealth.

After a courtship of twenty-eight days, Marie accepted his proposal. They had a civil ceremony in Paris and, on December 12, 1907, a lavish Greek Orthodox wedding in the cathedral in Athens. But the wedding night was hardly a triumph. Her husband took her virginity "in a short, brutal gesture," she recorded, and then apologized. "I hate it as much as you do," he said. "But we must do it if we want children." She soon bore him a son and then a daughter, but this only increased the distance between them. The new Princess of Greece and Denmark spent most of her time in Paris, and, even when her prince joined her there, they were emotionally distant.

Observing the close ties between George and his favorite uncle, she concluded that his apparent lack of interest in their sexual life had a deeper cause. Although she saw nothing to suggest that George had ever had a homosexual affair, she described his body as "adverse to female bodies, your body like your soul devoted to man, chastely but ardently fixed on one Friend." In other words, whether he knew it himself or not, he was attracted to men more than women. As she wrote later, "We were of different races. Not only by complexion and the color of the hair, but by the reverberations of the mind and heart."

It did not take Marie long to seek the company of other men who were more responsive to her reverberations. As Europe hurtled toward World War I, she wrote: "The only events, for a woman, are those of the heart: a tear, a kiss . . . What do I care if empires fall? He kissed my lips this evening"—without specifying whom she had in mind. She pointed out that "others have come and gone," alluding to a succession of short, mostly sexually frustrating affairs.

On March 18, 1913, King George I, her father-in-law, was assassinated in Salonika, but a few days later she was more preoccupied with her private life than with such historic events, even when they touched her family directly. "*My Husband*," she wrote. "He bores me, he keeps me in chains, but he is the only man who will love me until death." Despite their emotional incompatibility, she knew that he would never leave her. Her conclusion: "The oppression of marriage is a universal, if necessary malady"—even if, as she added, "I dare to believe there are more released widows than disconsolate ones."

Marie noted that she experienced "two great passions" in her life. The first, who "by his age and authority could have been my father," was Aristide Briand; he repeatedly occupied the post of France's prime minister between 1909 and 1929, along with a record number of other cabinet posts. They met in 1913 when Marie hosted a lunch for Rudyard Kipling. On that occasion, she found herself more fascinated by Briand, fifty-one at the time and already a four-time prime minister, than by the legendary writer. The long-running affair that followed was hardly exclusive on either side.

As he took up with Marie, Briand still spent time with his mistress Berthe Cerny, who knew of his divided loyalties. "Men! You teach them how to comb their hair and to hold a fork, and then they deceive you with royal highnesses!" she complained. Neither had Marie cut ties with Albert Reverdin, a young surgeon from Geneva or "the other lover," as she called him. There was also the lover that she simply called "X" in her notebooks, a famous physician married to one of her friends who helped her deal with the declining health of her father. He, not Reverdin, appeared to be the second "great passion" of her life, although keeping track of her passions was no easy task.

Passionate or not, all of Marie's affairs appear to have been diminished by her "frigidity"—her inability to achieve orgasms. In 1924, she published a lengthy article on the subject in the journal *Bruxelles medical* under the pseudonym A. E. Narjani. She pointed out that "frigid women console themselves for their misery by attributing their affliction to the whole feminine sex." In a distinctly autobiographical passage, she described what such women go through. "At the beginning of their sexual life they often blame this deficiency on the partner, accusing him of being too hasty and not knowing how," she wrote. "But these women may change lovers time and again, they may even meet one with whom the act lasts an hour, to no avail. They end up by understanding that the deficiency is in themselves . . ."

In the same article, Marie endorsed the notion that women like her might be saved by an operation performed by Professor Josef Halban. The Viennese surgeon experimented with moving the clitoris closer to the opening of the vagina, which was supposed to increase the chances for a woman to achieve orgasms. She reported that he had operated successfully on five women; whether true or not, her eagerness to believe those claims indicated that she was already thinking about undergoing a similar operation herself.

Long before she resorted to that desperate measure, Marie met René Laforgue, who had begun practicing psychiatry in his native Alsace and, in 1923, moved to Paris to take up a post at a psychiatric clinic. By then, he had been following Freud's writings for a decade and had started corresponding directly with him. Marie had started reading Freud's works as well, and soon she was seeing Laforgue regularly. When she asked the psychoanalyst to write to Freud so that she could seek his help, Laforgue obliged.

In a letter to Freud on April 9, 1925, he wrote: "The lady in question suffers from a rather pronounced obsessional neurosis, which, though it has not impaired her intelligence, has nevertheless somewhat disturbed the general equilibrium of her psyche." All of which was a polite way of saying that Marie was the kind of smart but neurotic woman who would be a perfect candidate for him. Laforgue concluded by saying that Marie was planning to go to Vienna, hoping that Freud could "undertake a psychoanalytic treatment of her."

Freud promptly replied, saying that he knew nothing about the woman but would be willing to accept her for analysis "if you can guarantee the seriousness of her intentions and personal worth." He pointed out some timing constraints and also insisted that she had to speak German or English because his French was quite rusty. Since she knew both languages, this was no obstacle.

In their subsequent correspondence, Laforgue explained that Marie had a "marked virility complex, and also many difficulties in her life," which made her eager to undergo intensive analysis for anywhere between six weeks and two months, "as often as possible *twice a day*." Aside from dealing with her condition, he pointed out, she was hoping to learn about psychoanalysis. Freud protested that he could not devote so much time to one person, especially when that person had no clear "didactic or therapeutic" goal. But after Marie wrote to him directly in German to plead her case, he agreed to see her in Vienna. On September 30, 1925, she wrote to Laforgue from the Bristol Hotel, her regular domicile in the Austrian capital, that she had met Freud for the first time that afternoon.

According to Marie, she had come to see Freud in Vienna hoping to find the "penis and orgiastic normality." Measured by that goal, her consultations proved to be a failure as indicated by her decision, after more than a year of them, to try the surgery on her clitoris that she had written about earlier. Professor Halban performed the short operation, which, not surprisingly, also failed to solve her problem. She did not hide what she had done from Freud, confessing that it was stupid of her to have attempted such a quick fix.

But if Marie remained frustrated by her inability to enjoy sex to the fullest, she was far from disappointed with her sessions with Freud. From the moment they met, she was awed by the man she quickly called "my great master Freud."

As Freud's biographer Peter Gay wrote, Marie proved to be his "most notable recruit of the 1920s." She freely admitted that she had always sought the approval of father figures—and Freud proved to be the ultimate father figure for her, deserving of every superlative she could muster. "What a marvelous, unique being, such as the world has not seen in a long time and will not see again!" she wrote. "The quality of his character equals that of his thought, and daily contact with such a mind is the greatest event in my life."

Freud, who had been wary at first about the demands that Marie might make on his time and not quite sure what someone who qualified as royalty would be like, was just as impressed by her. Martin Freud called her the "best and dearest friend of father's last years." He believed that they quickly recognized that they were kindred spirits. "For she had most of father's chief characteristics—his courage, his sincerity, his essential goodness and kindliness and his devotion to scientific truth," he added. "In this sense the similarity of character was startling."

As soon as he started treating Marie, the older Freud was struck by the fact that she had "no prudishness whatsoever." The princess, as he called her, talked freely about her love affairs and fantasies, not sparing him any details.

She was also eager to explore her childhood, showing him five notebooks that she had filled up with her thoughts between the ages of seven and ten—and then forgotten about until she discovered them among her father's belongings after his death in 1924. "The riddle of these little books was one among the reasons which prompted me . . . to seek an analysis with Freud," she declared.

Written in her English, which was still very much a work in progress, they contained such lines as these: "I am sad, It is because I am sad, Poor me? No, so sad, never I was . . . Wery sad am I! oh! Papa console me I will work I will . . . Oh! My leg! it hearts me very much!"

Freud helped her see that the notebooks indicated she must have witnessed the "primal scene" at an early age, probably her nursemaid with her lover, which accounted for her familiarity with the male anatomy. In a letter to Laforgue after the first sessions with Freud, Marie wrote: "The analysis is the most 'gripping' thing I have ever done." After Freud's death, she published *Five Copy-Books,* adding Freud's and her own commentaries about their content. According to Freud's theory that he shared with her, Marie's understanding of men stemmed from the fact that she was "bisexual" in nature, which meant she had a strong masculine component within her. This probably came as no surprise to Marie because Laforgue had claimed earlier that her frigidity, combined with her husband's latent homosexuality, indicated that she harbored similar feelings about her own sex. "No one understands you better than I," Freud said.

Impressed as he was by her openness about every aspect of her personal life, he felt freer to talk about himself than he usually did with his patients. He noted, however, that "in my private life, I am a petit bourgeois"—far more conventional in his outlook and lifestyle than she was. As examples, he pointed out that he would never want one of his sons to get a divorce or one of his daughters to have an affair. The other contrast that he did not shirk from emphasizing was how much older he was. He told her about his cancer of the jaw and how, at his age, "there are a few things that don't work anymore." He was alluding to the fact that, while he still slept in the same bed with his wife Martha, their sex life was probably well in the past by then.

Freud treated Marie as a close friend and colleague, almost like another daughter. But he cautioned her not to become too emotionally dependent on him. Marie cried and declared that she loved him. "To hear that when you're seventy!" he responded, visibly delighted by the warmth between them.

Looking back much later, Marie came to understand his role as a father figure. "All my life I was to attach a value to nothing but the opinion, the approval, the love of a few fathers chosen higher and higher, and the last of whom was to be my great master Freud," she wrote.

Marie not only kept spending more and more time in Vienna for further sessions with him, she also underwent a transformation from patient to a trainee in psychoanalysis, gradually blossoming into a serious practitioner of the new science. "Under father's guidance, the Princess made psychoanalysis one of her main interests in life," Martin Freud pointed out.

Martin grew especially fond of Marie, dedicating to her the novel he wrote based on his experiences fighting on the Austrian side in World War I. Marie even seemed to win over Martha Freud, who normally kept her distance from her husband's circle of patients and collaborators. "Mme Freud told me how much her husband's work had surprised and shocked her, in that it treated sexuality so freely," Marie recalled. "It was almost *on purpose* that she did not take cognizance of it." This was a rare case of Martha's baring her soul to someone outside the immediate family. As Freud told Marie, "My wife is very bourgeois."

The master and the princess shared much more than their purely professional interests, including a fascination with the kind of Egyptian, Greek, and Roman statues that decorated Freud's study, some of which she helped him find. Then there was their adoration of their pets. "Under the influence of the Princess, Sigmund Freud became a commonplace dog-lover," Martin wrote. Both of them favored chows, and Marie wrote a book called *Topsy* about her deep attachment to her chow by that name—and about her reflections on life and death. This, too, was a work of psychoanalysis. Near the end of his life, Freud demonstrated his devotion both to the breed and to his princess by translating, with Anna, the book into German.

Marie's consultations and growing friendship with Freud had an impact on her other relationships as well. When she returned to Paris from Vienna late in 1925, she saw "X" again, resuming their affair but still frustrated by her frigidity. She continued to be drawn to him, but she was not about to accept his advice about her life. While she was in Vienna, he had tried to persuade her to abandon her quest to become a practitioner of Freud's science. "It would be ridiculous for you, who are not a doctor but a society woman, to get involved in psychoanalysis," he argued. Recording that remark in her notebook, she wrote defiantly: "I will acquire the analytic technique."

Her husband, Prince George, who felt more distant than ever from Marie, tried to convince her to abandon her preoccupation with Freud and psychoanalysis as well—equally to no avail. Her son, Peter, and especially her daughter, Eugénie, who struggled with pleurisy and other illnesses, also resented her frequent absences.

It wasn't just Marie's focus on psychoanalysis that kept her apart from her family: there was a new man in her life, Rudolph Loewenstein, a Polish-born physician who studied and then taught psychoanalysis in Paris. This lover was sixteen years younger than her, and she promptly dubbed him the "lion." But while they shared a passion for Freud's teachings, their mutual passion did not last long. No matter how hard she tried with him, "X," or others, she noted, "work is easy and sexual pleasure difficult."

When she was back in Paris, Marie continued in her role as a society woman, mingling with the rich and famous. Shortly after Charles Lindbergh made his solo flight across the Atlantic, landing near Paris on May 21, 1927, she met the instantly famous twenty-five-year-old aviator whose feat had captured the admiration of not only her countrymen but people everywhere. Rather than ponder the meaning of his accomplishment, though, her thoughts turned to the question whether he was still a virgin.

———

Marie was increasingly both a part of Freud's inner circle and active in spreading his teachings in France. In Freud's home in Vienna, she attended the Wednesday evening gatherings of analysts, not just as a listener but also as a participant. On November 24, 1926, she took part in the official launch of the Paris Psychoanalytic Society; its first president was Laforgue and its secretary-treasurer was Loewenstein, while she was one of the founding members and a contributor and financial supporter of its publication, a French review of psychoanalysis. At Marie's insistence, the front cover contained the phrase "under the high patronage of Professor Sigm. Freud."

Marie also busied herself with translations of Freud's works, always a complicated and tricky task, and gave her own talks on some of them. She continued to pen her essays on psychoanalysis as well. And as she kept confiding in Freud, he confided more in her. When she began a discussion about the unconscious mind, he described a recurring dream that he had not been able to understand. In it, he stood in front of a beer garden but, unable to enter through its gate, he was forced to turn back. Later, he realized he had been stuck before a similar gate on a visit to Padua. As he explained to Marie, he had the same dream each time he was stymied by whatever issue he was unable to solve at the moment.

Whether she was in Vienna or Paris, Marie was the "energy devil," as Freud called her, seemingly inexhaustible in her enthusiasm for her new calling. In 1929, when Freud's publishing company was close to collapse, she saved it from bankruptcy—and she continued to provide it with essential financial support during the subsequent economic hard times. She attended meetings of the International Psychoanalytical Association. And, on Freud's seventy-fifth birthday, she gave a lecture about him at the Sorbonne, with about five hundred people in attendance.

At the same time, nothing—not even persistent complications from the operation on her clitoris that led Halban to perform further surgery and a hysterectomy—stopped her from continuing her affairs, even when the lovemaking was painful. She kept up her long-running relationship with "X" or the "Friend," as she called him, at times vacationing with him and his wife, who must have known that Marie was more than a friend and traveling companion. But it was Marie who appeared to be the jealous member of this threesome. As she noted, "His wife twice a week, me three times."

Nothing in the sexual realm was beyond contemplation for her. In his early twenties, her son, Peter, had also undergone psychoanalysis and he clearly had conflicted feelings about his frequently absent mother. Discussing those feelings with her in April 1932, he declared: "If I were to spend a night with you, it might cure me." Typically, Marie immediately consulted Freud, admitting that she, too, had briefly considered such a possibility. Freud warned her that the consequences of incest could be "stronger than we are prone to estimate; then the trespass is followed by feelings of guilt against one which is quite helpless."

Marie evidently agreed. In all probability she had dismissed the notion of actually committing incest before she wrote to Freud; as she noted, a day after Peter confided his thoughts about spending a night with her, any temptation she might have had to oblige "was extinguished in the arms of the Friend." It also would have been out of character for her to ignore Freud's advice in this case, which may have been one of the rare occasions when he gently admonished her about the dangers of acting upon her instincts.

Freud and his royal disciple did not agree on everything. Their most serious dispute concerned the paper trail Freud had left with Wilhelm Fliess, the ear, nose, and throat specialist in Berlin who had been one of his earliest and, as he put it, "intimate" friends. Their friendship had ended at the beginning of the century, and Fliess died in 1928. But, in late 1936, Marie heard some startling news: Fliess's widow had sold her husband's extensive correspondence with Freud, along with some manuscripts he had included, to Reinhold Stahl, a bookseller in Berlin. This meant that what Freud considered to be the very private record of their correspondence was still in existence and up for sale. The bookseller had contacted Marie, informing her that he had a bidder in the United States but that he would prefer to keep the collection in Europe. When Marie examined one letter to check its authenticity, she recognized Freud's handwriting right away.

Freud had no records of his own of their correspondence, and he offered to split the cost of the collection—Stahl wanted 12,000 francs, the equivalent of $500, for the letters—with Marie. As he explained to her, the letters were the "most intimate you can imagine," discussing everything from his early professional setbacks to how, after the birth of their fifth child, he and Martha abstained from sex for a year so that she could have a break before giving birth to Anna, their last child. Freud declared that he wanted "none of them to come to the notice of so-called posterity." His goal was to obtain and destroy them.

But Stahl had other ideas—and so did Marie. "The letters and manuscripts were offered to me on condition that I not resell them at any price to the Freud family, directly or indirectly, for fear of the destruction of the material which is so important to the history of psychoanalysis," she wrote to Freud. While she could discuss how they would be handled, including possibly blocking access to them for a specified period of time after his death, she added, "I have a curious aversion to the idea of the destruction of your letters and manuscripts."

Anticipating his objections, Marie combined flattery with reason to convince him that she was right. "You yourself, dear Father, perhaps do not feel all your greatness," she wrote. "You belong to the history of human thought like Plato, let us say, or Goethe." Nothing in the letters, she assured him, "could diminish you!" She pointed out that whatever failings they might reveal would only help present him as a fuller human being. "You yourself, dear Father, have written in your beautiful works against the idealization at all cost of great men."

Marie stashed the letters in a safe deposit box at the Rothschild bank in Vienna, but the Anschluss caused her to take them to Paris, where they survived most of the war deposited with the Danish legation there. The collection was finally sent to London in 1945. Before his death six years earlier, Freud had appeared to recognize that Marie's decision to save it was the right one and he never held her defiance on this matter against her.

As for Marie, there was no doubt that she was motivated by her complete devotion to Freud. After she had settled the issue of the Fliess correspondence, she wrote to Freud: "The greatest happiness of my life is to have met you, to have been your contemporary." And as intent as she was on saving his papers, Marie would soon prove to be even more focused on saving the man himself.

8.

"VIOLENT PAIN"

MAX SCHUR WAS ONLY EIGHTEEN AND HAD JUST STARTED medical school at the University of Vienna in 1915 when a cousin, who was unable to return home to Geneva because of the war, talked him into attending Freud's lectures with her. The series of talks that Freud gave on Saturday evenings during the 1915–1916 and 1916–1917 academic years were later published as the *Introductory Lectures to Psycho-Analysis*, a collection that attained the status of a basic textbook of the new science. But at the time, as Schur recalled, most of the audience for those Saturday sessions consisted of "Freud's students, 'intellectuals,' and curiosity seekers." Only a relatively small number of medical students like Schur were sprinkled in the mix—in all probability, the result of the still decidedly mixed feelings among the medical school's faculty about Freud's teachings.

The medical students had to get Freud's signature on their "Index," the record of their courses, to get credit for their attendance. The first time Schur did so he was struck by the way Freud exchanged a few words with each student and shook his hand. "Most impressive was the searching look which accompanied the handshake," he wrote.

"Little did I dream at that moment that thirteen years later I would become Freud's personal physician." Nor could he have dreamt then that he would be charged with his care for the final decade of his life, making him a vital member of Freud's rescue squad—and, apart from Anna and the rest of his family, its only Jew.

At that first and subsequent lectures during that period, all of which he unfailingly attended, Schur was mesmerized by Freud's performances. He spoke without any notes, but whatever he said barely had to be edited for the written record afterward. Schur confessed that he found it hard to comprehend everything Freud said at the time, but he was struck by the "total harmony of content and delivery which created the impact"—and by the "hushed silence" of the audience for the two hours that he held forth. "It is not easy to explain why this was such a unique, unforgettable experience," he wrote—but it undoubtedly was just that.

Schur specialized in internal medicine, not psychology, but he underwent personal analysis in 1924, seeking to better understand himself and the concepts that Freud expounded upon. Three years later, an older colleague asked him to take a blood specimen from one of his patients, Marie Bonaparte, who was on one of her frequent visits to Vienna. That encounter put him on the path to a whole new relationship with Freud.

During their first meeting, as Schur recalled, Bonaparte "was pleasantly surprised to meet a psychoanalytically oriented internist." When she became quite ill during another visit to Vienna in 1928, Schur treated her for several weeks, taking charge of her full care. As impressed as she had been by his interest in psychology, she became convinced that he was a highly competent doctor with an appealing personal touch. And, as it happened, she believed that Freud needed just such a person to take charge of his care as well.

Freud was treated by various doctors and specialists, but for several years he had not engaged a personal physician who could monitor and coordinate all aspects of his complicated care. This was a job that needed to be filled, Bonaparte maintained, and she strongly recommended Schur to Freud. As she saw it, he was ideally suited for the position.

Schur was more than eager for the job, but he realized that Freud might see him as too young and inexperienced, since he was only thirty-one then. While the fact that he had attended all of Freud's lectures strengthened his case, he had not quite completed his personal analysis yet. For this potential patient, it was important that his personal doctor, if he was to have one, had more than a superficial understanding of his outlook and teachings. The dynamics of such a relationship between a young doctor and a "towering father figure such as he was," Schur noted, would be extremely delicate.

Persuaded by Bonaparte, Freud agreed to try him out. At their first meeting in late 1928, Freud immediately put Schur at ease by praising the way he had handled Marie's treatment. "There was nothing patronizing in this meeting of the sage master with a young doctor more than forty years his junior," Schur recalled. But before proceeding to discuss his medical history, Freud laid out the ground rules for their relationship.

First of all, he insisted that Schur always had to tell him the full truth about his medical condition, since there had been "some unfortunate experiences with your predecessors." This was an allusion to Freud's anger that in 1923, when a growth was removed from his jaw, Felix Deutsch, his personal physician at the time, had not told him it was malignant at first—something Deutsch immediately realized. Trying to justify that decision later, Deutsch argued that Freud had been "insufficiently prepared" to deal with a cancer diagnosis at that point. According to Schur, Deutsch "was apparently under the impression that Freud was thinking of suicide," which was not the case. Since the patient no longer trusted his doctor, Freud and Deutsch parted company.

As Deutsch's wife, Helene, recalled, "Freud was angry because he believed my husband had underestimated his strength." Nor was Freud mollified by Jones, with whom Deutsch had shared this "most deadly secret," as the Welshman put it. When Jones later admitted that Deutsch had told him and a few others about his diagnosis while initially keeping his patient in the dark, Freud, "with blazing eyes," asked: *"With what right?"* It is a testament to the strength of the bond between Freud and Jones that this confession did not derail their friendship.

Freud was satisfied with Schur's assurance that he would always level with him. However, he had another major concern that prompted his second precondition for taking Schur on. "Promise me one more thing: that when the time comes, you won't let me suffer unnecessarily," he declared. According to Schur, he said this "with the utmost simplicity, without a trace of pathos, but also with complete determination." Since he regularly experienced pain as a result of the numerous operations on his jaw and the persistent difficulties with his prosthesis, Freud wanted a guarantee that Schur would grant his wish to end his life once it became unbearable. The two men shook hands in agreement.

According to Jones, "Schur was a perfect choice for a doctor. He established excellent relations with his patient, and his consideration, his untiring patience and his resourcefulness were unsurpassable." Those relations went both ways. "In the shortest possible time, he [Freud] showed his readiness to establish a patient–doctor relationship based on mutual respect and confidence," Schur noted.

Equally important, Freud's new doctor quickly won the trust and respect of the rest of the family, especially Anna, who acted as her father's primary caregiver on a daily basis. "He and Anna made an ideal pair of guardians to watch over the suffering man and to alleviate his many discomforts," Jones wrote.

There was only one point of minor friction at the beginning of this patient–doctor relationship. Freud had told Schur he did not want him to extend any professional courtesy in the form of discounted fees for his services. When Schur submitted his bill for 1929, the first full year when he attended to his famous new patient, Freud promptly complained that it was too low. "I feel that you have backed away from the contract upon which our formal relations are based," he wrote. "I do not want to pay this bill and suggest you send me a more appropriate one."

————

Schur's first task was to learn everything he could about his new patient's medical history. Freud, who had almost obsessively fretted about his health even when he was much younger, was more than willing to oblige by discussing the subject in detail. But the two men needed several meetings to go over everything, since the operations on Freud's jaw and the prosthesis he wore made speaking at any length difficult.

Aside from his jaw, there were plenty of other issues to discuss. Freud had been prone to fainting spells, always, as Schur recorded, in situations "of acute stress." Famously, one of those episodes took place during a lunch in Munich with Carl Jung in November 1912 as the tensions between them were leading to their outright break. On that occasion, Freud became convinced that Jung's growing opposition to his views signaled that he harbored a death wish against him. According to Jones, who was also at the lunch, Freud suddenly "fell on the floor in a dead faint." Jung picked him up and placed him on a couch, where he quickly recovered. In a subsequent letter to Jung, Freud, who was still hoping to patch up their differences, ascribed the incident to a "piece of neurosis."

In the 1890s, when Freud was writing regularly to Fliess, he frequently reported on his other health issues. He complained about "migraine attacks" and, as would continue to be the case in subsequent decades, gastrointestinal problems. His major worry was what he described as his "cardiac misery." All of these concerns sapped his morale at times. In a letter to Fliess on April 19, 1894, he wrote: "It is painful for a medical man, who spends every hour of the day struggling to achieve an understanding of the neuroses, not to know whether he himself is suffering from a reasonable or hypochondriacal depression."

Based on the evidence provided by Freud, Schur concluded that he had suffered from "repeated attacks of tachycardia," a heart rate more than one hundred beats per minute, with "most violent" arrythmia. Those episodes, which could last for several days, caused intense chest pain and a burning sensation down his left arm, plunging him into some of his darkest moods. It also prompted him to give up mountain climbing, as he wrote to Fliess, "with a heavy heart." On that subject, he still managed to add playfully: "How meaningful colloquial usage is!"

But the most serious—and most lasting—problem was the cancer in his jaw. After the first operation in 1923, Freud underwent a few X-ray treatments, which had little chance of success in such a sensitive area. "The radiation Freud received only caused tissue damage and violent pain," Schur concluded.

When Schur consulted the extensive notes of Hans Pichler, the oral surgeon who began treating Freud in 1923 and continued to do so until his departure from Vienna in 1938, he discovered just how much time and effort went into managing the pain in this troubled area. "I consulted Pichler's notes for 1926, a 'typical' year with no major surgical procedures, just the unceasing attempt to achieve a minimum of comfort," Schur wrote. It was also the year when Freud turned seventy.

"There were forty-eight office visits, one biopsy, two cauterizations, and constant experiments with three different prostheses involving attempts to preserve the remaining teeth."

Yet when Schur came aboard as Freud's personal doctor, he was encouraged by his initial findings. Although he ascribed Freud's digestive problems to "an irritable spastic colon," which Freud tried to calm during his regular visits to the spa in Karlsbad, the news was hardly all bad. "Freud's condition, apart from his oral cavity, was amazingly good," Schur reported. "He had disciplined himself to keep up good nutrition in spite of his great difficulty in chewing and swallowing. His heart showed no consequences of his anginal episodes. There was no marked enlargement of the heart and the aorta. Despite his heavy smoking, he had no chronic bronchitis or pulmonary emphysema."

Schur called Freud a "model patient" who rarely voiced any complaints. The doctor explained that the two of them established a "nonverbal form of communication," whereby "only an occasional tortured look, a pleading gesture indicated his suffering." Freud treated him as a member of his extended family, he added, always displaying his generosity of spirit. "This ability to love, to give, to feel stayed with him to the end," Schur reported.

While Freud was understandably preoccupied with his health, he made a conscious effort from the beginning to show some personal interest in his young doctor's life as well. When Schur invited him to his wedding in Vienna in the summer of 1930, Freud sent him a letter from Berlin, where he was undergoing further treatment, to let him know he would not be able to attend—and to offer him an eloquent expression of his best wishes for the couple's happiness. "Mindful of the rare kindness and conscientiousness that you have shown in caring for the remains of my physical self, I should like to endow my wishes with the power to enforce their fulfillment," he wrote.

Freud did not skirt the issue of his health altogether, but used it to reiterate his satisfaction with the way Schur had taken over his care. "This is hardly the occasion to bother you with medical reports," he concluded. "I only want to say that I will not forget how often your diagnoses have turned out to be correct in my case, and that for this reason I am a docile patient, even when it is not easy for me."

———

As cooperative a patient as Freud wanted to be, he had one serious addiction that he had repeatedly tried and failed to conquer: his smoking. As Schur noted, "I could recognize immediately that this was an area where, as Freud himself had realized, he could not establish 'the dominance of the ego.'" It wasn't a question of refusing to admit the dangers of smoking: Freud believed that his early cardiac problems were, at least in part, a result of that habit. And the surgeries on his jaw served as painful reminders of the escalating price he was paying for it. But he still resisted the notion that he could live—and, especially, work—without his beloved cigars.

On February 12, 1929, shortly after Schur took on the job of serving as his personal doctor, Freud responded to a questionnaire by providing a summary of his smoking history. "I began smoking at the age of 24, first cigarettes but soon exclusively cigars, and am still smoking now (at 72½), and very reluctant to give up this pleasure," he wrote. When he was in his thirties, he gave up smoking for more than a year because of his heart problems, he reported, although he concluded that the lingering effects of influenza might have contributed to them. "Since then, I have been faithful to my habit or vice, and believe that I owe to the cigar a great intensification of my capacity to work and a facilitation of my self-control." He added: "My model for this was my father, who was a heavy smoker and remained one till his 81 year"— the year of his death.

To a succession of friends and physicians, he argued that smoking was essential to his productivity. "It was Freud's contention, based on his own experience, which I could later only confirm, that he needed nicotine during periods of creative writing or the preparation for such activity," Schur reported. "And when was Freud not at such a stage?" In other words, he always needed to smoke because he was always working.

In Freud's view, masturbation was the "primary addiction," and the "other addictions, for alcohol, morphine, tobacco, etc., enter into life only as a substitute for and a withdrawal [symptom] from it." This insight into the connection between the primary and subsequent addictions did not help him break his smoking habit.

In going through his medical records, Schur came across the reports by the pathologist who examined the excisions from his mouth during successive operations and minced no words on the cause of his problems. "Specially noticeable this time is the widespread inflammation which covers the whole of the mucous membrane and is the consequence of excessive smoking," he wrote in one of those reports.

But when Schur showed Freud such findings and the medical literature warning of the dangers of nicotine, he merely shrugged his shoulders. On one occasion, Freud even offered him a Havana cigar, which Schur felt obliged to accept and light up. Seeing that Schur was not a smoker and was not enjoying it, he remarked how expensive such fine cigars were—and never offered him another.

In letters to his colleague Max Eitingon in Berlin, Freud discussed his sporadic efforts to break his habit. "For six days now I have not smoked a single cigar, and it cannot be denied that I owe my well-being to this renunciation," he wrote on May 1, 1930. "But it is sad." Subsequent letters attested to how short-lived such renunciations were, since he was soon asking Eitingon to keep sending him the brands of cigars that he could not find in Vienna. "I am again sinning more," he wrote, adding that his supply of cigars was "quite low."

Soon, too, Pichler, the oral surgeon, was back at work, removing new lesions that either he or Schur kept on finding. Some were precancerous, but they looked decidedly menacing. Noting the appearance of a new "soft, irregular, partly dark colored" tumor that had "supposedly grown fast and much" in April 1931, Pichler advised further "excision and grafting." In his letters to Eitingon in the same month, Freud admitted to "a persistent deterioration in the conditions surrounding the prosthesis and a marked decline in the level of my general condition."

Yet in a letter only nine days later, he once again turned to his favorite subject. "About the cigars, I still want to report that the small ones—Pearl—proved to be very satisfactory," he wrote, adding that his supply needed replenishment again. If Eitingon's regular source "cannot deliver the Soberanos, I am willing to accept the rather good Reina-Cabana which were once offered as a substitute," he concluded.

Eitingon complied with his requests, but with some reluctance, which he did not try to hide. In his replies, Freud tried to get Eitingon to understand that he was fully aware of the trade-off he was making. "Your question about the cigars induces me to confess that I am smoking again," Freud wrote on June 1, 1931. "Considering my age and the amount of discomfort which I have to bear day after day, abstinence and the prospect [of preventing new lesions] which it involves do not seem justified to me."

William Bullitt, who was working with Freud on the book about Woodrow Wilson, was furious when he discovered that his coauthor had still not given up smoking. Bullitt pointed out that he, too, had been a cigar smoker, but managed to break the habit. Schur appreciated such attempts to convince Freud to do the same, but seemed resigned to failure. Bullitt "accomplished as little as all the rest of us," the doctor wrote.

———

At times, Freud's attitude toward smoking could convey the impression that he was almost cavalier about his health, far more preoccupied with enjoying his cigars than with his longevity. During his friendship with Wilhelm Fliess, who also tried to convince him to stop smoking, Freud bluntly declared in a letter on November 17, 1893: "I am not following your interdict from smoking; do you think then it is so very lucky to have a long, miserable life?"

Such declarations were misleading: he was both determined to cling to his simple if dangerous pleasures and acutely conscious of his mortality, very much hoping for a life that could be stretched out as long as possible before becoming miserable. That entailed constantly thinking about his own death, calculating when it might occur, and making adequate preparations.

Sometime in the 1920s, he penned in his elegant looping script a draft of his death notice, which is now preserved in his papers in the Library of Congress. "On xx 192x in his 7xth year here died Prof. Dr. Sigmund Freud. The corpse was cremated on xx (day)," it read, followed by a listing of his family members. It ended with: "Vienna, on xx 192x." The idea was that his wife or children could then simply fill in the x's.

Long before he reached his seventies, Freud had begun referring to himself as an old man. Even when he did so sardonically, he left no doubt that he frequently thought of himself that way. On May 7, 1900, a day after his birthday, he wrote to Fliess: "Well, I really am already 44 years old, a rather shabby old Jew, as you will see for yourself . . ." He certainly knew he was not shabby, and he understood that he was not really old, but his subsequent rush to anoint Jung as his crown prince when he was still operating at full strength indicated that he saw himself as much older than he was.

That perception was fueled by his thoughts of death—or, to put it precisely—his attempts to calculate how much time he had left. "Freud cannot be characterized as an obsessional neurotic, but his preoccupation with the prospective date of his death had the character of an obsessive trait," Schur observed.

Among the evidence to support that conclusion: Freud's letter to Jung on April 16, 1909, where he offered a detailed glimpse into his thinking. "Some years ago I discovered within me the conviction that I would die between the ages of 61 and 62, which then struck me as a long time away. (Today it is only eight years off)," he wrote. "Then I went to Greece with my brother and it was really uncanny how often the number 61 or 60 in connection with 1 or 2 kept cropping up in all sorts of numbered objects, especially those connected with transportation. This I conscientiously note. It depressed me . . ."

He acknowledged that it was a "superstitious notion" that he would die at that age, and guessed that Jung would write his musings off as "another confirmation of the specifically Jewish nature of my mysticism." But he pointed out they coincided "with the conviction that with *The Interpretation of Dreams* I had completed my life work, that there was nothing more for me to do and that I might just as well lie down and die."

When he was close to the age of his predicted death, Freud wrote to his Hungarian colleague Sándor Ferenczi in a similar resigned vein: "The superstition that my life is due to finish in February 1918 often seems to me quite a friendly idea." He had determined the exact month by adding the nine months since he was conceived to his sixty-first birthday—another indication of his peculiar method of calculation, which he had picked up earlier from Fliess.

Freud was a long way from completing his life's work, but a part of him seemed to welcome the idea of thinking otherwise. When his father was dying in 1896, he wrote to Fliess: "By the way, the old man's condition does not depress me. I do not begrudge him the well-deserved rest, as he himself desires it. He is suffering very little now, and is fading with decency and dignity."

In reality, though, Freud could not imagine fading away so long as he could summon the strength to stay active. "I cannot face with comfort the idea of a life without work," he wrote in a letter to Oskar Pfister, a Swiss Lutheran minister who was also a psychoanalyst, on March 6, 1910. "Work and the free play of the imagination are for me the same thing, I take no pleasure in anything else . . . In the words of King Macbeth, let us die in harness." Although the operations on his jaw would disrupt his schedule at times, he always sought to resume his practice of seeing six patients a day as soon as possible.

Once Freud made it past his sixty-second birthday, he came up with a new theory about when he would die. Both his father and his older half-brother Emanuel, who had settled in Manchester and died in a train accident in 1914, had lived to the age of eighty-one and a half; he became convinced that death would await him at the same age. But if he had moved back the clock in his mind, he was far from certain that this maneuver was successful. Writing to Ferenczi at the time of his sixty-fifth birthday in 1921, he confessed that the "thought of death has not left me, and sometimes I have the impression that seven of my internal organs are fighting to have the honor of bringing my life to an end."

Right before his seventy-fifth birthday in 1931, Lou Andreas-Salomé described her feeling of helplessness upon hearing that Pichler had performed yet another operation on Freud's jaw. "You will not be free from pain and not without physical discomfort, and this thought is quite intolerable," she wrote. "One would simply like to set to and find a scapegoat on whom one could vent one's wrath. I realize how childish this sounds, but there is a limit to all things . . . I simply cannot write a proper birthday letter."

Freud responded that he was surprised and disturbed by her letter, since it indicated that she was violently indignant about his fate. "Why?" he asked. "Because I had taken a further step on the stony path out of this existence?" He added that his previous close calls with death only underscored the obvious point that each such procedure was only delaying the inevitable. "Indeed the provisional nature of the reprieve and the definitive nature of the final departure were never so clear to me as now," he wrote.

To Marie Bonaparte, who also sent birthday greetings, he responded: "I am still quite below par, and this time I have certainly taken a huge step out of the circle of life."

———

Freud freely discussed death, the rituals and myths it inspired—and the way most people avoided the subject altogether. Death was "natural, undeniable and unavoidable," he wrote in "Thoughts for the Times on War and Death," the essays he produced during World War I. "In reality, however, we were accustomed to behave as if it were otherwise. We showed an unmistakable tendency to put death to one side, to eliminate it from life. We tried to hush it up." When silence is no longer possible, he added, "Our habit is to lay stress on the fortuitous causation of the death—accident, disease, infection, advanced age; in this way we betray an effort to reduce death from a necessity to a chance event."

All such efforts to deny the reality of death are intensified when the subject is personal. "It is indeed impossible to imagine our own death; and whenever we attempt to do so we can perceive that we are in fact still present as spectators," he wrote. "Hence the psychoanalytic school could venture the assertion that at bottom no one believes in his own death, or, to put the same thing in another way, that in the unconscious every one of us is convinced of his own immortality."

The price for clinging to such an illusion was steep, Freud maintained. "Life is impoverished, it loses in interest, when the highest stake in the game of living, life itself, may not be risked. It becomes as shallow and empty as, let us say, an American flirtation, in which it is understood from the first that nothing is to happen, as contrasted with a Continental love-affair in which both partners must constantly bear its serious consequences in mind."

Written only six years after his trip to the United States, this passage once again underscores his condescending, even contemptuous, view of American life. But his main message was much broader in scope: anyone who wants to lead a full, meaningful life must accept the reality of death.

As Freud recalled, his mother had instructed him about death at age six. "I was expected to believe that we were all made of earth and must therefore return to earth. This did not suit me and I expressed doubts of the doctrine." To convince him, his mother "rubbed the palms of her hands together—just as she did when making dumplings, except there was no dough between them—and showed me the blackish scales of *epidermis* produced by the friction as a proof that we were made of earth."

Since then, he concluded, he had come to accept the idea expressed in the saying, "Thou owest Nature a death"—which was a slightly altered version of the line in Shakespeare's *Henry IV*: "Thou owest God a death." As an atheist, Freud was not about to invoke God.

In his 1927 publication *The Future of an Illusion*, Freud insisted that psychology, instead of what he called false religious beliefs, offered people the best means to cope with the forces of nature that include diseases and the "painful riddle of death, against which no medicine has yet been found, nor probably will be." The idea was to free individuals from their "senseless anxiety" about the things that were beyond their control. "We are still defenseless, perhaps, but we are no longer hopelessly paralyzed; we can at least react."

On another occasion, he recalled the familiar warning, "If you want to preserve peace, arm for war," to offer a new formulation: "If you want to endure life, prepare yourself for death."

None of that meant that he was minimizing the value of life—quite the contrary. "I could not see my way to dispute the transience of all things . . . But I did dispute the pessimistic poet's view that the transience of what is beautiful involves any loss of its worth," he declared in his short essay "On Transience." It was precisely the fleeting nature of life that makes it all the more beautiful, he argued. "A flower that blossoms only for a single night does not seem to us on that account less lovely."

Contrary to his assertions about how everyone denies the reality of death, Freud had no illusions on the subject. But he also wanted to enjoy the beauty of life as long as possible. He made that perfectly clear when Schur was examining him on May 6, 1933, his seventy-seventh birthday.

At the time, Helene Schur, who was also a physician, was awaiting the birth of their first child. She was overdue and she and her husband were understandably anxious, which is why Freud told Max to hurry to her side. "You are going from a man who doesn't want to leave this world to a child who doesn't want to come into it," he said.

That child was born three days later. Peter Schur, who would grow up in the United States and follow in his parents' footsteps by studying and practicing medicine, proudly noted that Freud honored his birth by giving him three Austrian gold coins. "Remarkably, I still have those coins," he reported in 2013. He held on to one for himself and gave one each to his two daughters. That way, Max Schur's granddaughters would be reminded "of the Schur–Freud connection that, in its small way, helped shape history," he explained.

In fact, Max Schur's role in the saga of Freud's final decade was anything but small. Schur kept Freud healthy enough to contemplate, however reluctantly, flight from Vienna when his life was indisputably in danger—and still seemed very much worth living. Schur, who recognized that danger much earlier than his famous patient did, would also delay his own family's escape until Freud's safety was assured.

1

Martha Bernays, who grew up in an Orthodox Jewish family near Hamburg, met Sigmund Freud in 1882. Shown here a year before their marriage in 1886, they had six children.

2

The Freuds' youngest child, Anna, was especially devoted to her father. She never left home and became a noted child psychologist. She also fearlessly faced the Gestapo. This photo is from 1913.

The American Dorothy Burlingham, from the wealthy Tiffany family, came to Vienna in 1925 seeking treatment from Anna for her troubled children. She and Anna embarked on a "precious relationship" that lasted until Burlingham's death in London in 1979.

Freud with his sons Ernst and Martin (right) in their Austro-Hungarian Army uniforms in 1916. The whole family considered themselves "stout loyalists" of the Habsburg empire.

5

In 1909, Freud made his only visit to the United States, lecturing at Clark University in Worcester, Massachusetts. He was grateful for the honorary degree and other accolades he received, but still dismissed America as "a gigantic mistake." Top row from left, Abraham Brill, Ernest Jones, Sándor Ferenczi. Bottom row: Freud, G. Stanley Hall, Carl Jung.

6

The Weimar congress in 1911 demonstrated the rapid growth of the psychoanalytic movement. Freud and Jung are in the center of the second row, but they would soon part company.

7

In his study at Berggasse 19, Freud was surrounded by his statues and antiquities, and usually accompanied by his beloved chow. Photo from 1936.

8

Napoleon's great-grandniece Marie Bonaparte sought Freud's help for her "frigidity" and became one of his most ardent disciples. She was also an invaluable member of his rescue squad.

William Bullitt, who served as U.S. ambassador to the Soviet Union and then France, teamed up with Freud to write a scathing biography of Woodrow Wilson. He, too, worked tirelessly to extricate Freud from Vienna.

Chancellor Engelbert Dollfuss, Austria's diminutive right-wing dictator, tried to protect his country's sovereignty by banning the Nazi Party. Local Nazis assassinated him in 1934, setting the stage for Hitler's takeover four years later.

After sending his troops into Austria in March 1938, Hitler received a tumultuous welcome in Vienna. He proclaimed the Anschluss, the incorporation of the country of his birth into the Third Reich.

Anton Sauerwald, here in uniform in 1939, was appointed by the Nazis to extort Freud's assets. He acted like a typical anti-Semite at first, but then played a surprising role by enabling Freud's departure.

13

A relieved Freud with Anna on the train as they arrive in Paris. "Now we are free," he declared.

14

Marie Bonaparte and William Bullitt met Freud in Paris, escorting him from the train. After a day at Bonaparte's house, the Freuds continued their journey to London.

15

Freud with his daughter Mathilde and Ernest Jones in London. Jones had secured British entry permits for everyone in the Freud party, a considerable feat.

16

Max Schur with Freud in London. The physician had promised his famous patient that he would not allow him to suffer unnecessarily at the end. Delivering on that promise, he injected him with the morphine that triggered his death on September 23, 1939.

"POLITICAL BLINDNESS"

As the 1930s dawned, the Great Depression set in, reinvigorating many of the radical political movements that had flourished during the previous economic crisis in the wake of World War I but lost momentum later in the decade. In Germany, Hitler's Nazi Party attracted the support of a mere 2.6 percent of the voters in 1928, which translated into twelve parliamentary seats, seemingly confirming its status as a fringe movement; in the September 1930 elections, it won 107 of 577 seats, making it the second largest party in the Reichstag after the Social Democrats. In July 1932, the Nazis won 37.3 percent of the vote, an outright plurality that gave them 230 seats. The stage was set for the dramatic events that would catapult Hitler to power on January 30, 1933.

President of Germany Paul von Hindenburg, the eighty-five-year-old general who had led his country's army to defeat in World War I, was not sure how to handle the Nazis' rise and the accelerating disarray of the Weimar Republic. He entrusted the task of negotiating a new arrangement with the squabbling political parties to Franz von Papen, who had briefly served as chancellor in 1932. Papen convinced

Hindenburg to appoint Hitler chancellor, satisfying the aspirations of his followers, while his own appointment as vice chancellor was supposed to mean that he would control the fiery demagogue who had never held political office. "We have hired Hitler," Papen told his friends. In the long litany of misjudgments about Hitler, this ranks at the top of the list.

For Freud, Germany was hardly a faraway place. Like so many of his Viennese contemporaries, he identified with both Austria and Germany. In an interview with the German-American writer George Sylvester Viereck in 1926, he declared: "My language is German. My culture, my attainments are German. I considered myself German intellectually, until I noticed the growth of anti-Semitic prejudice in Germany and German Austria. Since that time, I prefer to call myself a Jew."

Although such statements indicated Freud was keenly aware of the noxious fumes emanating from Hitler and the Nazis who were operating next door, his first instinct was to downplay the dangers—both for Germany and Austria. In the summer of 1923, he received a letter from a young German Jewish war veteran by the name of Levens who considered himself a fervent patriot but had conflicted feelings about German nationalism. "I would advise you against wasting your energies in the fruitless struggle against the current political movement. Mass psychoses are proof against arguments," he responded. "It is just the Germans who had occasion to learn this in the World War, but they seem unable to do so. Let them alone."

Freud coupled this counsel with a more specific, personal message: "Devote yourself to the things that can raise Jews above all this foolishness, and do not take amiss my advice which is the product of a long life. Do not be too eager to join up with the Germans."

This was more than a warning not to make common cause with German nationalist parties; it reflected Freud's natural inclination to shy away from direct involvement in politics and his skepticism about revolutionary movements in general. It also underscored his conviction that people needed to look inward, with the help of psychoanalysis in many cases, to find their way in life. Political crusades and manifestos, he believed, were likely to offer individuals only illusory solutions.

When Max Eastman, the editor of *The Masses*, visited him in 1926, the Bolshevik Revolution was still a much-debated topic. Eastman had lived in Russia for two years and defended the new rulers, which intrigued his host. "You believe in liberty and there you get just the opposite," Freud asserted. Eastman offered what he later admitted was a "glib explanation" that the Bolsheviks' dictatorial methods were only a transitional phase to be followed by a "more real and universal liberty."

Freud was not impressed. "People who are going to produce liberty some time in the future are just the same to me as people who are going to have it ready for you in a celestial paradise," he declared. "I live in this real world right here. This is the only world I am interested in."

When Eastman asked him how he defined himself politically, Freud replied: "Politically I am just nothing." He was certainly overstating the extent he felt detached from the political battles of his era, but not by all that much. It wasn't exactly the case that he was uninterested; rather, he was determined to keep politics at bay while he focused on the world of his own making.

———

Freud's "real world," especially after his multiple operations on his jaw that almost completely ruled out travel, was largely confined to the two apartments on the mezzanine level of Berggasse 19. The American poet Hilda Doolittle, better known by her pen name H.D., moved to Vienna in 1933 to undergo analysis with Freud, a process that spilled over into the following year. Like most patients and visitors, she immediately noticed the strict orderliness of his universe there, including the schedule that was assigned to her. She would see Freud four days a week from five to six, and one day a week from twelve to one.

From the ground floor of the building, the stone staircase led up to a landing with two doors. "The one to the right was the Professor's professional door; the one to the left, the Freud family door," Doolittle observed. This arrangement avoided confusion between the private Freud and the Freud who treated patients. "There was the Professor who belonged to us [patients and students], there was the Professor who belonged to the family."

Other visitors also noted how much the living and working arrangements reflected Freud's personality and taste. "Berggasse 19 was a big roomy house full of books and pictures, the whole mezzanine floor padded with those thick rich rugs in which your feet sink like a camel's in the sand," Eastman wrote. "I was not surprised to see beside Rembrandt's *Anatomy Lesson*, without which no doctor's office would be recognizable, a picture of *The Nightmare*—a horrid monster with a semi-evil laugh or leer squatting upon a sleeping maiden's naked breast."

What the visitors observed often reflected their own background and expectations. If Eastman, as a radical, was particularly struck by the plush rugs, Joseph Wortis, an American who was in training for a career as a psychiatrist, recalled his starkly different impressions when he started his analysis with Freud in 1934. Berggasse 19, he noted, was an "ordinary house, in an ordinary part of Vienna." This was also the address for a butcher shop located beside the entrance that led to the stairway to the Freud apartments.

That entrance "was dilapidated, like most entrances in Vienna during that period," Wortis continued. The walls of the cluttered waiting room to Freud's office "were covered with pictures, diplomas, and honorary degrees from many lands." The photos included group shots of Freud and Jung with their American hosts during their visit to Clark University in 1909, leaving no doubt that he was proud of the recognition he had received there—notwithstanding his chronic grumbling about the United States. There were also books in many languages, "many of them inscribed in flattering terms to Freud." All of which attested to Freud's accomplishments and international fame.

For newcomers like Wortis, Freud could be an intimidating figure. The young American referred to him as "my present lord and master" who sat "like a stern Old Testament Jehovah, and who seemed to take no special pains to act with hospitality or reassurance." As Wortis lay on the couch and talked, Freud, who as always was sitting behind him so he was not looking the patient in the face, frequently complained that he was not speaking loudly and clearly enough. "You're always mumbling like the Americans do," he said. "I believe it is an expression of the general American laxity in social intercourse." He also believed that this could be a form of resistance to his treatment. Wortis had a simpler explanation: he was convinced that Freud was "a bit hard of hearing, but did not admit it."

Freud was a stickler for punctuality as well. "The Herr Professor is always *sehr punktlich*—very punctual—in everything he does," a maid told Wortis when he showed up for the first time. It was an admonition that Wortis disregarded on occasion, which Freud also ascribed to his unconscious resistance to treatment.

When it came to payments, especially by Americans and others who were charged the highest rates, he was similarly uncompromising. As a student, Wortis had to convince Freud that his fellowship to study psychoanalysis was generous enough to cover his treatment by its founder. Freud proposed his daughter Anna instead, whom he described as a "very good analyst" and much more affordable than he was. Wortis had to scramble to get confirmation from his fellowship sponsors that no switch was necessary, noting with some irritation that Freud "was unwilling to start before the financial matter was settled."

For all his severity, though, Herr Professor leavened his observations with flashes of sardonic humor. His chow was usually present during their sessions, lying or sitting quietly nearby. On one occasion, she was left out of the room and started scratching the door. Freud let her in, and she lay down on the rug and promptly started licking her private parts. Unable to get her to stop, Freud declared: "It's just like psychoanalysis."

Despite his initial skepticism about Wortis, Freud warmed to him as he did to so many of those who came both for analysis and to learn from his methods. "I prefer a student ten times more than a neurotic," Freud told him with a laugh.

Freud also could be forthcoming on his personal views about subjects other than psychoanalysis. When pressed, he spelled them out in a way that undercut his claim to Eastman that he was politically "nothing" and had no knowledge of such epic events as the Bolshevik Revolution. "Really, it's all *terra incognita* to me. I don't know anything about it," he insisted. Yet he effectively countered Eastman's naive parroting of Communist propaganda about the alleged transition to a classless society.

With Wortis, who like Eastman accepted much of the contemporary leftist rhetoric at face value, he offered even more revealing insights into his thinking. "Don't you think there's a lot of admirable idealism behind the Russian Revolution?" Wortis asked. Freud responded: "Of course, but it's an empty idealism, it's based on vague abstractions . . . A person must have some incentive to work well. They can't expect a country to survive on empty idealism. A man wants to get something for his work." Most importantly, he added, "The cost of Communism to intellectual freedom is too great. Communism means an intellectual dictatorship; it is not compatible with psychoanalysis because it is too dogmatic."

Freud was also completely unapologetic about his support for the alternative system. "I find capitalism quite satisfactory," he said. "I think the discovery of money was a great cultural advance," although he conceded that "one ought to regulate the production and distribution of wealth more satisfactorily." But he insisted that government should not replace private enterprise. "Everything run by the government is bad," he declared, pointing out that the Italian government produced abysmal matches: "You can use three of them before you get a light." This was a matter close to his heart, as was Austria's tobacco monopoly, which produced such poor-quality tobacco that he had to look elsewhere for good cigars.

When Wortis pointed out that the American government did a good job running the post office, Freud was unconvinced. "Maybe," he said, "but I assure you a private concern would do no worse."

In such discussions, Freud once again demonstrated that his popular image as a revolutionary thinker in his field was often at odds with his traditional views on a wide range of other subjects. His self-confidence also meant he did not genuflect reflexively to the fashionable views of the moment, particularly among intellectuals.

Wortis observed that he found Freud to be "surprisingly conservative in his morality," and tried to challenge him by arguing for the need for equality of the sexes in marriage.

"That is a practical impossibility," Freud responded. "There must be inequality, and the superiority of the man is the lesser of two evils." He blamed the high American divorce rate on the confusion of many husbands and wives about their respective roles. "In Europe, things are different: men take the lead and that is as it should be," he said. Yet Freud was drawn to strong, intellectually assertive women such as Lou Andreas-Salomé and Marie Bonaparte, who were hardly subservient to men.

Wortis also asked him why there was so much hostility to homosexuality. "It was always so, even in ancient Greece," Freud replied, explaining that everyone has a homosexual component. "People repress their own homosexuality and if the repression is strong enough, they adopt a hostile attitude."

He described homosexuality as "something pathological" and "arrested development," but warned against the misuse of psychoanalysis in such cases. "The only homosexuals one can attempt to cure are those who want to be changed," he said. Without a trace of disapproval, he added: "One often has the experience of starting an analysis with a homosexual who then finds such relief in being and talking just as he is that he drops the analysis and remains homosexual."

In his early study of the patient known as Dora, Freud had explained his views in more detail. "The uncertainty in regard to the boundaries of what is called normal sexual life, when we take different races and different epochs into account, should in itself be enough to cool the zealot's ardor," he wrote. "We surely ought not to forget that the perversion which is most repellant to us, the sensual love of a man for a man, was not only tolerated by a people so far our superiors in cultivation as were the Greeks, but was actually entrusted by them with important social functions."

While Freud's use of the term "perversion" sounds jarring to the modern reader, his message was that this was society's definition; his own ideas were far more complex than that. "The sexual life of each one of us extends to a slight degree—now in this direction, now in that—beyond the narrow lines imposed as the standard of normality," he declared.

Like many of his patients, Freud could not be easily categorized: he always charted his own course.

———

One reason that Freud felt confident in doing so was that his fame was still very much on the ascendency—and psychoanalysis was firmly established in numerous countries. Recalling his time in Vienna in the early 1930s, the young American correspondent William Shirer, who would become famous in his own right, wrote: "Psychoanalysis was bursting into the world at that time and Freud was its prophet. No doubt he was a genius and he had an impressive impact on the twentieth century, but he could brook no criticism from the men he had trained and, who defying him, began to break away and question some of his theories and methods." Shirer was referring to Carl Jung, Alfred Adler, and others who had gone their separate ways.

In fact, Freud's brand of psychoanalysis had won widespread recognition even earlier in the interwar period, despite the internecine feuds. Psychoanalytic societies and institutes proliferated in Europe and North America, and Freud's theories and practices were discussed just about everywhere. They also attracted a fair share of imitators who were seeking to profit from their popularity. Jones spotted an advertisement by a dubious "English Psycho-Analytical Publishing Company" with the come-on: "Would you like to earn £1,000 a year as a psycho-analyst? We can show you how to do it."

There were similar shenanigans in the United States. "Most unfortunately for Freud's repute, his theories lend themselves with terrible ease to the uses of ignorance and of quackery," *The New York Times* wrote in 1926. Freud did not treat such imitation as the sincerest form of flattery: he denounced those who, without proper training, claimed to utilize his methods. But he recognized the futility of trying to prevent all those he considered to be imposters from profiting from his reputation.

Overall, though, the extent to which psychoanalysis had become a regular topic of conversation offered compelling evidence of the power of Freud's ideas. So did the fact that those ideas were seeping into the literature of the period.

H. G. Wells is mostly remembered today for his science fiction, but he also wrote comic novels about British society. In 1922, he published

The Secret Places of the Heart, whose main character, Sir Richmond Hardy, tries to sort out his problems with his wife and other women by traveling around the country with Dr. Martineau, a psychiatrist. Hardy is a stand-in for Wells, while Martineau serves as a proxy for Freud, whom Wells would meet for the first time in 1931. At the start of their journey, the doctor spelled out his approach. "If the trouble is in the mental sphere, why go out of the mental sphere for treatment? Talk and thought; these are your remedies," he declares. He also offers such Freudian nuggets as, "To analyze a mental knot is to untie it."

———

Another result of Freud's growing fame was that other celebrities of his era were anxious to meet him. At the end of 1926, Freud and his wife, Martha, traveled to Berlin to see their two sons and their families who were living there, arriving in time for Christmas and the New Year. It was Freud's first journey there since the operation on his jaw more than three years earlier. They stayed with Ernst, who was an architect, and Albert Einstein took the opportunity to come around with his wife before their return to Vienna on January 2, 1927.

Freud and Einstein talked for two hours, clearly enjoying each other's company. Freud described Einstein, who was twenty-three years younger than him, as "cheerful, sure of himself and agreeable," wryly adding: "He understands as much about psychology as I do about physics, so we had a very pleasant talk."

In fact, Einstein may have understood more about psychology than he let on, since his son Eduard, a medical student at the University of Zurich, hung Freud's picture in his bedroom and tried to apply his theories to analyze himself. The youngest of three children from Einstein's first marriage, Eduard was frail physically and emotionally. "It's at times difficult to have such an important father, because one feels so unimportant," he wrote shortly before the meeting between his father and Freud. He later tried to commit suicide; diagnosed as a schizo-phrenic, he ended up in an asylum near Zurich.

While pleased with his encounter with Einstein, Freud also re-flected on the differences between their careers. "The lucky fellow has had a much easier time than I have," he noted. "He has had the support of a long series of predecessors from Newton onward, while I have had to hack every step of my way through a tangled jungle alone. No wonder that my path is not a very broad one, and that I have not got far on it." Left unspoken was the fact that the younger Einstein had won a Nobel Prize in 1922, an honor Freud would never receive despite numerous nominations.

———

Although the two men never met again after their one encounter in Berlin, Einstein reached out to Freud in the summer of 1932, seeking his help. With the Nazis and other radical movements on the rise again, the League of Nation's International Institute of Intellectual Cooper-ation asked Einstein to choose another eminent person to exchange ideas with him about the "most insistent of all the problems civilization has to face," as he put it in his letter to Freud. "This is the problem: Is there any way of delivering mankind from the menace of war?"

Einstein was a self-proclaimed pacifist, and Freud's views had evolved a long way from his initial support for his side in World War I, starting with his 1915 essays "Thoughts for the Times on War and Death" that decried the conflict's "blind fury" and indiscriminate de-struction. Shortly before receiving Einstein's letter that summer of 1932, he had signed an appeal organized by the French novelist Henri Barbusse, a pacifist and member of the Communist Party, calling on medical professionals to attend a congress aimed at preventing a new world war. "As guardians of the peoples' health we raise our voice in warning against a new interminable carnage into which the nations are being driven, the consequences of which are unforeseeable," it declared. Although Freud did not attend the gathering, this was a rare brush with political activism for him.

Freud, however, did not consider himself to be either a political activist or thinker, which meant that Einstein had to appeal to him in a way that played to his primary interests. The physicist confessed that he had "no insight into the dark places of human will and feeling," and asked Freud "to bring the light of your far-reaching knowledge of man's instinctive life to bear upon the problem."

Einstein added that the most obvious solution was the creation of a "supranational organization competent to render verdicts of incontestable authority and enforce absolute submission to the execution of its verdicts." That would require the "unconditional surrender" by every nation of its sovereignty "in a certain measure." But he conceded that "strong psychological factors are at work which paralyze these efforts," including the ease with which nationalist passions can be turned into a "collective psychosis" that leads to armed conflicts.

Einstein deliberately larded his letter with such terms, since he feared that Freud might beg off, arguing that Einstein's request strayed too far from his field of expertise. In reality, Freud was flattered to be asked, and unlikely to turn down Einstein for any reason. But in his response, Freud declared that the question about ridding mankind of war "took me by surprise" and that he was "dumbfounded by the thought of my (of our, I almost wrote) incompetence; for this struck me as being a matter of practical politics, the statesman's proper study."

Recognizing that Einstein was not asking for policy proposals but seeking to understand "how this question of preventing war strikes a psychologist," Freud tried to elaborate on the theories he wrote about earlier and address the "gist of the matter" that Einstein spelled out in his letter: the obvious obstacles to empowering any institution to enforce the peace.

"Conflicts of interest between man and man are resolved, in principle, by the recourse to violence," Freud wrote. "It is the same in the animal kingdom, from which man cannot claim exclusion." New weaponry proved that intelligence was more important than brute force, but the ultimate aim—of eliminating foes in any dispute—remained the same. Most often, this meant killing them, which also "gratifies an instinctive craving," but in other cases it could lead to their enslavement. "Here violence finds an outlet not in slaughter but subjugation."

In his view, there were two instincts at work in all humans: the one that seeks to conserve and unify, which is called "erotic" or "sexual"; and the one that seeks to destroy and kill, otherwise known as the death instinct. Echoing Einstein, he argued that wars could be prevented only if there was widespread consent for a "central control which shall have the last word in every conflict of interests"—and which would be endowed with "adequate executive force."

But Freud was even blunter than Einstein in his conclusion that no such institution would win enough acceptance to achieve its purpose: "It is all too clear that nationalistic ideas, paramount today in every country, operate in quite a contrary direction . . . there is no likelihood of our being able to suppress humanity's aggressive tendencies."

Freud was not only thinking of the Nazis and other right-wing groups; he was equally dismissive of the Bolsheviks who "aspire to do away with human aggressiveness by ensuring the satisfaction of material needs and enforcing equality between man and man. To me this hope seems vain," he wrote. "Meanwhile they busily perfect their armaments, and their hatred of outsiders is not the least of the factors of cohesion among themselves."

Although he referred to "pacifists like us" who find war intolerable, Freud came across in his letter as less than fully committed to the pacifist cause. "All forms of war cannot be indiscriminately condemned," he declared, so long as almost every nation was preparing "callously to exterminate its rival." This meant that "all alike must be equipped for war."

The exchange of letters was published as a pamphlet in 1933, but Freud recognized that he had produced one of his less impressive pieces of writing. His pessimism about the possibilities of eliminating war was fully justified and he had revealed more about his political outlook than he usually did, but he had failed to meet the expectations of readers who wanted at least some guidance from him on how the death instinct could be brought under control.

Realizing that he had not added much to Einstein's initial ruminations, Freud remarked that this exchange of letters would not win the Nobel Prize for either him or Einstein—a barbed attempt at humor given his sensitivity on the subject of the prize that kept eluding him. In a subsequent comment, he referred to the "tedious and sterile so-called discussion with Einstein."

All of which underscored the fact that for Freud psychoanalysis was the center of his solar system, and almost everything else was peripheral. He could stray further afield at times, as he did at Einstein's request, but he was neither surprised nor visibly disappointed when such efforts produced meager results. His first priority was to strengthen the theory and practice of psychoanalysis, no matter what was happening politically and economically. That was the way he measured his success or failure.

———

That was also why Freud could devote so much time and energy to seemingly minor disputes with some of his followers while Europe plunged deeper into crisis. Sándor Ferenczi, his longtime Hungarian associate, had begun experimenting with new techniques in his sessions with his patients, including playing the part of a loving parent by showing affection for them. This ran contrary to Freud's insistence on avoiding any emotional entanglements between analysts and patients, and he warned Ferenczi that he was proceeding "in all sorts of directions which do not seem to me to lead to any desirable goal." Troubled by the signs of an emerging rift between them, Ferenczi visited Vienna in late October 1931, so that they could discuss their disagreements.

Their talk was amicable as always, but it failed to resolve anything. Freud was still unhappy with Ferenczi's new course, and Ferenczi was in no mood to back down—as he made clear in a letter a few weeks after their meeting. In his reply dated December 13, 1931, Freud was equally clear about his objections. "I see that the differences between us come to a head in a technical detail which is well worth discussing," he wrote. "You have not made a secret of the fact that you kiss your patients and let them kiss you; I have also heard that from a patient of my own."

Anticipating a counter-accusation, he added: "Now I am assuredly not one of those who from prudishness or from consideration of bourgeois convention would condemn little erotic gratifications of this kind." But he argued that Ferenczi could be opening the door to much more dangerous practices. "Now picture what will be the result of publishing your technique," he continued. "There is no revolutionary who is not driven out of the field by a still more radical one. A number of independent thinkers in matters of technique will say to themselves: why stop at a kiss? Certainly one gets further when one adopts 'pawing' as well, which after all doesn't make a baby." Then, contradicting his claim that he was not motivated by prudishness, he luridly envisaged "peeping and showing" and "petting parties" as the next step if that process went unchecked.

For Ferenczi, this sweeping reprimand must have come as a shock. But Freud insisted that his sole purpose was to urge him to abide by the basic rules of behavior—avoiding the temptation to tinker with them in any way. "We have hitherto in our technique held to the conclusion that patients are to be refused erotic gratifications," he declared. To Max Eitingon in Berlin, the president of the International Psychoanalytical Association at the time, Freud complained that Ferenczi was offended "because one is not delighted to hear how he plays mother and child with his female patients."

None of this led to an open break between the two men, but their relations were distinctly cooler than before, which was the case until Ferenczi died in Budapest on May 22, 1933.

———

As much as Freud was focused on such internal disputes, he could not ignore the broader economic and political crisis in Europe that was casting a dark shadow everywhere. This was especially visible in Germany, a country that up till then had played a major role in the spread of his teachings and practice. Along with Karl Abraham, who died in 1925, Eitingon, the son of a wealthy businessman who owned a fur store in New York, was responsible for much of those early successes. In 1920, he had cofounded and financed the launch of Berlin's psychoanalytical clinic, which both treated patients and offered training for psychoanalysts. The facility's interior was designed by Freud's youngest son, Ernst, who had settled in the German capital after the war.

Thanks to Eitingon's generosity in underwriting the Berlin Psychoanalytic Institute, psychoanalysis was doing particularly well in Berlin. Between 1920 and 1930, according to one report, the facility had conducted 1,955 consultations, almost a third of which led to psychoanalyses. The patients were treated by ninety-four therapists, the majority of whom became members of the International Psychoanalytical Association. As the institute's reputation grew, it acted as a magnet for aspiring psychoanalysts, not only from Germany but also from Britain, France, Sweden, the United States, and other countries. This created a multiplier effect, since some of the returning graduates launched their own institutes.

When the stock market collapsed in 1929, Eitingon's father lost his fortune and died three years later—and Max was no longer able to keep making generous contributions to the institute in Berlin and the *Verlag*, the publishing arm of Freud's movement in Vienna. Even the sales of Freud's books, which had been a considerable source of income, shrank dramatically. In January 1932, Eitingon visited Freud in Vienna to discuss the future of both the Berlin institute and the publishing operation. He was alarmed not just by the financial problems but also by the growing power of Hitler's Nazi movement, and he was already contemplating a possible move to Palestine. Freud was focused more narrowly on the financial problems, at that point still not recognizing the greater danger that was looming. As a result, his advice to Eitingon was to keep the Berlin institute going as long as possible, effectively urging him to stay put.

To keep the Verlag afloat, Freud's oldest son, Martin, took over the job of manager and asked the creditors for a moratorium on its payments, while cutting back on costs. In April, Freud wrote an appeal to the International Psychoanalytical Association and the national societies for help. Since Eitingon suffered from what was described as a "slight cerebral thrombosis" at about the same time, the always energetic Ernest Jones stepped in to oversee the translation, distribution, and follow-up. Freud was far from optimistic about what could be achieved in the midst of the global depression. "I do not expect any result from it," he asserted. "Perhaps we are only repeating the ridiculous act of saving a birdcage while the whole house is burning."

As Jones noted, Freud was proven wrong in his prediction, since his appeal met with an "immediate and gratifying response," particularly from across the Atlantic. "What saved the situation was the generosity of the American colleagues, for which they deserve all praise," he reported.

Although this staved off the immediate threat of bankruptcy, the overall outlook for Freud's movement, especially for its heavily Jewish practitioners and Jews in general, was increasingly perilous. As much as Freud did not want to contemplate the bigger political picture, he could not completely ignore it. But he still wanted to cling to the belief that there was no reason for panic. During Bullitt's visit to Berlin in 1930 to work on the book about Wilson, Freud told him: "A nation that produced Goethe could not possibly go to the bad."

Soon, however, Freud felt the repercussions within his own family. In 1932, Oliver, who like Ernst had settled in Berlin, lost his job as a civil engineer and his father had to support him during his remaining time in the German capital. Even before Hitler came to power in January 1933, the exodus of Jewish psychoanalysts from Europe started gaining momentum, with some of them looking to begin new lives in the United States, Palestine, or elsewhere.

But Freud had no intention of moving. This was primarily the result of his attachment to his life in Vienna and his conviction that he was too old and ill to contemplate anything of the sort. That did not mean that he dismissed the Zionist movement, which was attracting more attention because of increasing anti-Semitism in Europe. After all, along with Einstein, he was a member of the first Board of Governors of the Hebrew University of Jerusalem, and in principle he supported the idea of finding a new home for many Jews. As he wrote to the translator of his books in Jerusalem in late 1930, "Zionism has awakened in me my strongest sympathies." It was "something that the present-day situation seems to justify," he added, although "I should like to be mistaken about this."

But Freud had more conflicted feelings about Zionism than he let on. During the previous year, there was an outbreak of violence between Arabs and Jews in the Holy Land, which cost the lives of 130 Jews. Afterward, Chaim Koffler, the Vienna representative of Keren Hayesod, a fundraising group organized by the Zionist movement to help Jewish immigrants in Palestine, wrote to Freud, asking him to declare his support for their cause. "I cannot do as you wish," Freud responded in a letter dated February 26, 1930. "Whoever wants to influence the masses must give them something rousing and inflammatory and my sober judgment of Zionism does not permit this."

Politely but firmly, Freud explained that, while he sympathized with the Jewish victims of the riots, "the baseless fanaticism of our people is in part to be blamed for the awakening of Arab distrust." More broadly, he declared: "I do not think that Palestine could ever become a Jewish state, nor that the Christian and Islamic worlds would ever be prepared to have their holy places under Jewish care. It would have seemed more sensible to me to establish a Jewish homeland on a less historically-burdened land. But I know that such a rational viewpoint would never have gained the enthusiasm of the masses and the financial support of the wealthy."

This was not the response Koffler was hoping for, and he wrote in pencil on the letter, "Do not show this to foreigners." According to the National Library of Israel, which has preserved a copy, the letter was not published for sixty years.

———

On January 27, 1933, three days before Hitler was named chancellor, Eitingon paid another visit to Freud in Vienna to discuss the implications for their movement. By then, Jones had replaced Eitingon as president of the International Psychoanalytical Association, but Freud still relied on Eitingon, as his man in Berlin, to try to preserve whatever he could in Germany. In a letter on April 3, he urged Eitingon to hang on as long as he could in Germany while acknowledging that the ripple effects of the Nazi takeover were being felt in Vienna as well. "There is no lack of attempts to create panic, but just like you I shall leave my place only at the very last moment and probably not even then," he wrote.

At that point, it was certainly easier to avoid panic in Vienna than in Berlin, where the Reichstag fire on February 27 served as an excuse to suspend civil liberties and grant Hitler full dictatorial powers under the terms of the innocuously named Enabling Act. As Jones had written to Freud on March 3, "You must be glad that Austria is not a part of Germany."

In the new scheme of things, anti-Semitism became official policy, with the medical profession an early target. Non-Aryan doctors, including psychoanalysts, could no longer participate in private or public health insurance programs, effectively preventing them from making a living. Eitingon was also compelled to resign his position as the director of the Berlin Psychoanalytic Institute, replaced by Karl Boehm, one of only two "Aryan" members of its board.

By the end of the year, Eitingon emigrated to Palestine, promptly organizing the Palestine Psychoanalytic Society. Most other Jewish psychoanalysts in Germany fled abroad as well. In London, Jones helped organize some of those departures, even paying out of his savings for the resettlement of the widow and daughter of Karl Abraham. He also consulted regularly with Anna Freud in Vienna, who was the secretary of the International Psychoanalytical Association, and reached out to his colleagues elsewhere both to sound the alarm and seek their help. In April, he described the overall situation in a letter to Smith Ely Jelliffe, a New York psychoanalyst:

> We are having a hectic time over here with political refugees. Some seventy thousand got away from Germany as the blow was falling. Among them are most of the German Psycho-Analytical Society . . . The persecution has been much worse than you seem to think and has really quite lived up to the Middle Ages in reputation.

The Nazi propaganda machine took direct aim not just at the German psychoanalysts but also at the broader movement—and its founder. "Psychoanalysis is an impressive example of the fact that nothing good for us Germans can ever come from a Jew, even when he [Freud] produces 'scientific achievements,'" the magazine *Deutsche Volksgesundheit aus Blut und Boden* [German Public Health from Blood and Soil] wrote in its August/September 1933 issue. "Even if he gave us 5% that was novel and apparently good, 95% of his doctrine is destructive and annihilating *for us.*"

On the evening of May 10, thousands of students joined a torchlight parade that wound up at a square opposite the University of Berlin. There, they set fire to a huge pile of books and kept adding more volumes. These were by authors the Nazis hated, everyone from Thomas Mann, Erich Maria Remarque, and Lion Feuchtwanger to H. G. Wells, Jack London, and Helen Keller. And, of course, Freud figured in that list as well. Before his books were added to the bonfire, the announcer offered a customized explanation: "Against the soul-destroying overestimation of the sex life—and on behalf of the nobility of the human soul—I offer to the flames the writings of one Sigmund Freud!"

Addressing the students, Propaganda Minister Joseph Goebbels declared: "The soul of the German people can again express itself. These flames not only illuminate the final end of an old era; they also light up the new." Similar book burnings took place in other German cities, too.

Freud's first impulse was to make light of these chilling spectacles. "What progress we are making," he told Jones. "In the Middle Ages, they would have burnt me; nowadays they are content with burning my books." As his biographer Peter Gay noted, "This must have been the least prescient bon mot he ever made."

But Freud understood at least some of the implications, especially for those who were close to him and still living in Germany. He agreed with the decisions of Eitingon and other colleagues to leave before the Nazi regime began restricting emigration, especially for Jews. And he was fully supportive of the decision of both of his sons in Germany to flee as well. Writing to his nephew Samuel in Manchester, he reported that for them "life in Germany had become impossible." Ernst, the architect and interior designer, moved to London, while Oliver, the civil engineer, went to France.

———

Alarmed by events in Germany, several of Freud's friends and colleagues began urging him to emigrate as well. "In our circles there is already a great deal of trepidation," he reported in a letter to Marie Bonaparte on March 16, 1933. "People feel that the nationalistic extravagances in Germany may extend to our little country. I have even been advised to flee already to Switzerland or France." But all such advice was "nonsense," he insisted. "I don't believe there is any danger here and if it should come I am firmly resolved to await it here. If they kill me—good. It is one kind of death like another. But probably that is only cheap boasting."

Responding ten days later to Bonaparte's subsequent invitation to come live in her house in the Parisian suburb of St. Cloud, he thanked her but wrote: "I have decided not to make use of it; it will hardly be necessary. The brutalities in Germany seem to be diminishing"— providing another example of his wishful thinking. In the same letter, though, he was realistic enough to recognize that the "systematic suppression of the Jews, depriving them of all positions, has as yet scarcely begun." He also argued that "persecution of the Jews and restriction of intellectual freedom are the only features of Hitler's program that can be carried out. The rest is weakness and utopianism."

From Budapest, Sándor Ferenczi, in his last exchange of letters with Freud before his death in May, was particularly adamant that Freud needed to flee Vienna as soon as possible. But Freud was equally adamant in his response, rejecting what he called the "flight motif," just as he had with Bonaparte. "I am glad to be able to tell you that I am not thinking of leaving Vienna," he wrote on April 2. He enumerated several practical reasons for his decision: "I am not mobile enough, and am too dependent on my treatment, on various ameliorations and comforts; furthermore, I do not want to leave my possessions here. Probably, however, I should stay even if I were in full health and youth."

The crux of the matter was that Freud wanted to believe he could continue living in Vienna for whatever time he had left in his life, no matter what was happening in Germany. "There is no personal danger for me," he maintained to Ferenczi, "and when you picture life with the suppression of us Jews as extremely unpleasant do not forget what an uncomfortable life settling abroad, whether in Switzerland or England, promises for refugees. In my opinion flight would only be justified by direct danger to life."

Four days after the burning of his books in Berlin, Freud wrote to Lou Andreas-Salomé in a more reflective vein, hinting that he wasn't quite as sanguine as he normally sounded about the supposed lack of immediate danger: "With us things are as might be expected in these mad times. Even Anna is depressed at moments."

The popular Austrian-Jewish writer Stefan Zweig, whose books were also thrown into the bonfire in Berlin, discussed the "horrors of Hitler's world" with Freud on several occasions. "As a humane man, he was deeply distressed by that terrible outbreak of bestiality, but as a thinker he was not at all surprised," Zweig recalled. Since Freud "denied the supremacy of culture over our instinctive drives," he added, the rise of the Nazis "confirmed in the most dreadful way—not that he was proud of it—his opinion that it is impossible to root the elemental, barbaric destructive drive out of the human psyche."

Freud could analyze events in that detached manner yet fail to draw the logical conclusions for his situation. In this respect, he was hardly alone, especially in Austria where the illusion persisted that the dangers of the barbaric, destructive drive could be kept at bay. "We are none of us very proud of our political blindness at that time, and we are horrified to see where it has brought us," Zweig wrote later. "Anyone trying to explain it would have to level accusations, and which one of us has any right to do so?"

Although some German Jews like Einstein, who left for the United States in December 1932, on the eve of Hitler's ascension, recognized the magnitude of the danger early, they were the exception rather than the rule. Reviewing the record, Zweig wrote: "I must admit that in 1933 and 1934, none of us in Germany and Austria would have contemplated the possibility of one hundredth part, one thousandth part of what was about to break over us a little later."

But Zweig could have also pointed out that his political blindness did not last nearly as long as Freud's did. Unlike Freud, he soon concluded that Austria would not be spared from Hitler's horrors, and he emigrated to England in 1934. In 1940, he and his second wife moved briefly to the United States before settling in Petrópolis, Brazil. He felt lonely and isolated there, depressed by the early German victories in the war, and he could all too vividly imagine what was happening back in Nazi-controlled Europe. The result was that both he and his wife took an overdose of barbiturates on February 22, 1942. In his suicide note, Zweig explained that now that "my spiritual homeland, Europe, destroyed itself," which included his German-speaking world, he no longer had the strength to carry on.

10.

"THE AUSTRIAN CELL"

FREUD'S CONVICTION THAT HE COULD CONTINUE LIVING AND working in Vienna was based on one premise: Austria's leaders were committed to following a separate path, which meant they would safeguard the country's independence, no matter what was happening next door. Hitler had consolidated his power with breathtaking speed, transforming Germany into a totalitarian state dedicated to enforcing his doctrine of racial purity, and his writings and speeches left no doubt that he was intent on pursuing his grandiose vision for a new German empire. Yet Freud chose to believe that Austria would not drown in the swelling Nazi tide.

"Despite all the newspaper reports of mobs, demonstrations, etc., Vienna is calm, life undisturbed," he reported to Jones on April 7, 1933. "We can expect with certainty that the Hitler movement will spread to Austria, is indeed already here, but it is very unlikely that it will present a similar danger as in Germany."

He argued that the Nazis would likely be only one part of an alliance of right-wing parties that were pushing the country in the direction of a "rightist dictatorship," which would signal the death of "social democracy." But while that development "will not make life pleasant for us Jews," he continued, any "legalized persecution" of Jews would trigger the intervention of the League of Nations. Besides, as he had already explained to Marie Bonaparte, "Our people are not quite so brutal." Only Germany's annexation of Austria could seriously endanger its Jews, he maintained, but France and its allies would not permit such a step.

In a letter to Jones on July 23, Freud wrote: "We too will get our fascism, party dictatorship, elimination of opposition, applied anti-Semitism. But we should retain our independence, and the peace treaty makes it legally impossible to strip minorities of their rights." That was reassurance enough, he insisted, to allow him to stay in Austria. His faith in the power of treaties looks stunningly naive in retrospect, but at the time he was far from alone in believing that the "witch's cauldron in Germany"—and, in particular, its leader—could be kept from boiling over.

Yet Freud occasionally let slip that he could envisage other, darker possibilities. "The world is turning into an enormous prison," he wrote to Bonaparte that same summer. "Germany is the worst cell. What will happen in the Austrian cell is quite uncertain."

———

The Austrian cell, as Freud called it, was widely viewed as a rump state: it was all that was left of the old, sprawling Austro-Hungarian Empire that had been dismantled by the victors at the end of World War I. With a population of 6.5 million, as opposed to the 50 million inhabitants who had lived under Habsburg rule, Austria was an even bigger loser than its German ally, a country that was far more vociferous in its protests about the peace terms imposed by the Treaty of Versailles. Despite the loss of 13 percent of its European territory and about 10 percent of its population, Germany remained largely intact.

The two former allies experienced many of the same problems in the early interwar period: hyperinflation, widespread social unrest, and the rise of radical right-wing and left-wing political parties, buttressed by paramilitary forces, who fought each other and undermined the fragile coalition governments trying to maintain a degree of order. The politicians in both Berlin and Vienna kept taking turns at the helm, with new chancellors rising and falling with bewildering speed, almost before they could become household names.

But Austria had its definite peculiarities and a political dynamic that did not necessarily follow the same trajectory as Germany. For one thing, the Austrians could still make fun of their situation, no matter how dire it looked. According to a Viennese saying of that era, "The situation in Germany is serious but not hopeless; the situation in Austria is hopeless but not serious." The survival of that kind of wry humor, accompanied by the sense that much of daily life in the capital remained civil and charming, helped nurture Freud's belief that he could ride out whatever storms were in the offing.

Even the divisions in Austrian society did not neatly parallel the ones in Germany. The capital was known as "Red Vienna," because it was the bastion of the Socialists, who fielded a paramilitary force known as the *Schutzbund*. Most of the city's 175,000 Jews, roughly 10 percent of its population, were among their most reliable supporters. The smaller cities and countryside were the stronghold of conservative Catholics, whose paramilitary force was called the *Heimwehr*. At times, the two de facto armies clashed directly; at other times, the small federal army, which was torn between its conflicting loyalties, participated in the conflicts. After a court acquitted three right-wingers who fired upon Socialist demonstrators, killing a worker and his seven-year-old son in July 1927, protesters set fire to the Palace of Justice and tried to stop firefighters from putting it out. The police responded with numerous salvos, killing eighty-four people and wounding about five hundred more.

But what each side hoped to achieve was far from clear, especially when it came to the essential question of Austria's existence. The Socialists were more tied to the notion of a common German identity than the conservative parties. Karl Renner, who served as Austria's first chancellor after World War I, was both a Social Democratic leader and a passionate advocate of unification with Germany. "The Austrians were never a nation by themselves and never could be," he argued in 1928. Germany and Austria floated the idea of a customs union between them in 1931, triggering the withdrawal of French credits for Austrian banks and deepening the economic crisis. At that point, Paris was still determined to enforce the separation of the two German-speaking countries.

Austria stumbled from crisis to crisis and the unemployment rate rose to 27 percent by February 1933. At the same time, Hitler's ascension to power in Germany did not bode well for the land of his birth. In *Mein Kampf*, the Nazi leader had declared that his "ardent love for my German-Austrian homeland" was accompanied by his "deep hatred for the Austrian state" and the realization "that Germanism could be safeguarded only by the destruction of Austria." In other words, the only acceptable outcome was Anschluss, the annexation of Austria by Germany to form one German state. The small Austrian Nazi Party was meant to be his tool to achieve that goal.

In theory, most Austrians were receptive to the idea of Anschluss. The American correspondent John Gunther, who was based in Vienna at the time, estimated that, in 1932, 80 percent of them fell into that category—but that quickly changed. "By the end of 1933 it was at least 60 percent against," he wrote. "Reason: the Hitler terror." Instead of waiting to win over popular opinion in Austria, the Nazis had launched a campaign of terror that included bombings, shootings, and other acts of violence. This alarmed a wide range of groups, including on the right, triggering a strong backlash.

Most significantly, a new political leader had emerged in Vienna to orchestrate the growing resistance to the Nazis. In May 1932, Engelbert Dollfuss, the minister for agriculture and forestry, was tapped for the job of chancellor by the Christian Social Party. He was chosen largely because many of the more seasoned politicians did not want to take on the seemingly hopeless task of trying to steer the country through its multiple crises. Only forty, he was hardly an imposing figure. An illegitimate child of a peasant Catholic family, he fumbled awkwardly through his speeches and stood all of four feet eleven inches tall, making him the butt of numerous jokes. One example: the police foiled an attempted coup against him by locating and removing the mousetrap smuggled into his room. Yet, according to Gunther, "He became David to the Goliath of the Nazis."

Hitler had been ratcheting up the pressure on Austria, jeopardizing tourism by imposing a new fee on Germans who wanted to travel there, along with continuing the terror campaign by both Nazis inside Austria and the "Austrian Legion," the Austrian Nazi paramilitary forces in Bavaria who launched cross-border attacks. On June 19, 1933, one person was killed and twenty-nine wounded in a grenade attack at Krems in the Wachau wine valley of the Danube. Dollfuss responded by banning the Nazi Party in Austria, rallying his countrymen, including the Socialists, to defy Hitler and drop their talk of an Anschluss.

This was action born of conviction. "Dollfuss really believed in Austria," wrote the Jewish writer George Clare, who grew up in Vienna before the Anschluss and ended up serving in the British Army during the war. "He did not see his country as just another German province."

The diminutive chancellor felt emboldened to take such decisive measures for two reasons. First of all, he had taken advantage of the resignations of three leaders of the parliament the previous March to dissolve that body while he assumed full dictatorial powers. He banned all political parties and launched a "Fatherland Front," which was billed as a broad patriotic movement. Secondly, he had allied himself with Benito Mussolini, his Italian counterpart, who at that point was determined to maintain Austria as a buffer state between his country and Hitler's Germany.

All three leaders may have qualified as Fascists, but their interests did not coincide then. Worried about the loyalty of his German-speaking subjects in the South Tyrol, Mussolini did not want to do anything that might encourage them to seek the backing of Hitler. As Gunther put it, this meant that the Italian dictator "became to all intents and purposes the Lord High Protector of Austria."

It wasn't just Dollfuss who wanted to encourage Mussolini in that role. Many Austrians welcomed the support of anyone who might help thwart Hitler's designs on their country. A curious incident suggests that perhaps Freud was one of them. In 1933, the Italian psychoanalyst Edoardo Weiss brought one of his patients to Freud for a consultation. The patient's father, who accompanied him and was a close friend of Mussolini, asked Freud to give him a gift for the Italian dictator with a dedication. Freud agreed, presenting him with a copy of *Why War?*— his exchange with Einstein, which in itself amounted to a pointed commentary. His inscription read "with the devoted greeting of an old man, who recognizes the cultural hero in the ruler."

Weiss believed that Freud was alluding to Mussolini's support for Italy's ambitious archeological excavation projects, which offered him a diplomatic alternative to saying anything that smacked of a political endorsement. But while Freud had no sympathy for Fascist dictators, there is another possible interpretation: like Dollfuss, Freud took the view that Mussolini was on Austria's side in this period, which was well before the Italian dictator and Hitler formalized the alliance that would bind them together during World War II. Freud also recognized that, in Austria itself, it was the right-wing Catholic politicians who were trying to fend off Hitler. As he wrote to Lou Andreas-Salomé later, "it is only this Catholicism that protects us from the Nazis."

———

Dollfuss continued to face opposition on two fronts—from the Socialists and the Nazis. Both Mussolini and the leaders of the Heimwehr, which the chancellor treated as an auxiliary army, were eager to eliminate the Socialists first. In February 1934, new battles erupted in Vienna and the provinces, with the Heimwehr, the federal army, and the police taking on the Socialist paramilitary units, the Schutzbund. The Karl-Marx-Hof and the Goethehof, huge worker housing complexes in the capital, were shelled; after the defenders surrendered, nine Socialist leaders were hanged and many others were imprisoned. In those and other battles around the country, nearly a thousand people were killed.

With the Socialists defeated, the Nazis stepped up their campaign of terror. Hitler was angered by the so-called Rome Protocols, an agreement between Italy, Austria, and Hungary, also a country with an authoritarian regime, to coordinate their foreign policies. To the German leader, this smacked of another effort by Dollfuss to safeguard Austria's independence. On July 25, Austria's Nazis attempted to overthrow him, with at least Hitler's tacit blessing if not outright support.

Alerted that his government was in danger, Dollfuss suspended a meeting of his cabinet in the federal chancellery at noon. During a changing of the military guard less than an hour later, 144 Nazis charged in, rounding up any officials they could find. Dollfuss, who was in his private study, managed to order the army to stay loyal, and then tried to escape from the assailants. But a group of them spotted him, and their leader, Otto Planetta, shot him twice at close range, hitting him in the armpit and neck. During the next two and a half agonizing hours, Dollfuss bled to death while his assassins refused to call a doctor or even a priest. The Heimwehr and the police finally came to help—but confusion reigned outside the chancellery as they debated what to do, not knowing what was happening inside.

Ironically, the death of Dollfuss did not mean victory for the Nazi putschists. Vastly outnumbered and without any signal from Hitler that he would come to their rescue, they asked for safe passage to Germany. Believing they had secured that promise, they surrendered in the evening. But Minister of Education Kurt von Schuschnigg, a dour Dollfuss loyalist who had also held the post of justice minister and was appointed as Dollfuss's successor the next day, had other ideas. Thirteen of the Putschists, including Planetta, were hanged and the others imprisoned.

Schuschnigg's ascension meant that the government remained committed to the policies of his assassinated predecessor: a right-wing dictatorship at home, but one that would continue to resist a Nazi takeover. The new chancellor, who had started his career as a lawyer in Innsbruck, was more ambivalent about the notion of an Austrian— as opposed to a German—identity, and he hoped to reach some sort of accommodation with Hitler. Nonetheless, he continued to rely on Mussolini to help stave off an Anschluss, and he incorporated the Heimwehr into the Fatherland Front to end the divisions within his armed forces.

For Freud and other Austrian Jews, the situation continued to look chaotic and unpredictable—but not necessarily alarming. During the violence in February 1934, Freud wrote to his son Ernst in London that "it is probably not easy to learn from the papers what is really happening in a city where shooting is going on." He added: "The future is uncertain: either Austrian fascism or the swastika. In the latter event, we will have to leave; native fascism we are willing to take in stride up to a certain point; it can hardly treat us as badly as its German cousin."

This mention of the "latter event" indicated he knew that a German takeover could not be ruled out, but he was still clinging to his belief that it would not happen.

Referring to the fate of Dollfuss, Clare—the Jewish writer who was a teenager in Vienna at the time—declared: "The murder of the little chancellor was a warning, but for us this warning was still invisible. We were no better than the Jews of Germany in reading the first signs pointing to their destiny."

———

The immediate concern for Jones, Freud, and others was the imperiled status of their movement in Germany. Although most of the Jewish psychoanalysts had fled that country, some remained. They were still members of the German Psychoanalytic Society in the early days of Hitler's rule, but it was becoming increasingly difficult for them to continue practicing their profession. Rather than fighting that trend, Jones, as president of the International Psychoanalytical Association, felt that he should seek to salvage whatever he could of psychoanalysis in Germany. He flew to Berlin to preside at a meeting of the society on December 1, 1933, where, as he put it, "the few remaining Jewish members volunteered to resign so as to save the Society from being dissolved."

It turned out that some of them could hang on a bit longer. But on September 15, 1935, the Nazis announced the sweeping Nuremberg race laws, which stripped Jews of all their rights, codifying their racist doctrine. The following month they arrested Edith Jacobson, a Jewish analyst at the Berlin Institute, for treating Communist patients instead of denouncing them to the Gestapo. Jones made another trip to Berlin, where he discussed not only her case but also what the other Jewish psychoanalysts should do. Along with Jones, they were still undecided whether they should resign from the society. But upon his return to

London, he cabled one of them: "Urgently advise voluntary resigna-tion." He had concluded that such a step might save the German so-ciety.

The last remaining Jewish members resigned on December 1. Ja-cobson remained in prison, but in 1938, when she fell ill and was hos-pitalized, she managed to escape, and later emigrated to the United States.

Although the Nazis scorned Freud and his theories, they did main-tain an interest in what they called psychotherapy. In particular, Mat-thias Göring, the cousin of Hitler's right-hand man Hermann Göring, launched the German Institute for Psychological Research and Psy-chotherapy in Berlin. When Jones met with the lesser known Göring in 1936, he found him to be a "fairly amiable and amenable person," although he soon concluded that Matthias Göring was not in a po-sition to deliver on his promises to respect anyone who did not fully submit to Nazi doctrines.

Karl Boehm, the president of the German Psychoanalytic Society, visited Freud in January 1937, trying to explain to him how he and the other Aryan psychoanalysts needed to operate in the new envi-ronment. They had to replace such terms as the Oedipus complex, he reported, to avoid reminding the Nazi authorities of the fact that their profession was grounded in the theories of its Jewish founder.

After Boehm had held forth for three hours, Freud broke in with a blunt statement. "Quite enough!" he said. "The Jews have suffered for their convictions for centuries. Now the time has come for our Chris-tian colleagues to suffer in their turn for theirs. I attach no importance to my name being mentioned in Germany so long as my work is pre-sented correctly there."

In reality, however, Göring's institute soon swallowed up the tat-tered remains of the German Psychoanalytic Society and its institute. The Nazi-controlled organization was hardly committed to presenting Freud's ideas, or even some newly labeled approximation of them, correctly. It was supposed to promote an Aryan brand of psychiatry to treat Germans, rejecting Freudian theories, although an undercurrent of his influence remained.

The books the formerly free German society had published, which were stored in Leipzig and included publications of the Vienna society, were confiscated. The fifteen Jewish psychoanalysts who had failed to join their numerous colleagues who had fled Germany when that was still possible soon died in the concentration camps.

———

Despite all the unsettling developments of the early and mid-1930s, Freud did not allow them to disturb his daily routine and intellectual pursuits. He continued to see his patients, and, as always, he was meticulous in responding to almost anyone who wrote to him. In 1935, for instance, he received an anonymous letter from an American mother who was seeking advice about her son, whom she considered deeply troubled. Responding in English on April 9, Freud wrote: "I gather from your letter that your son is a homosexual," adding that he was struck by the fact that she had avoided using that term herself.

Asking her why she was so reluctant to do so, he echoed the points he had made in his earlier discussion with his American analysand Joseph Wortis. "Homosexuality is assuredly no advantage, but it is nothing to be ashamed of, no vice, no degradation," he maintained. Instead of considering it an illness, "we consider it to be a variation of the sexual function, produced by a certain arrest of sexual development." As before, he invoked some of the famed homosexuals of earlier eras—Plato, Michelangelo, Leonardo da Vinci. "It is a great injustice to persecute homosexuality as a crime—and a cruelty, too."

The woman had requested his help, which Freud took to mean she was hoping he could "abolish homosexuality and make normal heterosexuality take its place." While each case was different, he explained, "in the majority of cases it is no more possible." But analysis might bring her son "harmony, peace of mind, full efficiency, whether he remains homosexual or gets changed." He even offered to accept her son for analysis with him—but only if she brought him to Vienna, which he knew was unlikely. "I have no intention of leaving here," he pointed out. He was in his element in such exchanges; he enjoyed sharing his opinions and insights, particularly when he thought they might help someone like this American mother.

Freud also derived more satisfaction than he let on from the recognition he received from many quarters. On May 26, 1935, he reported to Jones that the Royal Society of Medicine had unanimously voted to make him an honorary fellow. "As this cannot have happened 'because of my beautiful eyes,' it must be proof that respect for our psychoanalysis has made great progress in official circles in England," he wrote. His playful tone accentuated his delight, which was only heightened because he was a longtime Anglophile.

As much as he might have wanted to, however, he could not immerse himself completely in his own world, ignoring the sinister forces at work almost everywhere around him. "The times are gloomy," he admitted to the German writer Arnold Zweig (no relation to Stefan Zweig) on May 2. But he added: "Fortunately, it is not my job to brighten them."

On occasion, too, he offered advice that suggested he was particularly concerned with how quickly Germans, including many intellectuals, were acquiescing to Nazi rule. The novelist Thomas Mann had first visited Freud in Vienna in 1932, and he left Germany the following year when Hitler took power. The two men had stayed in touch and, in June 1935, Freud wrote to him on the occasion of Mann's sixtieth birthday. "I wish to express the confidence that you will never do or say anything—an author's words, after all, are deeds—that is cowardly or base, and that even at a time which blurs judgment you will choose the right way and show it to others," he declared.

Freud's life was brightened and made easier, no matter what his physical ailments and broader political worries, by his daughter Anna's constant devotion to his needs. "I of course rely more and more on Anna's care," he wrote to Lou Andreas-Salomé two weeks later. Quoting Mephistopheles (In the end we depend / On the creatures we made), he noted that "it was very wise to have made her."

Jones fully understood how dependent Freud was on Anna, and took it as a good sign when she joined him and Max Eitingon for a meeting in Paris that summer to discuss training methods. "Freud was evidently well enough to get on without her ministrations for a couple of days—a rare possibility," Jones observed.

With his eightieth birthday looming on May 6, 1936, Freud discouraged others from planning any kind of lavish celebration. "No, the times are not suited to a festival," he wrote to Jones. To Marie Bonaparte, he added: "The rumors that reach me about preparations for my birthday annoy me as much as the newspaper gossip about a Nobel Prize." He also claimed to know that the "attitude toward me and my work is really no friendlier than twenty years ago."

That was hardly the case: Freud's renown and influence were taken for granted by then, no matter how much he complained that he was underappreciated. And an occasion such as his big round number birthday was not about to slip by unnoticed. A stream of congratulatory messages and gifts arrived—most notably, a tribute to him signed by 197 writers and artists, including Thomas Mann, Romain Rolland, Virginia Woolf, H. G. Wells, and Stefan Zweig. Jones was convinced that its style "unmistakably" indicated that it was drafted by Mann.

An unabashed paean to Freud, the document described him as a "courageous seer and healer . . . a guide to hitherto undreamed-of regions of the human soul." From there, the praise only intensified, reaching its crescendo in the concluding paragraphs:

> In all spheres of humane science, in the study of literature and art, in the evolution of religion and prehistory, mythology, folklore and pedagogics, and last not least in poetry itself his achievement has left a deep mark; and we feel sure, if any deed of our race remains unforgotten it will be his deed of penetrating into the depths of the human mind.
>
> We, the undersigned, who cannot imagine our mental world without Freud's bold lifework, are happy to know that this great man with his unflagging energy is still among us and still working with undiminished strength. May our grateful feelings long accompany the man we venerate.

———

Freud frequently pointed out that his strength was hardly "undiminished," but this adjective was still accurate when employed in describing his resolve. He was determined to remain intellectually engaged and productive so long as he could cope with his physical limitations and infirmities. Once that would become too difficult and painful, as he had made clear to Max Schur, he had no desire to prolong his existence. In his letter to Thomas Mann in June 1935, he wrote: "My most personal experience . . . tends to make me consider it a good thing when merciful fate puts a timely end to our life span."

But Freud had at least one major project left that he was eager to complete before meeting his fate. Ever since he first saw Michelangelo's statue of Moses in the church of San Pietro in Vincoli in Rome in 1901, he found himself fascinated by the central figure in the Exodus story of the Jewish people. He published an anonymous study of the statue in 1914, rejecting the common interpretation that the artist had presented a Moses "agitated by the spectacle of his people fallen from grace and dancing around an idol [the golden calf]"—and about to smash the Tablets with the Ten Commandments that he had brought down from the mountain. Instead, the "tremendous physical power" of the statue "becomes only a concrete expression of the highest mental achievement that is possible in a man, that of struggling successfully against an inward passion for the sake of a cause to which he has devoted himself." In other words, Moses has tamed his anger so that he could save his people.

Not surprisingly, this was very much a psychological interpretation of both Moses and Michelangelo. "The artist felt the same violent force of will in himself [as he portrayed in his subject]," Freud wrote. While protesting that he was a mere "layman" when it came to the technical questions about works of art, Freud also explained that they "do exercise a powerful effect on me"—and it was evident that he had a far more sophisticated appreciation of them than he let on.

It was also evident that Freud's preoccupation—or, more accurately, obsession—with Moses was fueled by far more than his interest in the arts. He had often mulled over the possibility of writing more extensively about him, but it wasn't until the 1930s that he began to formulate how he would tackle this subject. In a letter to Arnold Zweig on September 30, 1934, he described what he considered to be his eureka moment, which was tied to the surging anti-Semitism of that era. "Faced with the renewed persecutions, one asks oneself again how the Jew came to be what he is and why he has drawn upon himself this undying hatred," he wrote. "I soon found the formula: Moses created the Jew." The result would be what he initially described as a "historical novel," which would reinterpret the biblical story and offer insights into its broader religious and historical context.

Freud understood that the three essays on Moses that he envisaged, particularly the third one that would spell out his views not just on Judaism but the other monotheistic religions—Christianity and Islam—would come across as "something fundamentally new and shattering to the uninitiated." Living as he was "in an atmosphere of Catholic orthodoxy," he explained further to Zweig, such a document could trigger a ban on psychoanalysis in Vienna and all of its publications. To avoid such an outcome, his plan was to write the essays, but to withhold the third, most controversial one from publication for the foreseeable future.

The first two essays, published in German in the psychoanalytical magazine *Imago* in 1937, were controversial enough. This was where Freud presented his thesis that Moses had not been a Jewish child adopted by the Egyptian royal family, as presented in the Bible; instead, he was an Egyptian who became the leader of the Jewish people. He also was drawn to a generally dismissed theory that the Jews had not only turned against Moses but possibly killed him, which would fit neatly into his notion of parricide and the ensuing legacy of guilt. Freud knew full well what kind of backlash could await him. His first sentence says as much: "To deny a people the man whom it praises as the greatest of its sons is not a deed to be undertaken light-heartedly—especially by one belonging to that people."

Freud was willing to accept Moses as a historical figure, not a mythical one. But he concluded that Moses had drawn upon the beliefs of Akhenaten, an Egyptian pharaoh who enforced a "strict monotheism, the first attempt of its kind in the history of the world." This was in stark contrast to all the other pharaohs who demanded the worship of multiple deities. In other words, Moses was not only an Egyptian: his teachings were Egyptian as well, even if they reflected beliefs that were atypical for the Egyptians of that era. This contradicted both Jewish and Christian teachings about the origins of their belief in one God.

The title of the second essay, "If Moses was an Egyptian . . . ," makes clear that Freud realized how shaky some of his assumptions were.

He was attracted to what he characterized as the "psychological probabilities," while recognizing that they "lacked objective proof." That could make them look like an "iron monument with feet of clay," he admitted. "Even if all parts of a problem seem to fit together like the pieces of a jigsaw puzzle, one has to remember that the probable need not necessarily be the truth and the truth not always probable." During his remaining time in Vienna, he struggled with his ideas for his third essay, which would spell out his broader theories on religion, but it wasn't until he made it to London that he wrote it.

Whatever the strengths and weaknesses of Freud's decidedly contrarian, idiosyncratic, and, at times, labyrinthine essays on this subject, the very fact that he found himself so preoccupied with it in the final years of his life reveals a great deal about his state of mind. It wasn't only a case of completing his study and reflections on Moses; it was also a way for him to escape facing the mounting evidence that his contemporary world was plunging into a nightmare.

————

In a letter to Arnold Zweig on October 14, 1935, Freud described Max Schur as a "very able physician, [who is] so deeply indignant about what is going on in Germany that he will not prescribe any German drugs." Along with another Jewish doctor at the hospital where he worked, Schur called for a general boycott of German medicines, and they drew up a list of Swiss, Austrian, and French drugs that could be substituted for them. This led to their blacklisting by the Nazi cell in their hospital, Schur recalled. In the event of a Nazi takeover of Austria, this also meant, as he put it, that they were "destined for a concentration camp."

It is striking that Freud sounded almost bemused by Schur's political stance. His view that his fellow Austrians would never resort to such brutal behavior as the Germans, in turn, bemused Schur. "He forgot that Hitler was an Austrian," he sardonically remarked. More seriously, he concluded: "It would seem that Freud, who had uncovered the force of the aggressive drive in the individual, could not believe that this force could be unleashed in an entire nation."

Unlike his patient, Schur was genuinely alarmed and not willing to let events take their course before taking action on his own. He started looking at the possibilities for emigrating and applied for jobs abroad, including Cairo. In 1937, he applied for visas for his family to the United States. Thanks to the fact that Schur was born in a part of the Austro-Hungarian Empire that was incorporated into interwar Poland, he was eligible to do so under the Polish quota—and the visas came through. But because Freud was insistent on staying in Vienna, Schur remained there with him, delaying any decision about fleeing while he kept trying to encourage his patient to consider a similar course.

Schur was far from alone in his mounting concern that his most famous patient could be in danger. William Bullitt, the coauthor of the still-unpublished book about Woodrow Wilson, shared Schur's fears and was eager to help protect him in any way he could. When he had served in Moscow as the first U.S. ambassador to the Soviet Union, a tour that lasted from 1933 to 1936, he had been swiftly stripped of his illusions about the raw brutality of that totalitarian state. When he subsequently took up the post of U.S. ambassador to France, he needed little convincing that the other rising totalitarian power in Europe, Nazi Germany, was also a dangerous threat.

In the summer of 1937, Bullitt's strong recommendation led to the appointment of John Wiley, his former number two at the embassy in Moscow, as the U.S. Consul General in Vienna. At least in retrospect, this looks like a carefully planned maneuver on the European chessboard, which allowed Bullitt to slide his knight to a position where he could spring into action if his coauthor Freud found himself at risk.

Long afterward, Bullitt explained his role to Schur. According to the physician, Bullitt told him he had arranged for Wiley's posting in Vienna "with the special 'assignment' of keeping a watchful eye and, within diplomatic limits, a protecting hand on Freud and his family."

In a letter to Freud from Paris on September 7, Bullitt announced the imminent arrival of "my close friend, Mr. John C. Wiley" in Vienna. "Mr. Wiley served with me as Counselor of the American Embassy in Moscow and you will find him an unusual fellow," he wrote. "I have asked Mr. Wiley to have a talk with you as soon as he arrives in Vienna."

Bullitt also mentioned the other Parisian who was close to Freud. "I hear news of you occasionally from Marie Bonaparte and she tells me that you are in excellent form," he wrote. Bullitt's light, upbeat tone notwithstanding, there was little doubt that his letter was more than a perfunctory note of introduction. It was a signal that, with the assistance of Wiley, he would be ready to respond if the dangerous cascade of events precipitated by Hitler dictated action to save Freud.

———

In contrast to his predecessor who had paid with his life for his defiance of the Nazis, Chancellor Schuschnigg was eager to ease the pressure on his country by cutting a deal with Germany. Franz von Papen, the German politician whose disastrous maneuvers had facilitated Hitler's rise to power, survived the subsequent initial round of bloodletting by serving as the Nazi regime's ambassador in Vienna. In that capacity, he worked assiduously to set the stage for a German takeover without sparking the kind of resistance that had led to the collapse of the attempted putsch in 1934. The idea was to lull the Austrians into making concessions, allegedly in the name of peace and compromise, only to trap them later.

By June 1936, Freud appeared to understand the looming danger.

"Austria's approach to National Socialism seems unstoppable," he wrote to Arnold Zweig. "All the fates are conspiring with the rabble. I am waiting, with ever decreasing regret, for the curtain to fall for me." Yet he would still cling to the hope that Schuschnigg could arrest the drift toward Nazi domination.

The Austrian chancellor believed that he was doing just that when, on July 11, he signed the Austro-German agreement that he had negotiated with von Papen. In theory, it offered something for both sides and normalized relations between the two countries, but its deliberately ambiguous wording and specific terms left no doubt that von Papen had emerged with almost everything he wanted.

One part of the agreement sounded reassuring. "Germany has neither the intention nor the desire to interfere in Austrian internal affairs, to annex Austria or to make it part of the German Reich," it blithely declared. The other part should have been deeply unsettling. "The Austrian Federal Government will base its policies in general and those concerning Germany in particular on the fundamental fact that Austria acknowledges itself to be a German state." Once again, it looked like the Austrians themselves could not decide who they really wanted to be. Schuschnigg also agreed to free most of the imprisoned Nazis in Austria, which came to about 17,000 people, and to offer individual Nazis the chance to join the Fatherland Front—effectively, allowing them to infiltrate government bodies. As John Gunther wrote, this represented a triumph of von Papen's "suede glove" approach: "His policy was based on the fact that there was no use ravishing a girl whom you are to marry next week."

One reason Schuschnigg felt he had to accept von Papen's terms was that he knew that Mussolini could not protect him. The Italian dictator had been a strong supporter of his predecessor, but the murder of Dollfuss struck a blow to his prestige, and, more significantly, to his aspirations of maintaining Austria as a buffer state. Hitler's growing power meant that Mussolini now looked like the smaller, weaker dictator by comparison. Schuschnigg's one remaining hope was that this round of concessions could still preserve Austria as a separate German state, as promised by his agreement with von Papen—no matter how inherently contradictory and increasingly naive all this sounded.

—

Even when Freud came closest to acknowledging the perilous nature of the times, or perhaps especially in those moments, he was eager to turn his gaze elsewhere. Late in 1936, Marie Bonaparte provided him with just such an opportunity by sending him the manuscript of the book that would later be published in English with the title: *Topsy: The Story of a Golden-Haired Chow*. Attached as he was to his own chow, Jofi, Freud was immediately entranced by Bonaparte's account of her ties to Topsy and her frantic efforts to save the dog from cancer.

"I love it; it is so movingly genuine and true," he wrote to her on December 6. "It is not an analytical work, of course, but the analyst's thirst for truth and knowledge can be perceived behind this production, too." He was enraptured by her reflections on why she—or he— could love their dogs "with such extraordinary intensity." As Freud summed up her thesis: dogs offered the "simplicity of a life free from the almost unbearable conflicts of civilization." And despite the differences in their "organic development," they engendered "that feeling of an intimate affinity, of an undisputed solidarity."

Freud was so taken with the manuscript that he and Anna offered to translate it into German. As Anna explained, he was eager to do this as a "favor in gratitude for her [Bonaparte's] unflagging helpfulness." The French edition was published in 1937, and the Freuds completed their translation in April 1938.

But Freud was motivated by far more than his desire to repay Bonaparte for her loyalty and support. Her book was as much about life and death, whatever the species, as it was specifically about dogs. This was familiar terrain for Freud. His first chow, a gift from Dorothy Burlingham in 1928, had lived with him for only fifteen months before she disappeared in the Salzburg train station and was then found dead on the tracks. His subsequent chow, Jofi, underwent an operation in January 1937 for the removal of two ovarian cysts, and she suddenly died from a heart attack a week later. Those losses were especially painful since, as Jones pointed out, Freud's affection for dogs was a "sublimation of his very great fondness for young children which could no longer be gratified." And, as Bonaparte wrote, "Dogs are children that do not grow up, that do not depart."

At least that is the serene vision that dogs provide—until they fall ill or die. When Topsy developed a tumor under her lip, one that in a few months was likely to condemn her to the "most atrocious of deaths," Bonaparte made an immediate decision: "Topsy, if she can be healed, has as much right to life as I." She proceeded to have her undergo X-ray treatments at the Curie Institute in Paris, an all too familiar setting for Bonaparte. "Twelve years ago another body also lay under the rays: my father, whom a similar affliction, though differently placed, was destroying," she wrote. "But then I knew that the rays penetrated him in vain day after day."

In Topsy's case, the X-rays cured her, offering her owner new hope. "A power seems to emanate from Topsy, as from a talisman of life," Bonaparte declared. But the whole experience made her reflect on her own mortality. "My life, like yours, Topsy, is declining, and when you will no longer be guarding the door of my room, it will be Death . . ."

In response to such passages, Freud wrote: "If you, at the youthful age of fifty-four, can't help thinking so often of death, are you surprised that at 80½ I keep brooding on whether I shall reach the age of my father and brother . . ." In a letter on August 13, 1937, he urged her to "let me live in your friendly memory—the only form of limited immortality I recognize." But as if to leaven those thoughts about death, he added: "Does Topsy realize she is being translated?"

———

Decades after the death of her father, when Anna Freud discussed this period with the American child psychiatrist Robert Coles, she offered her perspective on events in that critical period. "By 1936 it was clear that nothing would stop Hitler from seizing Austria—or, I should add, Austria from joining Germany," she said, emphasizing that this was the family's perception at the time, not something she was saying with the benefit of hindsight. "We were not denying what was likely, but we were not surrendering to fear and apprehension."

So why did they not leave Vienna then? "The answer was quite simple: my father was quite sick, he was in pain a lot of the time; he was nearing the end of his life—over eighty, with cancer; and he could not imagine any 'new life' elsewhere. What he knew was that there were only a few grains of sand left in the clock—and that would be that." Somewhat defensively she added, "It is always easy in retrospect to know what was right, to know what should have been done, and when it should have been done."

Anna was fully justified in pointing out the dangers of passing judgment with the benefit of hindsight. She was also right to identify her father's age and health as the overriding concerns for the family. But she may have been guilty of overstatement, or at least employing hindsight more than she was willing to admit, in her assertion that by 1936 it was clear to Freud that Nazi Germany would swallow up Austria. It certainly should have been clear by then, but he was still reluctant to accept the inevitability of such an outcome.

Or, to put it more accurately, Freud could be clear-eyed in his political diagnosis on some occasions while still trying to track increasingly illusory rays of hope, which were prone to distort his vision.

Writing to Jones on March 2, 1937, Freud admitted that the "invasion of the Nazis can probably not be checked," and that his hope was that "one will not live to see it oneself." He compared the situation to 1683, when Ottoman Turkish troops besieged Vienna. The city was saved by the winged hussars led by King Jan Sobieski of Poland, who defeated the invaders. No such miracle was in the cards this time, Freud continued, no one was going to ride to the rescue. "If our city falls, then the Prussian barbarians will swamp Europe," he concluded. "Unfortunately, the power that has hitherto protected us—Mussolini—now seems to be giving Germany a free hand."

But as late as February 6, 1938, when Hitler was closing in on Austria, Freud still wanted to believe Chancellor Schuschnigg might have a chance of averting the dark vision he had presented to Jones. In a letter to Eitingon, he declared: "Our brave and in its way decent government is now more energetic than hitherto in keeping the Nazis at bay, although in view of the latest events in Germany, no one can be sure what is going to happen."

Schuschnigg and his countrymen, including Freud, were about to find out.

11.

"OPERATION FREUD"

On March 10, 1938, about a month after Freud had praised Austria's "decent government" and its efforts to keep the Nazis "at bay," the telephone rang in his apartment at Berggasse 19. When the housekeeper Paula Fichtl picked it up, she did not recognize the voice of the caller—and he did not introduce himself. "Tell the Herr Professor that Hitler is coming tomorrow!" he said before hanging up. Fichtl reported the terse message to Freud, whose only response was, "That will be bad, Paula."

In fact, Schuschnigg's efforts to preserve Austria's independence had effectively begun to collapse a month earlier—on February 12, to be exact, although most of his countrymen, including Freud, were not aware of it then. On that date, the Austrian chancellor met with Hitler at Berchtesgaden, the German dictator's Alpine retreat. But as soon as the visitor offered some standard compliments about the picturesque setting and lovely weather, Hitler cut him off. "We did not gather here to speak of the fine view or the weather," he declared.

Instead, Hitler launched into a furious denunciation of his guest, accusing him of doing "everything to avoid a friendly policy." Making clear that he was incensed not just by Schuschnigg but also by the very existence of an Austrian state, he branded the "whole history of Austria" as "one uninterrupted act of high treason." He added ominously: "I am absolutely determined to make an end to all this. The German Reich is one of the great powers, and nobody will raise his voice if it settles its border problems."

Stunned by this frontal assault, Schuschnigg tried to remind Hitler of Austria's contribution to German history, but Hitler dismissed it as "absolutely zero." He also ignored his visitor's efforts to defuse the palpable tension in the room by assuring him that Austria would seek to "remove obstacles to a better understanding" between the two countries. Berating his guest for allegedly ordering the fortification of its border with Germany, Hitler proceeded to deliver a direct threat: "I have only to give an order, and in one single night all your ridiculous defense mechanisms will be blown to bits. You don't seriously think you can stop me for half an hour, do you?"

In case Schuschnigg was hoping for outside help, Hitler was intent on disabusing him of that notion, too. "Don't think for one moment that anybody on earth is going to thwart my decisions. Italy? I see eye to eye with Mussolini . . . England? England will not move one finger for Austria." As for France, he pointed out, it had failed to stop his troops from marching into the Rhineland two years earlier, violating the provision of the Versailles Treaty that designated the territory as a demilitarized zone. French forces were strong enough then to force a German retreat, Hitler admitted, but this was no longer the case. "Now it is too late for France," he said.

Handed off to Foreign Minister Joachim von Ribbentrop and Franz von Papen, who had just been dismissed as Germany's envoy to Austria but was still eager to participate in Hitler's power play, Schuschnigg found himself presented with a list of demands that he was supposed to accept as part of an "agreement" between the two governments.

They included numerous measures that would ensure a Nazi strangle-hold on the Austrian state: the appointment of Arthur Seyss-Inquart, a pro-Nazi lawyer, as minister of interior, giving him control of the police; the end to the ban on the Austrian Nazi Party; and the "assimilation" of the Austrian economy by Germany. Feeling he had no other choice, Schuschnigg accepted von Papen's patently false assurances that this agreement would prevent any "further difficulties for Austria" and signed it.

But the Austrian chancellor had one card left. As he told Hitler, the agreement would not be valid unless President Wilhelm Miklas accepted it as well. The ensuing delay, caused by Miklas's opposition to some of its provisions, allowed Schuschnigg to try to mount a rear-guard action to stop or at least delay a German takeover. Infuriated, Hitler ordered his generals to stage troop maneuvers on the border and ratcheted up his threatening rhetoric. Speaking to the Reichstag on February 20, he insisted he would not tolerate an assault on the "general rights of self-determination" of Germans who happened to live outside of Nazi Germany's borders and who were allegedly suffering persecution because of their desire for "unity with the whole nation." This statement was directed at both Austria and Czechoslovakia's Sudetenland with its largely ethnic German population.

Summoning up his remaining resolve, Schuschnigg responded by pointing out that Austria was willing to make concessions but only "thus far and no further." On March 9, he also announced that the country would hold a plebiscite on March 13. Austrians would be asked to respond to this question: "Are you in favor of a free and German, independent and social, a Christian and united Austria?" This formulation acknowledged the Germanic heritage of the Austrian people but its purpose was to give Austrians the opportunity to support the continued existence of their own state.

Knowing that most Austrians were likely to respond positively, Hitler had no intention of waiting for them to do so. He ordered his troops to prepare to march into their country. It was then that the anonymous caller delivered the warning for Freud.

———

On March 10, the same day as the phone call, Freud noted in his diary: "Wiley from American embassy." He was referring to John Wiley, the diplomat whose posting to Vienna was arranged by Bullitt. Wiley's visit to Berggasse 19 was the first signal that the members of Freud's nascent rescue squad were preparing to respond to the looming danger.

The following day, German troops closed the border with Austria and, under intense pressure from Hitler's minions, Schuschnigg called off the plebiscite and decided to resign. In a farewell broadcast that evening, he denounced as lies the false reports of widespread unrest and the "shedding of streams of blood," referring to the pretexts the Nazis were already lining up to justify their pending invasion. "We are not prepared even in this terrible hour to shed blood," he said. "We have decided to order the troops to offer no resistance." He wrapped up his short address with the plea, "God protect Austria!"

In the early morning hours of March 12, German troops poured across the border. Given the Austrian government's earlier capitulation, it was hardly surprising that some of their own customs officials helped dismantle the barriers at the border right before Hitler's soldiers showed up. At 4 a.m., William Shirer, the CBS correspondent in Vienna, wrote in his diary: "The worst has happened! Schuschnigg is out. The Nazis are in. Hitler has broken a dozen solemn promises, pledges, treaties. And Austria is finished. Beautiful, tragic, civilized Austria! Gone."

Shirer was stunned by the scenes he witnessed in Vienna even before Hitler's troops reached that city. Emerging from the subway at Karlsplatz, he found himself "swept along in a shouting, hysterical Nazi mob . . . The faces! I had seen these before at Nuremberg—the fanatical eyes, the gaping mouths, the hysteria." Following the crowds singing Nazi songs, he spotted a group of policemen looking on, already wearing red-black-white swastika armbands. "So they've gone over too," he noted. And there were the immediate attacks against Jews: "Young toughs were heaving paving blocks into the windows of Jewish shops. The crowd roared with delight."

Shirer and a colleague went to see Wiley at the American legation. Shirer observed that the diplomat "was standing before his desk, clutching his invariable long cigarette-holder, a queer smile on his face—the smile of someone who has just been defeated and knows it." Wiley quietly stated the obvious to his visitors: "It's all over."

As German troops marched into Austria without a shot fired in opposition, Freud echoed that sentiment by penning his famous diary entry: *"Finis Austriae."* On that same afternoon, the inhabitants of Berggasse 19 could hear the excited shouts of newspaper sellers from the street below. "Quick, Paula—get me the *Abend*," Freud told the housekeeper, referring to the afternoon newspaper that had reliably supported Austrian independence. When Fichtl returned, Martin watched his father as he reached for the paper, scanned the headlines, crumpled it up, and, without saying a word, threw it into a corner of the room. This rare display of emotion, Martin pointed out, only underscored his "disgust and disappointment."

When the younger Freud picked up the discarded paper and smoothed it out, he immediately recognized that this tragedy for the country would have its most immediate impact on one group of people. "We, Jews, would be the first victims," Martin concluded. The paper was already filled with shrill anti-Semitic propaganda.

On the following evening—Sunday, March 13—Germany announced the Anschluss, the transformation of Austria into a "province of the German Reich," as the new law proclaimed. On the same day, the board members of the Vienna Psychoanalytic Society gathered in Berggasse 19 to figure out what they should do. They concluded that all of them should flee Vienna and its new Nazi masters, and that the society should be relocated later to wherever its founder ended up.

Freud responded by recalling the destruction of the Temple in Jerusalem by the Roman emperor Titus, and how Rabbi Jochanan ben Sakkai disagreed with the Jewish zealots who wanted to die fighting rather than surrender to Roman rule. The rabbi not only survived but managed to convince the Romans to allow him to open a new school in the Galilee where Jews could study the Torah. "We are going to do the same," Freud vowed. "We are, after all, used to persecution in our history, tradition and some of us by personal experience." He was not drawing an exact analogy since he realized that the Nazis were not about to tolerate a new center for his brand of psychoanalysis, but he was emphasizing the need to save rather than sacrifice themselves.

If all that appeared to signal Freud's willingness to accept the necessity of abandoning his longtime home so that he could continue with psychoanalysis elsewhere, Ernest Jones, the president of the International Psychoanalytical Association, and his other foreign colleagues were far from convinced that he had experienced a genuine change of heart—or that they could prevail upon him to do so. "Knowing how strong was this reluctance, and how often in the last few years he had expressed his determination to stay in Vienna to the end, I was not very hopeful about the outcome," Jones recalled.

His pessimism was understandable. As Martin Freud pointed out, his father "could have left Vienna at any time during the many secure years before the Hitler shadow began dimming the city's gay sky; but he never did, nor did he, as far as I know, ever seriously contemplate emigrating." Following the Anschluss, the challenge of extricating Freud was far more daunting. Convincing him to go along with any such plan would be only the first step—but still a tricky one. Jones realized he needed all the help he could get to overcome that first obstacle. He needed to mobilize his troops.

———

While Hitler was making his triumphant journey to Vienna with ecstatic crowds cheering him on, Jones engaged in a frantic round of phone calls from London to those colleagues who might be able to help. He talked with Dorothy Burlingham, who, as he noted, "was by now almost one of the Freud family." The American heiress of the Tiffany fortune resided two floors above the Freud apartment on Berggasse 19, where she could be close to Anna Freud, her partner for the rest of her life. Burlingham was in touch not only with Jones, but also with Marie Bonaparte in Paris—and, most importantly, John Wiley, Bullitt's man in Vienna.

The scene on the streets on March 14, the day Hitler arrived in Vienna, underscored the need to prepare for the worst. Georg Klaar, the Jewish writer who was seventeen at the time and soon became known as George Clare, later described his impressions of the reception the German dictator received. "The city behaved like an aroused woman: vibrating, writhing, moaning and sighing lustfully for orgasm and release," he wrote.

Burlingham was ill and mostly bedridden at the time, but she was ideally prepared for her role as a go-between and early warning system for "Operation Freud," as it could be called. Since she had set up a direct phone line between her bedroom and Anna's bedroom downstairs, Anna—or Paula, the housekeeper—could reach her or one of her children at a moment's notice. Dorothy, in turn, could relay information to the others whenever she believed Freud was in danger.

On March 15, the day when Hitler addressed the huge gathering of his supporters from the balcony of The Hofburg, Vienna's imperial palace, and Nazi gangs looted Jewish stores and hunted down Jews on the streets, Jones rushed to Vienna, as he explained, "to make a final effort to persuade Freud to change his mind." Burlingham had told him that Freud was still balking at leaving, and the Welshman was convinced he had to make that appeal in person. Marie Bonaparte promised to follow him to Vienna shortly.

Since there were no flights from London to Vienna that day, Jones flew to Prague, and from there he hired a small monoplane that took him the rest of the way to the city that was no longer the capital of an independent Austria. According to Hitler's speech at The Hofburg, it was now the "youngest bulwark of the German nation." Jones's first impressions confirmed the extent of the Nazi takeover. "The airfield was stacked with German military planes and the air was full of them assiduously intimidating the Viennese," he recalled. German tanks rumbled down the streets where there were frequent shouts of "Heil Hitler!"

Contacted by Anna Freud, Jones took her advice and headed straight to the Verlag, the International Psychoanalytic Publishing House, which was located at Berggasse 7 and already a target of the new rulers. Martin Freud, who served as the manager of the operation, had gone there that morning, determined to destroy what he realized would be taken as incriminatory evidence against his father and other clients who used his services as a lawyer. In particular, he had maintained bank accounts abroad for them, investing in foreign currencies that were more stable than Austria's. This had been perfectly legal up until the Anschluss, he noted, "but I knew that it would be a crime in the eyes of the dollar-hungry Nazis."

One client came over personally that morning to repossess his documents and delayed Martin in getting to the other records. Before the younger Freud could do much, a group of about a dozen armed thugs burst into the premises. They were "an odd medley, shabbily dressed," most of them carrying rifles, and there was no clear leader. The most aggressive member of the group was a small, haggard man who was armed only with a pistol. Whenever Martin appeared reluctant to comply with their orders, he recalled, this man "displayed a blood-thirsty spirit by drawing his pistol and noisily pulling out and pushing in the magazine as he shouted, 'Why not shoot him and be finished with him? We should shoot him on the spot.'"

Two of the men kept their rifles pressed against Martin's stomach as others pulled money from the safe and cash drawers. Soon, the table was stacked with bills and coins in different currencies. Left un-touched, though, were the papers that Martin had managed to grab just before the gang arrived, and which now lay unnoticed on a shelf. He was anxious for the opportunity to make them disappear alto-gether, but nervous about the pistol-waving member of the contingent who, as he put it, "might be controlled by a hysterical impulse if not treated carefully."

When Jones showed up at the Verlag, he encountered the sight of the armed "villainous looking" invaders who were counting the money from a drawer while Martin was seated nearby under guard. The new arrival had hoped he might impress the thugs by explaining that the publishing house was an international venture, but instead they also detained him. His appeal that they allow him to communicate with the British embassy was scornfully rejected, making him reflect on "how low my country's prestige had fallen after Hitler's successes." But in about an hour they released him, and Jones hurried down the street to Berggasse 19 to check on Freud and the rest of the family.

Back at the Verlag, Martin remained a prisoner, although the num-ber of men holding him steadily decreased during the afternoon once they no longer found new stashes of money. When only one guard was left, who, according to Martin, looked like a seedy, unemployed head waiter, the threatening atmosphere began to dissipate. The guard stopped pointing his rifle at him and allowed him to get up and stretch. Then he began talking about his difficult economic situation—and Martin immediately got the not-so-subtle hint. Reaching into his pockets that the others had not bothered to check, he handed over some gold coins and notes.

Having earned his captor's gratitude, Martin asked to visit the toilet. The man obliged, escorting him down a passageway where the documents Martin wanted to destroy were piled up. As they walked through there, Martin surreptitiously grabbed what he could and, once inside the toilet, tore them up and flushed them away. Pleading the need for subsequent visits, he managed to repeat that exercise several times.

During those walks down the hallway, other thugs drifted back in at times, sneaking some of the money that had been piled up earlier on the table. It turned out that a Nazi neighbor was observing these proceedings through the window and alerted the nearby headquarters of the S.A., the paramilitary brownshirts. The district commander came running over and made sure that Martin's captor surrendered the money he had taken from him—although not to Martin. In that chaotic first day of break-ins, there was more improvisation than planning, more intimidation and snatching of valuables than organized extortion. For the targets of these raids, this meant improvising as well.

———

While Martin was still detained in the Verlag, a group of armed brownshirts showed up at the Freud residence nearby. Trying to shield her husband, who was resting, Martha Freud decided to treat the intruders as if they were normal guests, inviting them to be seated and to store their rifles in the hallway stand that was normally used for umbrellas. They turned down those offers, but were thrown off balance by her courtesy—and even more so by her subsequent maneuver. She brought out some money she had in the house, placed it on the table, and asked politely: "Won't the gentlemen help themselves?" Anna then led them to the safe in another room and opened it, pulling out 6,000 shillings, the equivalent of $840. The invaders were delighted by their haul.

It was in the midst of these proceedings that Freud appeared in the doorway, looking frail but fixing them with one of his withering looks. Jones, who was still at the apartment after leaving Martin at the Verlag, noted, "He had a way of frowning with blazing eyes that any Old Testament prophet might have envied." This group of intruders was more disciplined than the ones at the Verlag, but they were unnerved by the sight of the imposing old man. Their leader addressed Freud by the title "Herr Professor," and they soon backed out of the apartment—but not before promising: "We'll be back."

Once they left and Freud learned how much money they had taken, he offered another display of his sardonic sense of humor. "Dear me," he said, "I have never taken so much for a single visit."

In the meantime, Martin had been released from the Verlag and had gone straight to check on his parents. He was relieved to see that the brownshirts there "had not behaved at all badly," apart from their seizure of the family's available cash and the confiscation of their passports; they even left a receipt for the money they took. But it was clear that both invasions signaled only the beginning of the actions by the new authorities.

Jones certainly understood as much, and he immediately had a "heart to heart talk" with Freud. Despite all of the drama earlier that day, Jones recalled, "As I had feared, he was bent on staying in Vienna." When the Welshman pointed out that he was not alone in the world and that so many people were concerned about him, Freud replied: "Alone. Ah, if I were only alone I should long ago have done with life."

But recognizing that Jones was right in asserting that he had more than himself to think about, he trotted out other arguments for staying put. He was too weak to travel, he said, and, more tellingly, he said that, given the strong opposition to accepting immigrants almost everywhere in Europe, no one would take him. As Jones noted, widespread unemployment meant that every country was "ferociously inhospitable" to would-be immigrants; left unsaid was that much of that aggressive inhospitality was directed at Jews looking for safety. But he told Freud that he would return to England to see if he could convince officials there to make an exception in his case.

While Freud did not directly object, he offered an additional justification for his reluctance to emigrate: he could not leave Austria any more than a soldier could leave his post. Jones countered by invoking the case of Charles Lightoller, the second officer on the *Titanic*. He was saved from drowning as the ship was going down when a boiler exploded and a blast of hot air from the airshaft propelled him to the surface. As he explained during the subsequent interrogation, "I never left the ship, Sir; she left me." Jones believed this proved to be the winning argument with Freud, convincing him to accept the necessity of emigration if it could be arranged.

That was a big *if* at that point. But the urgency of the challenge was no longer in doubt. Earlier on the same day, March 15, John Wiley, who was quick to learn about the raids on the Verlag and Freud's home, sent a terse cable to Bullitt in Paris: "Fear Freud, despite age and illness, in danger."

Bullitt immediately sprang into action. He called President Roosevelt in Washington, and the next day Secretary of State Cordell Hull sent a telegram to Wiley. "In accordance with the President's instruction," he wrote, he had asked Hugh Wilson, the American ambassador in Berlin, "to take this matter up with the appropriate German authorities and to express the hope that arrangements might be made by the appropriate authorities in Austria whereby Dr. Freud and his family might be permitted to travel to Paris where the President is informed friends are anxious to receive him." Hull added that he understood that it was "probably impossible" for Wiley to take similar steps in Vienna, but he urged him to provide updates on Freud's situation there and to report on "what arrangements, if any, are being made or can be made for them to leave Austria."

At the same time, Bullitt wrote a personal telegram to Wilson in Berlin: "If Wiley should telephone or telegraph you with regard to assistance to Professor Freud and his immediate family who may seek refuge in Paris please render every possible assistance including financial for which I will be responsible." The last part of the message indicated Bullitt fully understood that the Nazis were likely to demand, in effect, ransom money, and he was ready to pay whatever would be necessary.

Given the heightened sense of danger for Freud, Bullitt and Wiley wanted to be sure that the Nazis understood that any overt move against him could backfire since his case was receiving attention at the highest levels. Bullitt called on Count Johannes von Welczeck, the German ambassador in Paris, to warn him that any mistreatment of Freud could spark an international outcry. According to Jones, Welczeck, who was a "man of culture and a humanitarian," conveyed the message to his higher-ups.

With Bullitt's encouragement, Wiley and his diplomats in Vienna made a point of showing the flag near Freud's apartment—literally so. Anytime Burlingham signaled possible danger, Wiley, his wife, Irena, or other members of his mission visited the Freud family, and one of their official cars was often parked outside, conspicuously adorned by the American flag. They knew the Gestapo would be watching, and they correctly assumed that, at this early stage of his drive for empire, Hitler wanted to avoid direct confrontations with America's envoys.

On March 17, another high-profile visitor showed up in Vienna to lend her support to the efforts to protect Freud and his family. As the Princess of Greece and Denmark, Marie Bonaparte represented royalty and she carried a family name that resonated everywhere; she could also tap into a broad array of personal contacts and draw upon her considerable personal wealth to help the cause. She stayed at the Greek legation and contacted diplomats at other foreign missions in Vienna, urging them to keep her assessed of any relevant information they might pick up. Most of all, her frequent visits to Berggasse 19 offered Freud, Anna, and the rest of the family strong moral support along with a guarantee of financial backing—and, once again, signaled the authorities that Freud was far from alone.

To underscore that point, Bonaparte physically positioned herself at times between the Freuds and anyone seeking to barge in on them again, sitting on the chilly staircase leading up to the apartment. Fichtl, the housekeeper, recalled how she would perch there in a black mink coat pulled tightly over her shoulders, holding light colored suede gloves, with a delicate hat on her head and a crocodile skin handbag at her side, engulfed by the powerful scent of her perfume. From time to time, Fichtl brought her tea or hot chocolate while she kept up her vigils there. The housekeeper believed that Freud was not aware of this particular act of dedication since he did not venture outside at that point, but he certainly knew that she was doing everything she could to protect him and the family. As he put it, "The princess is of inestimable value to us."

Jones explained that Bonaparte's arrival allowed him to feel less conflicted about leaving Vienna at that perilous moment so that he could return to London "for the urgent task of seeking permits in England." The importance of his mission was impossible to exaggerate: it had to succeed if Freud and his family were to be saved.

As soon as he made it back to London on March 22, Jones went on the offensive. The key figure he wanted to target was Sir Samuel Hoare, the home secretary. By chance, the two of them belonged to the same ice skating club, which meant they had met before, but they were hardly close acquaintances. Mindful of protocol, Jones decided against trying to contact him directly. Instead, he first asked his brother-in-law Wilfred Trotter, a surgeon who was a fellow of the Royal Society of Medicine, which had elected Freud as an honorary fellow in 1935, for a letter of introduction to Sir William Bragg, a physicist who was the president of that prestigious society. Jones planned on asking Bragg, in turn, for a letter of introduction to Hoare, who had the power to decide who would be granted entry to Britain.

It seemed like a perfectly choreographed approach, but Jones was startled when Bragg displayed his stunning naivete by asking him: "Do you really think that the Germans are unkind to the Jews?" Nonetheless, the physicist provided Jones with the letter of introduction to Hoare. When he called on Hoare, Jones was relieved to discover that the home secretary "without any hesitation displayed his usual philanthropic qualities and gave me carte blanche to fill in permits, including permission to work, for Freud, his family, servants, his personal doctors, and a certain number of his pupils with their families."

As Anna Freud put it, Jones "did the near impossible" by securing entry permits to Britain for a total of eighteen adults and six children. This was a result that exceeded even Jones's expectations. On March 25, after he saw Hoare's secretary and confirmed the details, he wrote exultantly in his diary: "Success!"

Jones had won approval for the Freud party to enter Britain far more quickly than expected, but that represented only a partial victory. The much more difficult task was to convince the Nazis to allow them to leave Vienna—and the signs did not look promising.

Following the first raids on the Verlag and the apartment, the Nazis began a more systematic campaign of intimidation and extortion. They were intent on extracting as much money as possible from any Jewish family seeking exit permits, but there was no guarantee that, even after the family navigated the maze of shifting requirements and paid whatever sums were required, they would be allowed to emigrate.

On March 22, the same day that Jones had returned to London, Anna was summoned to the Gestapo and Martin was expecting a similar summons at any moment. The two siblings went to see Max Schur to ask for something that would end their lives if they felt desperate. "They feared torture, and not without reason," the doctor recalled. He supplied them with a "sufficient amount of Veronal, a strong barbiturate," something that neither Schur nor the two of them admitted to their father.

Back at Berggasse 19, Martin watched through the window as four heavily armed S.S. men drove Anna off in an open car. "Her situation was perilous; but far from showing fear, or even much interest, she sat in the car as a woman might sit in a taxi on her way to enjoy a shopping expedition," he wrote later. In reality, as indicated by her and Martin's request to Schur earlier, she was afraid for herself—and, even more so, she worried that she might inadvertently say something under interrogation that could be used against her father. Still, she was determined not to show her fear either to the Nazis or to her anxious family.

Freud's diary entry for that day simply read: "Anna with Gestapo." Schur came over to Berggasse 19 to keep him company and to reassure him that his beloved daughter would return. "That was the worst day," he recalled. "The hours were endless. It was the only time I saw Freud deeply worried. He paced the floor, smoking incessantly." From her sickbed two floors up, an equally distraught Burlingham kept checking in for updates by phone. The ever-vigilant Wiley dispatched a cable to Bullitt via the State Department with the news of Anna's arrest.

While there would be other interrogations of both Anna and Martin, this was the longest one. Grilled on her role in the International Psychoanalytical Association, she was not allowed to return to the apartment until late that evening. With vast understatement, Schur wrote: "Freud who was rarely demonstrative in his affection, showed his feelings to some extent that evening." By at least one account, he was so relieved to see her that he wept. This was almost certainly the moment when Freud abandoned any remaining doubts about the need to emigrate. He recognized that he had to flee if at all possible, mainly for the sake of Anna who had so much longer to live—and who would not leave him under any circumstances.

———

The drama at Berggasse 19 was only one part of a larger tragedy. Like Freud, many Austrian Jews had believed that their countrymen would never express their anti-Semitism as viciously as the Germans did from the start under Hitler. But the scenes that Shirer and other correspondents witnessed on the streets after the Anschluss were echoed in a variety of settings, instantly stripping Jews of such illusions.

Edith Laub, who was sixteen at the time, recalled how some of her classmates, even those she had believed were her friends, shouted: "Open the windows, it stinks of Jews." Along with other Jewish women, she and her mother were soon ordered to scrub the floors in a Nazi headquarters, another act of deliberate humiliation.

From his family's apartment window, the Jewish teenager Georg Klaar witnessed an act of violence that he found particularly chilling. A neighborhood policeman, who had always been courteous to his father and him, was clubbing "some poor soul" who had dared to shout out a protest when he saw the crowds welcoming Hitler's troops. "Within minutes . . . that policeman, yesterday's protector, had been transformed into tomorrow's persecutor and tormenter," he wrote.

Those two teenagers were among the lucky ones who managed to flee Austria. Laub ended up in the United States, where she became editor-in-chief of *Mademoiselle* magazine in the 1970s, using her married name of Edie Locke. Klaar settled in England, became George Clare, and penned his widely acclaimed autobiography *Last Waltz in Vienna*.

Many other Jews were not nearly as fortunate. When Egon Friedell, a sixty-year-old cultural historian and essayist who was also a cabaret performer, heard storm troopers coming upstairs to his apartment on March 16, he jumped from a window to his death. About five hundred Austrian Jews chose suicide that spring rather than arrest, a one-way ticket to a concentration camp, or whatever else the new authorities might have had in mind for them, usually starting with the confiscation of their assets. The Nazis were concerned enough about rapidly spreading rumors citing even larger numbers of suicides that they issued a revealing denial: "From March 12 to March 22 ninety-six persons committed suicide in Vienna of whom *only* [my italics] fifty were directly connected with the change in the political situation in Austria."

To offer a veneer of legitimacy, the Nazis held a plebiscite on April 10 seeking approval for the Anschluss, ostensibly making up for the forced cancellation of Schuschnigg's plebiscite earlier. Now that they were in total control, there was no risk they would be rebuffed by the voters. At a Vienna polling station that Shirer visited, he reported, "wide slits in the corner of the voting booths gave the Nazi election committee sitting a few feet away a good view of how one voted." In rural districts, he added, most people did not even bother stepping into a booth, choosing instead to cast their ballots in the open for everyone to see. Not surprisingly, the authorities reported that 99.75 percent of Austrians voted for the Anschluss.

Confident of their consolidated power, the Nazis intensified their drive against Vienna's Jews, particularly the wealthy ones. "The treatment of the Jews has exceeded anything that took place in Germany," Wiley cabled Bullitt. "It has been an economic pogrom; burglary in uniform."

The searches and interrogations of the Freuds indicated that the Nazis saw them as one of their most important targets.

———

Following the Anschluss, the Nazis appointed the people who were supposed to oversee the plundering of Jewish assets that Wiley was referring to. Known as trustees or commissioners, they were assigned to Jewish families and expected to proceed on the assumption that their wealth and businesses were all "improperly acquired," as the Nazi newspaper *Der Angriff* had explained when Hitler came to power in Germany.

But if that meant that the property of Jews was fair game, what would happen to the rich Jews themselves was not yet clear. In this period before the full machinery of the Holocaust was set in motion, the trustees were the ones who could determine their fate. They could make it relatively easy for Jews, in essence, to bribe their way out of the country—or they could strew their paths with so many additional obstacles that they would be doomed to failure, which in the long term was likely to mean not only the loss of their property but also their lives. The choice of a particular trustee could prove to be a choice for life or death.

On March 15, Anton Sauerwald assumed his duties as the trustee for the Freud family, which meant overseeing their holdings, including the Verlag. The initial impression Sauerwald made could not have been more chilling, with Schur, Freud's doctor, recalling that he came across as the "tough brute."

At his first meeting with the board of the Verlag, Sauerwald acted very much like the stereotypical Nazi spewing anti-Semitic abuse. Singling out two non-Jewish psychoanalysts, he demanded to know why they were keeping company with "Jewish pigs." He announced that he was now taking charge of the operation, and he ordered the group to show him all the financial records. There was little reason to expect any leniency from their new overlord.

But Sauerwald, who was thirty-five at the time, soon began to demonstrate that he was no ordinary representative of the Nazi regime. The son of a pharmacist, he had studied chemistry at the University of Vienna under Josef Herzig, who was a friend of Freud. Despite his seemingly uncritical embrace of Hitler's anti-Semitism, Sauerwald had been an admirer of his elderly Jewish professor who had died in 1924. As Jones concluded, he may have then transferred some of those feelings to Freud, who was only three years younger than Herzig. After the Gestapo had paid one of their visits to Berggasse 19, Sauerwald was downright apologetic about what he saw as their rude behavior. "What can you expect?" he told Anna. "These Prussians don't know who Freud is."

What Sauerwald was really saying was that, by contrast, he understood Freud's importance; after all, he was an Austrian German not a Prussian, and a very well-educated one at that. But he was still under pressure to squeeze whatever money he could out of the Freud publishing operation and household. In April, for example, Matthias Göring, Hermann's cousin who was intent on promulgating his own brand of "psychotherapy," explained in a letter to Sauerwald that they needed money to retrain those Viennese psychologists whom he viewed as tainted by their surroundings. "I believe in Vienna also in Aryan circles you can still feel the Jewish influence without people being aware of it," he wrote, an obvious reference to Freud's teachings.

Yet during his long stints on the premises of the Verlag and the apartment, Sauerwald methodically read many of Freud's works, and he found himself increasingly impressed by his erudition and theories about psychoanalysis. According to Schur, "As a result, he became extremely helpful and used all his considerable influence with the Nazis to facilitate the emigration of Freud, his family, and his immediate group."

How did Sauerwald explain his contradictory behavior—on the one hand, espousing Nazi racial doctrines and, on the other, treating Freud with respect? Schur was particularly interested in understanding him, and he discussed that question with Alexander, Freud's younger brother, in London in 1939. Sauerwald had visited that city after the Freuds and Schur had settled there, and met with Alexander. As Schur summed up the report he heard on their conversation, Sauerwald still maintained that Jews were not a "reliable element of the population" and, therefore, they had to be "eliminated"; he added that "this might be deplorable, but the end justifies the means." Nonetheless, an individual Nazi could "alleviate hardship in selected cases," he said. By that, Sauerwald was clearly alluding to his own handling of Freud.

That was not the only surprise to come out of that talk. Sauerwald, who had run a chemical laboratory in Vienna earlier in the decade, purportedly told Alexander that he had been utilized as an explosives expert by the city's police during the period before the Anschluss when Nazi terror attacks were commonplace. He also made the startling claim that he had supplied the Nazis with the bombs for those attacks in the first place. For that reason, he could easily identify the type of explosives that were used in them, ingratiating himself with both the Nazis and the police. This would suggest that Sauerwald reveled in duplicity, something that continued once the Nazis put him in charge of the Freud case. But a recent study by Austrian historian Christiane Rothländer pointed out that no documentary evidence exists to back up this version of events that was presented by Schur and also reported in the Austrian press after the war. The Municipal and Provincial Archives of Vienna confirm that they have no such documents.

Whatever Sauerwald had really done up to that point, he found himself in a critical role as Freud's fate hung in the balance after the Anschluss. He soon came across the kind of evidence that could have prevented Freud from emigrating, which would have almost inevitably meant that he would have later perished in the Holocaust. Everything depended on what Sauerwald would or would not do, on his willingness to allow Freud to slip away from the Third Reich.

———

During the initial Nazi raid on the premises of the Verlag on March 15, the Nazis had seized several documents that Martin Freud knew would be viewed as incriminating and that made him, in his words, "a certain candidate for a concentration camp." But he managed to buy back some of them from an ex-convict who had been appointed vice president of the police force; in the chaotic early days of the Anschluss, wealthy Jews could still bribe their way out of a number of perilous situations. The same corrupt newly minted police official promised to warn Martin whenever he might be targeted for arrest.

Not all problems could be solved that way. Martin and Marie Bonaparte tried to negotiate a deal to salvage most of the books of the Verlag, knowing that the new authorities had the opposite idea. But they failed. "Indeed, the Nazis were not satisfied to destroy the books remaining in Vienna," Martin recalled. "They arranged to have returned a much larger number which I had sent to Switzerland for safe keeping." It was particularly galling that the official who ordered this action displayed a "strange sense of humor when he debited father's account with the quite considerable cost of the books' transportation to their funeral pyre in Vienna."

Any Jews seeking to leave Austria at that point had to pay a "flight tax," and to satisfy a long list of other requirements, some of which were arbitrarily imposed. The key factors were how much money they had and whether there was evidence that they were violating the new rules. As he reviewed the records of the Verlag and the Freud household, Sauerwald came across information that would have constituted more than adequate proof of that.

According to Jones, Freud's will, which Martin had not managed to destroy, mentioned funds that he kept abroad. In a letter after the war to her cousin Harry, the son of her uncle Alexander, Anna wrote that Sauerwald had also acquired the records about "our affairs in Switzerland." This suggested that, aside from the books, other funds were stashed there. Sauerwald kept those documents "safely locked up until we were gone," she reported, adding that "he did not misuse his power and very few people are able to withstand such a temptation." Her point was that Sauerwald could have tried to impress his Nazi bosses by exposing such activity, but he did not do so.

At the time, however, the Freuds could not be sure that Sauerwald would maintain his silence. With the help of their lawyer, they also had to navigate the complicated procedures required of anyone trying to emigrate. Anna took the lead in those battles with the Nazi bureaucrats and the thugs who were always ready to supply the muscle, trying at all times to shield her father from any direct involvement by arguing that he was too old and ill to participate; she also tried to help those acquaintances who found themselves in similar circumstances. As her father put it in a letter to Jones, "Anna is untiringly active not only on our behalf but also for innumerable others."

Adolf Eichmann, who was already on the rise as a putative expert on the "Jewish question," admitted that the situation in Vienna was particularly confusing then. "Because of the complicated system, obtaining the necessary paperwork for a passport can take up to two or three months," he reported. "For example, a certificate confirming that one does not have a criminal record may take 6-8 weeks to obtain. Rich Jews therefore employ Aryan lawyers to get the papers." He added that some of the required documents would expire before the Jews could obtain other necessary documents. "These Jews had to go through the same process several times until they could emigrate," he wrote after setting up the Central Office for Jewish Emigration in Vienna that summer. "This caused heavy workloads for the authorities," he added, leaving no doubt that this was far more troubling to him than the ordeals of the Jews themselves.

While trying to make headway with those authorities, Anna and Marie Bonaparte combed through Freud's massive collection of papers and correspondence, burning the documents that they felt were expendable to try to reduce the volume to a manageable amount for what they hoped was an imminent departure. Bonaparte also regularly checked Freud's wastepaper basket, often retrieving papers that he had discarded. She not only was determined to save Freud but also as much of his legacy as possible. According to Fichtl, Bonaparte repeatedly smuggled items out of the apartment. "She was hiding everything under her skirt and went every day to her [Greek] embassy with it," the housekeeper recalled. Those documents were then sent to Paris with the diplomatic mail, shielding them from inspection and likely confiscation.

Even Sauerwald participated. Along with Bonaparte, he packed up some of the books on psychoanalysis that had eluded the earlier sweeps and took them to the Austrian National Library, where the director agreed to store rather than destroy them. Miraculously, they survived the war there.

———

On May 12, Freud wrote to his son Ernst, who had been living in London with his wife and children since they had fled Berlin in 1933. "I am writing to you for no particular reason because here I am sitting inactive and helpless while Anna runs here and there, coping with the authorities, attending to all the business details," he reported. The family was hoping to receive the "all clear" on the tax issues and other matters, he added, leaving no doubt that the uncertainty of the long wait was taking its toll. "Two prospects keep me going in these grim times: to rejoin you all and—to die in freedom."

Freud sounded philosophical about what would await him in a new country, assuming they succeeded in leaving Vienna. "Compared to being liberated nothing is of any importance," he wrote. "Anna will certainly find it easy to manage, and this is the main thing, because for us old people between seventy-three and eighty-two the whole undertaking would have made no sense." By old people, he was referring to his sister-in-law Minna, his wife, Martha, and himself.

Bonaparte and Bullitt were both ready to help with the payments the Nazis were demanding before Sauerwald would sign their exit visas; Bullitt was willing to put up $10,000, a huge sum at the time. But since the American remained at his ambassadorial post in Paris, it proved easier for Bonaparte to handle whatever transactions proved necessary. Freud's own local funds had been either confiscated or frozen at that point, while Sauerwald was continuing to maintain his silence about his foreign holdings. As Fichtl recalled, "The Princess [Bonaparte] paid for everything"—although Freud insisted on repaying her once they were free.

Even without factoring in his foreign accounts, Freud's assets, which included everything from his money and furniture to his artwork and books, were valued at 125,318 Reichsmarks, roughly $50,000; adjusted for inflation, this would be the equivalent of about $950,000 today. That translated into a 25 percent flight tax of 31,329 Reichsmarks. Bonaparte was their savior—but not just because she provided the largest portion of the money they needed; she also kept up their spirits. As Martin Freud pointed out, "I think our last sad weeks in Vienna . . . would have been quite unbearable without the presence of the Princess."

Some members of the family left Vienna before Freud could do so, taking advantage of the fact that they were issued new German passports to replace the confiscated Austrian ones. On May 4, Minna was the first to receive an exit visa, and, since she was ill, Dorothy Burlingham took her to Switzerland; later, they would both continue to London. Warned by his police contact of plans for his arrest, Martin took the train to Paris on May 14, joining his wife and two children whom he had dispatched there a few days earlier. His sister Mathilde and her husband, Robert, followed suit on May 24. But Freud was still stuck in Vienna, awaiting the declaration certifying that the authorities had no further claims on him.

Then there was the question of Freud's four elderly sisters in Vienna (another sister, Anna, had emigrated to the United States as a young woman). According to Martin, Freud and his brother Alexander "had supplied them with ample means to live in comfort for the rest of their lives," in all likelihood with Bonaparte's help. This suggests that they were willing to stay behind, perhaps under the misimpression that they would be in less danger than their famous brother. A simpler explanation may have been that there was not enough time to fight the bureaucratic battles and negotiate the separate ransom payments that would have been required to obtain permission for them to leave as well. In any case, they remained—although Bonaparte was soon alarmed enough to try to get them out. Tragically, that effort failed.

———

Once it became apparent that Sauerwald intended to approve the Freud party's departure, Bonaparte returned to Paris and everyone busied themselves with the remaining preparations. As always, Martha was a model of efficiency, attending to all the details of household. She even helped Fichtl, the housekeeper who was going with them, conceal the silver and gold coins she had received over the years as gifts from the family by sewing them into her coat since she did not want to part with her "treasures."

On June 2, Freud finally received the *Unbedenklichkeiterklärung*—the "declaration of no impediment"—that confirmed he had fulfilled all his obligations to the tax authorities. But the Nazis demanded that he also attest to the fact that he had been well treated. To that end, they presented him with a declaration to sign:

"I Prof. Freud, hereby confirm that after the Anschluss to the German Reich I have been treated by the German authorities and particularly by the Gestapo with all the respect and consideration due to my scientific reputation, that I could live and work in full freedom, and I could continue to pursue my activities in every way I desired, that I found full support from all concerned in this respect, and that I have not the slightest reason for any complaint."

Freud knew he had no choice in the matter, but he could not resist asking the Nazi official who was waiting for his signature whether he could add one sentence: "I can heartily recommend the Gestapo to anyone."

Fichtl overheard this exchange and held her breath. But, as she recalled, "The policeman only looked angrily at the Professor and, without a word, rushed out the door."

On June 4, Fichtl served Freud, Martha, and Anna their last breakfast at Berggasse 19. They had tickets for the Orient Express departing for Paris that afternoon. Anna's final request during breakfast was for Fichtl to serve her father a glass of vermouth to fortify him for the journey. At the last minute, Max Schur, who was supposed to be on the same train with his family so that he could monitor his patient, was unable to join them because he required an emergency appendectomy. Anna told him it was too dangerous for her father to wait, and they arranged for another doctor, Josefine Stross, to take his place on the train. Still recovering from his operation, Schur managed to get out with his family on June 10—as he wrote, "probably just in the nick of time."

The Freuds had two compartments on the train at their disposal: one was for Sigmund, Martha, and Anna, along with their beloved chow Lün, and the other was for Fichtl and Dr. Stross. As the train pulled out of the station, Fichtl was startled by a man who approached her to ask if she was part of the Freud party; her immediate assumption was that he was a Nazi. But it turned out he was a member of the U.S. legation who was to keep tabs on the Freuds until they safely reached France; he maintained a discreet distance from them during the trip and then disappeared. This was clearly Wiley's work, once again fulfilling Bullitt's wishes to protect the Freuds.

As the train rolled through Germany, via Munich and Dachau, the air of tension in both compartments was palpable. "Those were the worst hours of the trip," Fichtl recalled. Dr. Stross was particularly concerned about the elderly patient in her care and his heart's ability to cope with the stress. As Freud wrote to his friend Max Eitingon two days later, "She looked after me well for in actual fact the difficulties of the journey produced an effect of painful cardiac weariness on me, against which I took ample doses of nitroglycerine and strychnine."

When the train approached the border to France at 3:30 in the morning, Martha asked Stross and Fichtl to join her, Sigmund, and Anna in their compartment. "The Frau Professor wanted all of us to be together then," Fichtl noted. The feared customs inspection never happened, perhaps because the German authorities knew that an American representative was on the train. Similarly, the border guards glanced briefly at the passports and other documents that the Freuds handed over to them.

The train then crossed the Rhine, entering France. Visibly relieved, Freud leaned back in his seat. "Now we are free," he said.

12.

"THIS ENGLAND"

WHEN THE ORIENT EXPRESS PULLED INTO THE GARE DE L'EST in Paris early in the morning on June 5, 1938, Maric Bonaparte, William Bullitt, and Ernst Freud, who had come over from London, were waiting on the platform to greet the arrivals from Vienna. As Fichtl recalled, Bonaparte was outfitted in a flowing designer dress, her sable wrap draped over her shoulders, while Bullitt sported an elegant tie and a handkerchief planted in the front pocket of his single-breasted gray suit, with a jauntily tilted homburg completing the picture of the consummate diplomat.

The welcoming party was accompanied by a swarm of reporters and photographers who were frantically clicking away as soon as the Freuds, looking slightly dazed, emerged from the train. With Bullitt's help and Ernst Freud running interference, Bonaparte took charge, leading them through the assembled journalists and a growing number of people stopping to see what the commotion was all about. In front of the station, Bonaparte's two chauffeur-driven cars, a Bentley and a Rolls-Royce, were waiting to whisk them away to her villa in St. Cloud on the western edge of the city.

The Freuds spent the day at her house resting, talking, playing with the dogs, and greeting visitors, mostly on the terrace or in the garden, where a sofa was ready for the guest of honor, with wool blankets to keep him warm. He was flanked by Martha and Anna, who were seated in comfortable chairs. As Freud wrote to Eitingon the next day, Bonaparte "surpassed herself in tender care and attention, returned to us part of our money and refused to allow me to continue the journey without some new Greek terracotta figures." She also filmed the gathering, capturing the memorable images of the Freuds who were finally able to relax after the months of tension. (Bonaparte's films are now preserved in the Library of Congress.)

Long before the Anschluss, Freud, whose savings were wiped out by the hyperinflation after World War I, had been putting aside gold coins as a hedge against any recurrence of that situation. Along with the documents and other personal items Bonaparte had smuggled out of Berggasse 19, the princess had taken some of that money as well, sending it out of the country in the Greek legation's diplomatic pouch. In Paris, she informed Freud that he was better off financially than he had assumed, which explained his reference to her returning "a part of our money." The terracotta figures he also mentioned referred to the statues and antiquities Freud loved to surround himself with. Bonaparte surprised him further by presenting him with the bronze Roman statue of Athena that had stood on his desk in Vienna; this, too, she had managed to smuggle out of Berggasse 19.

"The one day in your house in Paris restored our good mood and sense of dignity," Freud wrote to Bonaparte afterward. "After being surrounded by love for twelve hours we left proud and rich under the protection of Athena."

That same evening the Freud party embarked on the last leg of their journey, crossing the channel by night ferry. In those days, the train carriages were loaded directly onto the ferry, which allowed Freud to stay put throughout the crossing. His first view of the sea came when they were landing at Dover, where he had to part with Lün, his chow, for the six-month quarantine that Britain mandated for all dogs arriving from out of the country. But special arrangements had been made in advance for Lün to be kept by a "friendly vet," with Freud granted visiting rights whenever he could make use of them.

To avoid another commotion at London's Victoria Station, Freud's train was routed to a different platform than the usual one, where a large group of journalists had been waiting for him. Lord De La Warr, the Lord Privy Seal, had also arranged for the Freuds to receive diplomatic privileges, which meant they did not have to go through customs. Instead, Ernest Jones, along with his wife, Katherine, and Freud's son Martin and daughter Mathilde, greeted them upon arrival and led Sigmund and Martha to his waiting car "for a quick get-away." Anna, Ernst, and Paula Fichtl followed in two taxis with everyone's luggage.

Jones drove the Freuds across town to the furnished house that Ernst had rented at 39 Elsworthy Road at the foot of Primrose Hill; this would serve as their temporary home until their furniture arrived and they could find something permanent. As they passed such landmarks as Buckingham Palace, Piccadilly Circus, and Regent Street, Freud eagerly pointed them out to Martha. But the excitement he felt about his return to a city he had first visited and admired in his youth was tempered by the circumstances of his departure from Vienna. He opened up about those conflicting emotions in his letter to Eitingon. "The feeling of triumph on being liberated is too strongly mixed with sorrow, for in spite of everything I still greatly loved the prison from which I have been released," he wrote.

Yet his spirits were on the rise. From the window of his room in the house, he continued in his letter to Eitingon, "I see nothing but greenery, which begins with a charming little garden surrounded by trees." Referring to his beloved rustic neighborhood on the outskirts of Vienna, he added, "So it is as though we were living in Grinzing." He was not even put off by the fact that, since the bedrooms were upstairs, Anna, Paula, and his son Ernst, who lived nearby, had to carry him downstairs every day and then back up in the evening because he was too weak to handle those trips on his own.

The best indication of his vastly improved mood was his revived sense of humor. He took his first walk in the garden with Jones, who became a regular visitor. "I am almost tempted to cry out 'Heil Hitler,' " he said. Fichtl, the housekeeper, overheard Freud going on in the same vein to Jones on another early occasion. "We thank our Führer that he forced us to emigrate here," he declared.

Such feelings were only reinforced by the enthusiasm of his hosts. His arrival was given huge play in the British press, and the medical journals were especially effusive as they welcomed him. The *Lancet* pointed out that his teachings had always been extremely controversial, often stirring hostile emotions the way Darwin's did. "Now, in his old age, there are few psychologists of any school who do not admit their debt to him," it asserted. "The medical profession of Great Britain will feel proud that their country has offered an asylum to Professor Freud, and that he has chosen it as his new home."

Freud wrote to Bonaparte in Paris that the result of all this coverage was an avalanche of flower deliveries and letters. A few of the letter writers were seeking his autograph, he explained, but the majority were "from strangers who only wish to say how happy they are that we have come to England and that we are in safety and peace."

Writing on June 22 to his brother Alexander, who was still in Switzerland, he sounded somewhat dazed by the displays of adulation: "Our reception was cordial beyond words. We were wafted up on the wings of a mass psychosis." While numerous academic and Jewish societies offered him honorary memberships, he also noted that he was besieged by "hordes of autograph hunters, cranks, lunatics, and pious men who send tracts and texts from Gospels which promise salvation." Sounding more bemused than irritated, he wrote: "In short, for the first time and late in life I have experienced what it is to be famous." This was not exactly accurate, since he had been famous for a long time before then; however, most Viennese had taken his fame in stride, without the fanfare that he encountered in London.

In that same letter to Alexander, he reflected more broadly—and more seriously—on his family's new situation and setting. "The fact is, things are going very well for us, too well I would say if it weren't for an injured heart and an irritated bladder reminding one of the impermanence of human happiness," he wrote. Anna "is as usual working for herself and others," he added, while Martha "is really enjoying her life." Jones confirmed Freud's observation about Martha. "Mrs. Freud never looked back to Vienna, only forward to her new mode of life as if she were twenty-seven years old instead of seventy-seven," he wrote. As she had at Berggasse 19, she insisted on doing her own shopping and was quickly on good terms with many of the shopkeepers. As Jones put it, "She was at once a capable and gracious mistress of the house, a charming companion, and a most gracious hostess."

Above all, Freud believed he had been proven right in his conviction that he had landed in the only place outside of Vienna where he could feel almost at home. "This England . . . is in spite of everything that strikes one as foreign, peculiar, and difficult . . . a blessed, a happy country inhabited by well-meaning, hospitable people," he asserted.

———

Once he was settled, Freud routinely turned down almost all invitations to venture outside of the house. But on June 10, shortly after his arrival in London, he showed up at the kennels where Lün was in quarantine. Supported by Anna, a visibly weary Freud made his way to the front door with great difficulty. According to Kevin F. Quin, the head of the kennels, Lün rewarded him for his effort by jumping with joy upon his arrival. "It was difficult to say which was more delighted," Quin told an Australian reporter. "I have never seen such happiness and understanding in an animal's eyes." Freud played and talked with the dog for a full hour, he added, and promised to return as often as possible. He later made good on that promise.

Freud did not make such exceptions often, not even for the Royal Society of Medicine that had made him an honorary fellow two years earlier. On June 23, three of its officials called on Freud at home so that he could sign their charter book. As *The Times* reported in its story headlined HONOUR FOR PROFESSOR FREUD, this was a "rare occasion" when that volume was taken off the premises of the Royal Society since Freud was not well enough to go there. Normally, this was an exception reserved for the King, the patron of the society who would sign the book at Buckingham Palace.

Marie Bonaparte, who was visiting London, and Anna Freud witnessed the signing. Anna pointed out to her father the other signature on the page he was asked to sign: it belonged to Charles Darwin, someone he viewed as an intellectual hero. Another signatory was Isaac Newton. "Good company!" he remarked later. According to the Royal Society's *Notes and Records*, "The simple, homely ceremony derived the dignity and pathos from the heart-felt gratitude of the exiled psychologist to the Society which had done him honour."

The prominent guests kept coming. Some he had met before, such as the British writer H. G. Wells, who had visited him in Vienna. The Austrian writer Stefan Zweig, who had emigrated to England four years earlier, was also eager to resume his friendship with him. "In all those years, a conversation with Freud had always been one of my greatest intellectual pleasures," he noted. At the same time, he knew that Freud was old and ill, and not sure quite what to expect. "I had been secretly a little afraid of finding Freud embittered or with his mind disturbed when I saw him again, after all the terrible trials he must have endured in Vienna, but I found him more at ease and happier than ever," he recalled. "As soon as you entered his room, it was as if the lunacy of the outside world had vanished."

On a visit on July 19, Zweig brought along Salvador Dalí, the surrealist painter who was in awe of Freud. While Dalí sketched him, Freud remarked: "In classic paintings, I look for the sub-conscious—in a surrealist painting for the conscious." Once the sketch was completed, Zweig recognized it revealed a harsh reality, which had not been immediately apparent to him. "I never dared to show it to Freud, because Dalí had prophetically shown death in his face."

But Freud was highly appreciative of the visit. "I really owe you thanks for bringing yesterday's visitor," he wrote to Zweig afterward. "For until now I have been inclined to regard the surrealists, who apparently have adopted me as their patron saint, as complete fools (let us say 95%, as with alcohol). That young Spaniard, with his candid fanatical eyes and his undeniable technical mastery, has changed my estimate."

Freud could still be a lively, provocative host. When the philosopher Isaiah Berlin called on him in October 1938, Freud personally opened the door and led him to his study. Born in Riga in 1909 into a Jewish family that emigrated to Britain after the Bolshevik Revolution, Berlin was the first Jew to be elected to a fellowship at All Souls, Oxford, and he quickly became an intellectual star. He was naturally curious about the new arrival from Vienna.

Either feigning ignorance or also genuinely curious, Freud asked his younger guest what he did. Berlin explained that he attempted to teach philosophy. "Then you must think me a charlatan," Freud declared, prompting Berlin to deny that he harbored such thoughts. When Freud described how he escaped from Vienna thanks to the help of Princess Marie Bonaparte, Berlin admitted he did not know anything about the Greek royal family. "I see you are not a snob," Freud observed with evident approval. Their conversation continued over tea in the garden, with Martha and their teenage grandson Lucian joining them. Berlin was immediately put at ease.

During such visits, Freud tried to avoid drawing attention to his physical decline, although this became increasingly difficult. Nonetheless, he still came across as an imposing figure. The legendary literary couple Virginia and Leonard Woolf met him only once, on January 28, 1939, after inquiring whether he would be willing to receive them. They were part of the circle of writers and artists known as the Bloomsbury Group. While Virginia achieved greater fame as a writer, Leonard assumed primary responsibility for the Hogarth Press, which published Freud's works and other books on psychoanalysis in English. When Freud extended the invitation to his home that they were hoping for, Leonard confessed that he went there with some trepidation.

"Nearly all famous men are disappointing or bores, or both," Leonard wrote later. "Freud was neither; he had an aura, not of fame, but of greatness." His cancer of the jaw was taking its toll, and "it was not an easy interview," Leonard continued. But Freud was "extraordinarily courteous in a formal old-fashioned way—for instance, almost ceremoniously he presented Virginia with a flower." He reminded Leonard of a "half-extinct volcano, something sombre, suppressed, reserved."

Yet no matter how much Freud was suffering physically, he remained engaged intellectually. When the discussion inevitably turned to Hitler and the Nazis, Virginia asserted that she and Leonard felt some guilt that the British side had triumphed in World War I. Perhaps, she ventured, a different outcome would have prevented Hitler's rise. Freud emphatically disagreed, arguing that Hitler and the Nazis would have come to power anyway and a German victory would have only made the overall situation much worse.

All of which left a strong impression on the visitors. "He gave me the feeling which only a very few people I have met gave me, a feeling of great gentleness, but behind the gentleness, great strength," Leonard wrote. When Leonard turned the subject to the popularity of his books, Freud said they had made him infamous, not famous. "A formidable man," Leonard concluded.

———

Ernst, the architect in the family who had settled in London earlier, was determined to help his parents find a permanent home, one that he could modify as much as needed to fit their needs—and in a way that would replicate the feel and key features of Berggasse 19 where they had spent most of their lives. On July 28, 1938, the family bought a house at 20 Maresfield Gardens in Hampstead, a part of London popular with psychoanalysts. With a mortgage of £4,000 from Barclays Bank, they could cover the total cost of £6,500. "You can imagine the demands its purchase made on our shrunken savings," Freud wrote to Jeanne Lampl-de Groot, a Dutch colleague.

But Freud, who saw the house for the first time two weeks later and would not move in until late September, was delighted by what he called "our own house!" Built in about 1920 in the Queen Anne Revival style, it was a red brick structure that was more spacious than Berggasse 19, with large rooms, and "far too beautiful for us," as Freud explained in his letter to Lampl-de Groot. He added that Ernst "has transformed this house into a ruin in order to restore it anew in a more suitable state for us." One of the younger Freud's additions was an elevator, which allowed his father to go from the bedrooms upstairs to the lower floor where his office and library were located. It was an equally critical addition for his aunt Minna, whose health had been steadily deteriorating.

Freud called his son's restoration and, in some cases, reconfiguration of the house "sheer sorcery translated into architectural terms."

In a letter to Eitingon, he similarly praised Ernst for how "splendidly" he had taken care of everything. "We have it incomparably better than at Berggasse and even than Grinzing," he wrote. "'From poverty to white bread,' as the proverb says." One example of Ernst's work was the floor-to-ceiling bookcase he designed to house most of his father's collection of books that had arrived from Vienna along with the family's other household items. Two of their Biedermeier cabinets, which were used to display many of Freud's antiquities, were incorporated into the bookshelves.

Other parts of his considerable collection of figurines, including new items received as gifts, were laid out on a table or housed in additional display cabinets. Paula Fichtl meticulously arranged the ones that came from Vienna according to the way they had appeared in Berggasse 19. All of which prompted Leonard Woolf to observe that Freud's study was "almost a museum," although everything "seemed very light, shining, clean, with a pleasant open view through the windows into a garden."

When Freud first inspected his new quarters and office once his belongings were installed there, he declared, "Everything is here again, except me." That remark contained a typical mix of irony and self-deprecating humor, reflecting his recognition that his aging body could not be refurbished as easily as his new abode. And despite the tremendous effort by Ernst, Paula, and others to reproduce an approximation of his living conditions in Vienna, Freud was acutely conscious of his status as an outsider, no matter how many accolades he received.

He was highly appreciative of England and its people, but he was now an émigré, no longer living in the country that he had always called home. "Everything here is rather strange, difficult, and often bewildering, but all the same it is the only country we can live in," he wrote to Marie Bonaparte on October 4. For older émigrés, such conflicting feelings were hardly unusual, and Freud was no exception in that regard.

Then, too, Freud was more troubled than he usually let on about events in Germany. In September, Hitler's belligerent rhetoric about Czechoslovakia had looked like it might trigger a new war. As Dorothy Burlingham, who had also moved to London to be close to Anna, recalled, "You should have seen the parks, suddenly they were dotted with guns pointed to the skies . . . You can imagine our friends the immigrants, all so unhappy that they had chosen England, all so frightened what would happen to them."

On September 30, Prime Minister Neville Chamberlain had returned from his meeting with Hitler in Munich, boasting that he had achieved "peace for our time" by ceding the Sudetenland to Germany—triggering a jubilant response from most of his countrymen. But in his letter to Bonaparte, Freud somberly noted that "now that the intoxication of peace has subsided, people as well as Parliament are coming back to their senses and facing the painful truth. We too of course are thankful for a bit of peace, but we cannot take any pleasure in it."

The news only got worse from Germany. On November 10, his diary entry read simply: "Pogroms in Germany." This was a reference to *Kristallnacht*, the "night of broken glass," when the attacks on Jews and their shops, businesses, synagogues, and homes throughout the country signaled a major escalation in Hitler's increasingly violent anti-Semitic campaign.

Like other émigrés, Freud was particularly worried about the family members he had left behind, four of his sisters. "The latest horrifying events in Germany aggravate the problem about what to do with the four old women between seventy-five and eighty," he wrote to Bonaparte on November 12. He reminded her that he had given them a considerable sum of money, but worried that it may have been confiscated. He also speculated whether there might be a way to get them to southern France. "But would this be possible?" he asked. He did not sound optimistic.

Freud did not live long enough to learn what happened to those sisters. In the summer of 1942, all four were deported from Vienna to Theresienstadt, which masqueraded as a showcase ghetto but primarily served as a transit camp for inmates who were usually murdered elsewhere. Three of the sisters—Rosa, Marie, and Pauline—were dispatched in a transport to the Treblinka II death camp on September 23, where they perished in the gas chambers. Adolfine, or Dolfi as she was known, remained in Theresienstadt for a few more days but died there on September 29. Martin Freud wrote that she starved to death.

———

As always, Freud was also preoccupied with his work—and troubled by what he viewed as his vastly diminished productivity as a result of his waning physical condition. But he kept treating patients, who would lie on his famous couch that had followed him from Vienna. Once he was installed in the new house, he could see up to four patients a day when he felt well enough to do so. Visitors kept showing up as well, and, as Schur reported, he remained an avid reader.

While Anna continued to act as her father's primary caregiver, she had also attended the fifteenth International Psychoanalytic Congress in Paris in the summer of 1938, the last one that would be held until after World War II. Jones presided over that gathering, and the presentation of an extract from Freud's work-in-progress, *Moses and Monotheism*, allowed the founder to be there in spirit.

Knowing that his time was running out, Freud wanted to wrap up his uncompleted projects. When William Bullitt visited him in London shortly after he settled there, the American brought the manuscript of their biography of Woodrow Wilson with him, hoping to resolve their remaining differences. Specifically, Bullitt wanted his coauthor to agree to drop the passages he had added earlier. To his relief, Freud accepted his advice and approved the text without them. Since they had also agreed not to publish the book while Edith Wilson, the president's widow, was still alive, Freud knew he would not live to see that happen, but at least he could feel confident that it would be published someday.

He had different feelings about his book on Moses. The first two parts of this project, which was based on the controversial premise that Moses was an Egyptian, had appeared in the German psychoanalytic magazine *Imago* in 1937, which meant it was already attracting critical attention. But he needed to write the third section to prepare it for publication as a book. Only a few days after Freud arrived in London, however, Abraham Shalom Yahuda, a noted Biblical scholar, called on him in a bid to convince him that he should not publish it at all.

Yahuda was far from alone in his opposition. Writing to the German-Jewish writer Arnold Zweig, Freud mentioned a letter he had received from a young American Jew "in which I am asked not to rob his poor unfortunate people of the only comfort left to them in their misery." He explained that this "well-meaning" letter overestimated his influence. "Am I really to believe that my dry essay would diminish the faith of even one . . . person . . ." he asked. Given his prominence not just as the founder of psychoanalysis but also as a leading thinker, this was not, to put it mildly, the most compelling counterargument.

Although Freud was unwilling to bow to such attempts to muzzle him, they may have contributed to his difficulties in tackling the concluding section about the monotheistic religions. Before leaving Vienna, he had confessed in a letter to Jones that the book "torments me like a *ghost not laid.*" Those last three words were written in English; he presumably was trying to say something like a "ghost that cannot be banished." In his actual text, he wrote about the "inner misgivings as well as external hindrances" that dogged him throughout his work on the Moses book.

Yet he was determined to finish the manuscript as soon as possible after his arrival in London. On July 15, his diary entry read "Moses sold to America," which he found very encouraging for two reasons: American sales were vital for the success of the English version, and he hoped that this would bring in money to help cover the family's expenses. Two days later, he reported in his diary: "Moses finished."

Freud had started writing the final section in Vienna while he was still uncertain whether he would ever release it. In the portion he wrote in London, he felt the need to explain why his thinking had changed. "Formerly I lived under the protection of the Catholic Church and feared that by publishing the essay I should lose that protection and that the practitioners and students of psycho-analysis in Austria would be forbidden their work," he wrote. "Then, suddenly, the German invasion broke in on us and Catholicism proved to be, as the Bible has it, 'but a broken reed.'" Since he knew that he would be persecuted "now not only because of my work, but also because of my 'race,'" he had been forced to seek refuge in England.

In the country that had afforded him the "kindliest welcome," he felt liberated from the threat of persecution, free to publish a work that he knew would hardly meet with universal applause. "I dare now to make public the last part of my essay," he announced. He knew it would offend many of his fellow Jews, but he was at pains to explain that he was not rejecting Judaism as a whole. In reply to a letter from the Committee of the Yiddish Scientific Institute, he wrote: "You no doubt know that I gladly and proudly acknowledge my Jewishness though my attitude toward any religion, including ours, is critically negative." In another letter, he added: "We Jews have always known how to respect spiritual values. We preserved our unity through ideas, and because of them we have survived to this day."

While Freud admitted in *Moses and Monotheism* that belief in one God was central to the values and survival of the Jewish people, he juxtaposed that belief—not just of Jews but of others as well—with what he saw as the reality that no such God exists. "The religious argument is based on an optimistic and idealistic premise," he wrote. "The human intellect has not shown itself elsewhere to be endowed with a very good scent for truth, nor has the human mind any special readiness to accept truth."

Stefan Zweig visited Freud shortly after his volume on Moses was published. According to his account, he found Freud remorseful that his book had come out "in the middle of the most terrible hour in Jewish history." Zweig quoted Freud as saying: "Now that everything is being taken away from the Jews I come along and take away their great man as well"—referring to his argument that Moses was an Egyptian. Yet Freud's actions and words suggested that, as a newly free man, he did not really regret confronting others with what he viewed as the truth while he still had the strength to do so.

Moses and Monotheism would prove to be his last complete work, but he also embarked on a short new book titled *An Outline of Psycho-Analysis*, which aimed to summarize his ideas on his chosen field. It was published posthumously although he was not able to finish it. His illnesses began taking their final toll before he could do so.

———

Six days after the Freud party left Vienna, Max Schur showed up with his wife and two children at the train station in that city. Freud's physician was still in a wheelchair, wrapped in bandages after his last-minute appendectomy, and he had to be helped on board the train to Paris, something that his then five-year-old son Peter remembers to this day. They, too, were greeted by Marie Bonaparte in the French capital, and Schur spent three days recuperating at her house. "Recuperating of course meant more than the healing of my abdominal wound," Max Schur recalled. "What an unbelievable contrast it was to be out of the world of madmen."

Catching up with Freud in London, Schur resumed his familiar role as his primary physician. The Home Office allowed him to do so even before he passed the required British medical examinations. At first, he was encouraged by the "amazing" way Freud had weathered the journey from Vienna to London, and pleased to see his dedication to his work that summer. But Schur also knew that his patient was vulnerable to new lesions in his mouth. In the past, most of the lesions were precancerous but, as he noted, "the tendency of the past two years had been towards full-fledged malignancy."

By August, Schur was concerned enough about the appearance of new lesions that he contacted Hans Pichler, the oral surgeon who had operated on Freud in Vienna, asking him to come to London to treat his famous patient again. Anna Freud fully backed this appeal, although her father initially felt they were being unduly alarmist.

On September 7, Pichler arrived and operated on Freud the next day. "Excision of large pieces of very hard, firm tissue," he reported. While the surgery was successful, Freud's recovery was slow and painful. In a letter to Marie Bonaparte on October 4, he wrote: "This operation was the worst since 1923 and has taken a great deal out of me. I feel dreadfully tired, and feel weak when I move." The recovery, he added, was supposed to take six weeks, which meant that he had two more to go. Nonetheless, he had started seeing patients again.

Schur believed that this period marked the "end of Freud's creative activity," which was how he described his writing. In another letter to Bonaparte on November 12, Freud appeared to agree. "I am still quite unproductive. I can write letters, but nothing more," he declared. Even his voice betrayed his waning strength. On December 7, the BBC recorded a statement from him at his home. They were hoping that he would read the introduction from one of his books, but he only spoke briefly in a muffled voice. His final words: "At the age of 82 I left my home in Vienna as a result of German invasion and came to England where I hope to end my life in freedom."

Following the discovery of an inoperable oral lesion in February

1939, Freud was started on radiation treatments, weakening him further. On April 28, he reported to Bonaparte that Anna could no longer travel to Paris for meetings. "I am growing increasingly incapable of looking after myself and more dependent on her. Some kind of intervention that would cut short this cruel process would be very welcome." Yet he still managed to enjoy his eighty-third birthday on May 6, strolling around the garden where family members and guests had gathered. Fichtl, the ever-devoted housekeeper, tied greetings around the necks of the dogs, who delivered them to Freud.

If Freud accepted the fact that he did not have long to live, he still had one ambition: he wanted to become a British citizen. As his son Martin noted, "Father loved England." In a letter to H. G. Wells on July 16, 1939, Freud explained that "since I came over to England as a boy of eighteen years, it became an intense wish phantasy of mine to settle in this country and become an Englishman."

Wells lobbied for an Act of Parliament that would have granted Freud's wish, but the parliamentarians were unwilling to waive the five-year residency requirement for anyone seeking to become a naturalized citizen. As they saw it, this was a question of not setting a precedent. But both Wells and Freud knew that he had no chance of living long enough to qualify.

———

Although he was dedicated to caring for his famous patient, Schur had his own ambitions as well. By not immediately taking advantage of the visas the United States had approved for him and his family in 1937 and then repeatedly putting off any action on them, he risked jeopardizing his chances for settling in that country. Unlike Freud, he was not content to live the rest of his life in England—and he did not share Freud's disdain for the United States. After the Munich crisis, he reapplied for U.S. visas, only to learn that the previous applications were still considered valid. There was a catch, however: he had to make use of them by the end of April or he would lose them.

When it looked like the radiation treatments were producing an improvement in Freud's condition, Schur decided to go with his family to the United States, setting sail on April 21, 1939. He planned on getting his "first papers" to settle there, take the New York State boards for his medical license, and then return as quickly as possible to London to resume his care for Freud until the seemingly imminent end of his days.

Schur arranged for another doctor to fill in for him during the time he would be away, but he knew that Freud "did not quite approve" of his trip. "He was used to me and in a sense dependent on me, and he probably felt that I was deserting him, or worse, giving up on him," Schur wrote later. Nonetheless, Freud helped him with some of the formalities and wished him success on his mission. From New York, Schur was in regular touch with the substitute doctor and Anna, and he was initially encouraged by their reports that the radiation treatments were still helping Freud.

But in a letter to Bonaparte on April 28, Freud rejected that view. "People are trying to lull me into an atmosphere of optimism by saying that the carcinoma is shrinking and the symptoms of reacting to the treatment are temporary," he wrote. "I don't believe it and don't like being deceived."

Intent on making good on his promise to return to Freud in London as soon as possible, Schur used every connection he could to expedite the bureaucratic process in the United States. Thanks to the intervention of Julian Mack, a federal judge who was the father of Ruth Mack Brunswick, an American psychiatrist who had studied and worked with Freud in Vienna, he was awarded his "first papers" on June 15. Schur then passed his medical boards at the end of that month and sailed back to England with his family on the *Île de France*, arriving on July 8.

Rushing over to Maresfield Gardens, Schur was startled by the sight of his patient. "I found Freud looking much worse," he recalled. "He had lost weight and was somewhat apathetic, at least as compared to his normal mental vigor." There was some discoloration of the skin over his right cheekbone, and he had lost part of his beard during his radiation treatments. Examining his mouth, Schur was struck by the tenderness of the bone in the affected area and the foul odor emanating from it. The two men knew each other too well to pretend that the situation was anything but extremely serious. "He knew what I thought; I knew what he knew," Schur noted.

There was not much that anyone could do except try to alleviate the pain. Since Freud "hated barbiturates and opiates" and thought of morphine only "as a last resort," Schur wrote, he and Anna applied Orthoform, a powder that served as a local anesthetic but did nothing to repair the damaged bone in his mouth. Anna, who was also juggling her practice and her efforts to rescue more analysts who were still on the continent, had to tend to him at night. She kept applying more Orthoform since the pain kept waking him.

By August, Freud could not see patients anymore, which forced him to put an end to his lifetime occupation. He needed more and more rest; he slept in his study, no longer going back upstairs in the evenings. He could see the garden and its flowers from there, which was a small consolation, but even his beloved chow no longer wanted to be by his side. As Schur recalled, the dog "could not tolerate the smell" emanating from the wounds in his mouth and crouched in the far corner if he was brought into the room. Freud knew why and "looked at his pet with a tragic and knowing sadness," Jones wrote.

Marie Bonaparte visited Freud for the last time in early August, and later in the month his fifteen-year-old granddaughter Eva, his son Oliver's only child, came from France as well. As Schur wrote, "He showed a special tenderness towards this charming girl," knowing full well that he would not see her again. Jones and others were also making their final visits.

On September 1, Germany attacked Poland, igniting World War II. Schur moved into the Freuds' house at the same time and sent his family to safety outside of London. On September 3, when Britain and France issued their declarations of war against Germany, Martha, Minna, and Anna joined Schur in Freud's study, which had been converted into something akin to a hospital room. In those earliest days of the war, Fichtl pointed out, the elder Freuds maintained a stoic calm, while younger members of the family were often in a near-panic as the first air raid sirens started going off.

The patriarch observed the precautions that everyone was taking on such occasions, especially the ones that were meant to safeguard his manuscripts and art collection. But, as Schur put it, he was already "far away," increasingly detached from the swirl of events around him. When Schur asked him what he thought of the old assertion from World War I, which was repeated in a radio broadcast about the new conflict, that this was going to be the "last war," he replied: "Anyhow it is my last war."

In his personal war with his chronic pain, Jones recalled, Freud never showed any signs of impatience. "The philosophy of resignation and acceptance of unalterable reality triumphed throughout." When Jones visited him for the last time on September 19, Freud was dozing but then opened his eyes and waved his hand, which the Welshman took as a sign of greeting and farewell.

Two days later, Freud took his doctor's hand and told him in German: "My dear Schur, you certainly remember our first talk. You promised me then not to forsake me when my time comes. Now it's nothing but torture and makes no sense anymore."

Schur assured him that he had not forgotten his promise, and Freud thanked him. He also told him: "Tell Anna about this." Schur did so, and, with her agreement, gave Freud an injection of two centigrams of morphine the next morning that put him into a "peaceful sleep," as Schur recalled. He followed up twelve hours later with a second dose that put him into a coma. At 3 a.m. on September 23, 1939, Freud died.

His family was largely reconciled to that outcome. As Anna explained to a friend later, "I believe that there is nothing worse than to see the people nearest to one lose the very qualities for which one loves them. I was spared that with my father, who was himself to the last minute."

In a letter to Paul Federn, a longtime colleague of Freud who had served as vice president of the Vienna Psychoanalytic Society before also fleeing in 1938, Martha struck an equally philosophical note. "I cannot even complain, for I have been granted more than a lifetime in which I have been allowed to look after him, to shield him from the troubles of everyday life," she wrote. "That my life had now lost sense and content is only natural."

On the morning of September 26, those family members and friends who could reach London gathered at Golders Green, where Freud's body was cremated. His ashes were placed in a Greek vase, which was another gift from Marie Bonaparte, who returned from Paris for the ceremony.

Ernest Jones delivered the eulogy. He talked about Freud's accomplishments and how his legacy would long survive him. "His creative spirit was so strong that he infused himself into others," he declared. "If ever man can be said to have conquered death itself, to live on in spite of the King of Terrors, who held no terror for him, that man was Freud."

It was not only Freud's calculated realism that accounted for his equanimity in the face of death. The other decisive factor was the devotion of all his rescuers, the men and women who had made it possible for him to die in freedom.

AFTERWORD

After Freud died, W. H. Auden wrote a poem that sought to capture the meaning of his life—and how his presence was still making itself felt. The key passage from "In Memory of Sigmund Freud":

> to us he is no more a person
> now but a whole climate of opinion.

This was particularly true for the members of Freud's rescue squad, who led lives that continued to be shaped by the "climate of opinion" he left behind. His ideas, spelled out in his writings, lectures, correspondence, and endless therapy sessions and conversations, kept hovering around them, insinuating themselves ever deeper into their thinking. His death provided them with a new impetus to try to carry on his legacy.

A glance at what happened to the main characters in this story:

———

Anna Freud lived for the rest of her life in the house at 20 Maresfield Gardens, where her father died. At first, she stayed there with her mother, Martha, and her ailing aunt Minna, without her partner Dorothy Burlingham, who had gone to New York for the birth of her first grandchild in August 1939. Due to the outbreak of World War II, she was not able to return to London until April 1940.

As long as Minna was alive, Dorothy lived on the same street as Anna but in a different house, 2 Maresfield Gardens. When Minna died in 1941, Dorothy moved in with Anna. Martha Freud died in 1951 at the age of ninety, leaving the two women—who, as Dorothy's biographer and grandson Michael Burlingham wrote, looked "much like a married couple"—to spend the next twenty-eight years of their lives together until Dorothy's death in 1979.

In 1941, Anna and Dorothy opened the Hampstead War Nurseries to care for and observe children who were left homeless as a result of the war. Based on those experiences, Anna wrote "Young Children in Wartime" and other studies that further enhanced her reputation as a leader in her field. After the war, she and Dorothy launched the Hampstead Child Therapy Course and Clinic, which was renamed the Anna Freud National Centre for Children and Families after her death. She also traveled frequently to lecture at Yale and other universities in the United States.

Her clinic attracted students from all over who looked up to her both as a major figure in her own right but also as the daughter of the founder of psychoanalysis. Jonathan Tobis, a medical student from the United States, recalled his stint at the clinic in the early 1970s—especially the general sessions where Anna Freud would discuss her work. "It was like sitting at the foot of the Buddha," he said. "Maybe 60 people in the room listening with rapt attention and awe as she discussed the subtleties between 'shame' and 'guilt.'"

Anna died in 1982 at the age of eighty-six, and her ashes were laid to rest in what is known as the Freud Corner in the Golders Green Crematorium, next to the Greek vase that contains the ashes of her father and mother. The house at 20 Maresfield Gardens is now the Freud Museum in London. Similarly, Berggasse 19, where the Freud family lived in Vienna, now houses that city's Sigmund Freud Museum.

———

Ernest Jones was president of the International Psychoanalytical Association until 1949, the post he had held since 1932 (and previously from 1920 to 1924). In the postwar years, he continued to see patients, but his main ambition was to write a full biography of Freud, examining not only his professional but also personal life.

"It is not a book that would have met with Freud's own approval," Jones wrote in his preface to the first of the three volumes he produced in the 1950s. In his own writings, Freud felt "he had divulged enough of his personal life" and he wanted "to keep private what remained," Jones explained. In order to write a truly authoritative biography, Jones needed to convince Freud's family to offer their full support, while cognizant that its subject had not wished for anything of the sort.

Jones managed to win the family over for two main reasons. First of all, his eloquent eulogy at Freud's funeral had left a strong impression, especially on Anna and Martha. Secondly, the biographies and articles published in the first decade after Freud's death usually irritated the family members, who felt they misrepresented him, distorting his ideas and presenting inaccurate information. Anna, Ernst, Mathilde, and Martin, Freud's children who were still in England, decided that Jones, who had known and worked with their father for so long, was the one person who could try to set the record straight.

Although Jones had turned seventy in 1949, he tackled his new project with his usual remarkable energy and enthusiasm. He made it a priority to interview Martha at length, who provided him with much of his information about the couple's early years, before she died in November 1951. He also scooped up every bit of Freud correspondence he could, and he appealed to Anna for copies of the deeply personal letters between her parents during their lengthy, long-distance courtship.

To convince her to agree, Jones showed her his draft of the first chapter soon after Martha's death. "I am simply amazed at the objective, factual and scientific approach to the whole subject," she wrote to one of her father's friends. After that, she helped in any way she could. When Jones published his opus, the dedication read: "*To Anna Freud, True Daughter Of An Immortal Sire.*"

Jones completed all three volumes before he was diagnosed with liver cancer. Hospitalized and in pain, he understood full well what was happening. On February 11, 1958, he asked his doctor for help in ending his life. Like Freud, he was insistent on making that final decision himself. His wife, Kitty, was at his side as his wish was granted.

———

Marie Bonaparte was not able to save Freud's four sisters, but she worked vigorously to help other Jews flee German rule. She funneled money to Jewish organizations that arranged the escapes of scientists and physicians, and she lobbied French politicians to grant transit visas or residence permits to them. Her biographer Celia Bertin estimated that she helped rescue nearly two hundred Jews, although she never advertised her involvement in such cases. She also floated far less practical ideas—for instance, proposing to William Bullitt, the U.S. ambassador in Paris, that his country should buy land in Mexico to establish a Jewish state there.

In the postwar era, Bonaparte continued her dual life as a practicing psychoanalyst and member of high society. Since she was the Princess of Greece and Denmark, it was only natural for her to attend the coronation of Queen Elizabeth II in 1953. That same year the English edition of her book on the topic that was always her major preoccupation was published. Its title: *Female Sexuality.*

She returned to London for such occasions as the inauguration of the clinic founded by Anna Freud and Dorothy Burlingham and Ernest Jones's unveiling of the plaque at 20 Maresfield Gardens honoring Sigmund Freud. She also participated in the major gatherings of her colleagues. In 1957, at the twentieth International Psychoanalytic Congress in Paris, she offered something close to a valedictory statement about everything that Freud had set in motion. Psychoanalysis, she declared, had led to the "liberation of the irrepressible sexual instincts; greater frankness with our children, greater sexual freedom for women." As a result, "Mankind has . . . become a little less hypocritical, and, perhaps, a little happier."

In the same paper that she read to the congress, she argued that psychoanalysis encouraged everyone to face reality, including the ultimate reality of their existence. Instead of seeking refuge in religions that denied the reality of death, people would be better off learning from Freud, who showed a "greater acceptance and therefore courage in the face of death, that inescapable enemy which it is better to confront than deny."

But she was far from philosophical about the death penalty, lobbying frantically on behalf of Caryl Chessman, a convicted rapist, kidnapper, and robber who sat on San Quentin's death row for twelve years before he was executed in 1960.

Informed that she had leukemia at the age of eighty, Bonaparte shared the diagnosis with her daughter. Marie expressed the hope that she might live longer, but seemingly was ready to accept the outcome. She died on September 21, 1962.

William Bullitt had always been extremely ambitious, and, after the fall of France in 1940, he returned from his ambassadorial post in Paris hoping for a leading role in the Roosevelt Administration. He had his proponents, such as presidential aide Harold Ickes, who urged his boss to appoint him secretary of state—to no avail. "He talked too much, and is too quick on the trigger," Roosevelt replied. Bullitt's dramatic resignation from the American delegation to the Paris peace talks at the end of World War I, followed by his strident denunciations of Woodrow Wilson and the Treaty of Versailles, earned him that kind of reputation.

While refusing to name Bullitt to any of the top jobs, Roosevelt still turned to him for advice on a variety of international issues, and Bullitt might have continued to play a significant role in Washington. However, after Under Secretary of State Sumner Welles propositioned two male conductors on a train trip back to the capital, Bullitt made a fatal blunder: on April 23, 1941, he warned the president that the hushed up incident could spark a "terrible public scandal," and urged him to fire Welles. It did not help Bullitt's cause that he was seen as envious of Welles's senior position. Roosevelt was more incensed at what he saw as Bullitt's vindictive streak than he was at the behavior of Welles, who managed to hang on to his job for another two years.

Bullitt was soon sidelined completely. In 1943, he was the Democratic candidate for mayor of Philadelphia but lost the election. After failing to get a commission in the U.S. Army on account of his age, he enlisted in the Free French Forces led by General Charles de Gaulle. He served as a top aide to the commander of France's First Army, and he was injured by a vehicle during the battle for Alsace. In Paris, he returned to the U.S. embassy where he had served as ambassador and unlocked the gates that had been closed for four years.

But no amount of heroics could salvage his diplomatic career back home. Given his opposition to Roosevelt's concessions to Stalin at the Yalta peace conference that allowed the Kremlin to control Eastern Europe, he became as strident a critic of the president, even after his death on April 12, 1945, as he and Freud had been of Wilson. Bullitt believed that both American presidents had caved to foreign pressure, setting the stage for new instability and, possibly, a new conflagration. In his 1946 book, *The Great Globe Itself*, he warned of the danger of the latest weapon, the atomic bomb. "After the next World War . . . there may be no after," he wrote.

Bullitt and Freud's book on Wilson was finally published in December 1966, and the reviews were overwhelmingly negative. Bullitt did not see them because he was back in Paris then, fighting a losing battle with chronic lymphatic leukemia. He died, at age seventy-six, on February 15, 1967, a deeply embittered man. Unlike Freud and most of the other members of his rescue squad, he never made peace with his fate.

———

Anton Sauerwald, the Nazi trustee who was in charge of dealing with Freud in Vienna after the Anschluss, remained a somewhat mysterious character in this drama. After Freud's departure for London, he visited Freud's sisters who had stayed behind, in all likelihood trying to shield them from his masters. But when he was called up during the war to serve as a technical expert for the Luftwaffe, he was no longer able to help them.

Captured by the Americans in March 1945 and held in a POW camp, he was released in June, a month after the war in Europe had ended. But when he returned to Vienna, he discovered that his troubles were far from over. Partly at the behest of Harry Freud, a U.S. Army officer who blamed Sauerwald for the persecution of his famous uncle, the newly formed People's Court took up his case. The prosecution charged Sauerwald with membership in the Nazi Party before the Anschluss, when the party was outlawed; they also accused him of financial fraud during the period when he was expropriating Jewish property.

Writing to Harry Freud in October 1945, Anna Freud contradicted his version of events, maintaining "that we really owe our lives and freedom to Sauerwald." On July 22, 1947, she wrote to Marianne Sauerwald, who had been desperately seeking help for her husband, to assure her that she and her mother had "in no way forgotten" what he had done to protect her father "in a very precarious situation."

The letter helped get Sauerwald out of prison, but the case still dragged on until 1949 when the court finally acquitted him. He died in 1970 in Innsbruck.

——

Max Schur took his family to the United States almost immediately after Freud died, fulfilling his long-held plans to settle there. But Atlantic crossings were highly dangerous in October 1939. "I remember how we picked up survivors in lifeboats from a U-boat sinking, and then saw British warships circle a burning vessel," Peter Schur, who was only six at the time, noted in a speech about his father to the Vienna Psychoanalytic Association in 1994. Their ship was then pummeled by a hurricane, and his physician mother had to perform an emergency appendectomy on one of the crew members while his father administered anesthesia.

In New York, Schur resumed his medical private practice and worked initially at Bellevue Hospital's Division of Syphilology and Dermatology. He also became a member of the New York Psychoanalytic Society, teaching and practicing psychoanalysis at the Downstate Medical Center of the State University of New York.

Schur stayed in touch with other members of Freud's rescue squad—Anna Freud, Marie Bonaparte, and Ernest Jones, who had helped save him as well as Freud. In 1964, he delivered a lecture to the New York Psychoanalytic Society on "The Problem of Death in Freud's Writings and His Life." Encouraged by Anna Freud, he wrote a fuller account of his relationship with Freud, finishing his manuscript before he died in 1969 at the age of seventy-two.

The book, *Freud: Living and Dying*, was published in 1972. Aside from providing numerous new details about Freud, it reflected the near adulation that Schur felt for his patient. "He was always a deeply human and noble man, in the fullest meaning of the word," he wrote. "And I saw him face dying and death as nobly as he had faced living."

ACKNOWLEDGMENTS

A FELLOW AUTHOR ONCE TOLD ME THAT THE HARDEST PART about writing books is the time between writing them. Unless you are one of those people who always think several steps ahead, you are suddenly adrift, disoriented, searching for the next project, and never sure you will come up with anything that will be as engaging as your last one. But when someone or something triggers an idea that looks not only plausible but truly compelling, you immediately feel energized, with a renewed sense of purpose. You are immensely grateful to that someone or something that put you back on track.

I remember exactly what triggered the idea for *Saving Freud*. Howard Estrin, a new acquaintance at the time, sent a copy of Stefan Zweig's *The World of Yesterday*, a beautifully written memoir about growing up in Vienna at the turn of the last century. I was intrigued by Zweig's evocation of the intellectual atmosphere in the mostly Jewish circles he moved in, and especially struck by his descriptions of his encounters with Freud in Vienna and later in London. I was hooked; if there was a eureka moment for this book, that was it.

Freud may be a familiar figure, but many people—myself included— knew very little about the circle of friends who ultimately extricated him from Vienna or about his intriguing mix of revolutionary theories and conservative views. To tell this story, I relied especially on the extensive writings and correspondence of Freud and his contemporaries, who recorded so many of their experiences, along with their biographers.

I am especially grateful to Randolph Bernays Randolph, the great-grandson of Freud's sister Anna (not to be confused with Freud's daughter by the same name), who provided me with the unpublished English translation of her memoirs. Teresa Radzinski, a friend in St. Augustine where we both live, introduced us to each other. I was also delighted to discover that Peter Schur, the son of Freud's doctor Max Schur, lives and still practices medicine in Boston; he shared his memories of his father with me, along with the text of the speech he delivered on "The Freud-Schur Connection" to the Vienna Psychoanalytic Association in 1994.

In Vienna, I was the beneficiary of generous help from Daniela Finzi and Natascha Halbauer at the Sigmund Freud Museum, and Karoline Gattringer and Niki Schobesberger at the Wiener Stadt- und Landesarchiv (Municipal and Provincial Archives of Vienna). I also want to thank Edward Serotta, Reinhard Engel, and Marta Halpert, all former journalistic colleagues and longtime Vienna residents.

In London, Bryony Davies at the Freud Museum (yes, there are two Freud Museums, one in Vienna and the other in London) and the archive of the Royal Society of Medicine fielded my requests for help in tracking down various aspects of the story. So did the National Library of Israel. During a period when Covid restricted travel, I especially appreciated their assistance.

In the United States, I want to thank Margaret McAleer at the Library of Congress, which houses an enormous Freud collection, and Michael Frost at Yale University's Sterling Memorial Library, which has William Bullitt's papers.

I regularly checked my translations from documents and books in

German with Margrit Kuehn, who is far more proficient in the language than I am. The psychologist John J. Hartman shared his research about Anna Freud, and Jonathan Tobis, who was my classmate at Amherst, vividly recalled his impressions of her when he was studying at her clinic in London.

For nearly two decades until her death in early 2020, my editor at Simon & Schuster was the wondrous Alice Mayhew; I am forever in her debt. Writers are understandably nervous about switching editors at any time, and I am no exception. But as soon as I started working with Bob Bender on this book, I realized that I had no reason for worry. He is the proverbial old-school editor—gracious and insightful, and right on target with his suggestions. Since I like to think of myself as an old-school writer, I consider that the highest recommendation for an editor. His talented colleague Johanna Li was also a pleasure to work with. I want to thank several other members of Simon & Schuster's remarkable team: Alison Forner, Rebecca Rozenberg, Julia Prosser, Stephen Bedford, Phil Metcalf, and Carly Loman, along with copy editor Kate Lapin.

Robert Gottlieb, my longtime agent, was, as always, a sounding board for ideas as soon as I began considering a new project, and his immediate enthusiasm for this one gave me the confidence to jump right in. His Trident Media Group colleagues Erica Silverman, Nora Rawn, and Marianna Sharp were equally supportive.

Of the friends who offered help, I'd like to single out David Satter, who as in the past served as one of the early readers of my chapters. I'd also like to thank Greg Dent, Michael Traison, and Frank Denton for their suggestions. There are many others whom I want to acknowledge for their friendship: Ardith and Steve Hodes, Eva and Bart Kaminski, Francine Shane and Robert Morea, Ania Bogusz and Ryszard Horowitz, Alexandra and Anthony Juliano, Sandra and Bob Goldman, Jerzy Kozminski, Grzegorz Jedrys, Grazyna and Bogdan Prokopczyk, Halina and Wojtek Wyczalkowski, Barbara and Antoni Moskwa, Monika and Frank Ward, Michael Keh, Cece and David Drysdale, Martha Poitevent, Peter Brown, Bill Faehnle, Michael Salley, Sarah Stern, Arlene Getz, Fred Guterl, Jeff Bartholet, and Carl Spadaro.

When it comes to my family, the list can get almost as long. It includes my sister Maria and her husband, Roberto, my other sister Terry, my cousins Barbara Wierzbianski and Christine Nagorski, Tom Nagorski and Anne Heller along with their children, Natalie and Billy, Adam Wierzbianski and Gail Mallen. My relatives-in-law include Eva Kowalski, Sylwia and Marek Socha and their daughter, Kinga. As with my friends, this is far from a complete list.

My wife, Christina, or Krysia as everyone calls her, and I have four children—Eva, Sonia, Adam, and Alex—who have all served as readers and critics, offering unstinting encouragement. Our lives are also enriched by our eight grandchildren: Stella, Caye, Sydney, Charles, Maia, Kaia, Christina, and Isabel. The eighth, Isabel, was delivered by Adam's wife, Agustina, just as I was completing my eighth book—a wonderful coincidence. We couldn't be happier to have Agustina as a daughter-in-law, along with Eran and Shaun as our sons-in-law.

The person at the center of this family—and the anchor of my life—is Krysia. I met her when I was an exchange student in Krakow, and I can't imagine the subsequent decades without her. I also can't imagine writing this book, or any of my previous ones, without her as my first editor. She offers constant advice, support, and insights on just about everything. Once I delved into Freud's universe, she even tolerated my attempts to analyze her dreams. But she was quick to remind me that I am not the slightest threat to the master.

NOTES

Epigraph

viii *"It is an iron"*: Stefan Zweig, *The World of Yesterday*, 383.

Chapter 1: "To Die in Freedom"

1 *"The oldest eastern"* and *Hitler in Vienna*: Gordon Brook-Shepherd, *The Austrians: A Thousand-Year Odyssey*, 328.

1 *The new arrivals*: Peter Gay, *Freud: A Life for Our Time*, 619–22. (Subsequent endnotes that read "Gay" are referring to his biography, not *The Freud Reader* that he edited.)

1 *"The city was"*: Eric Kandel, as quoted in his Nobel Prize speech in 2000: https://www.nobelprize.org/prizes/medicine/2000/kandel/biographical/.

2 "Finis Austriae": Michael Molnar, ed., *The Diary of Sigmund Freud 1929–1939*, 229.

2 *"Won't the gentlemen"* and *rest of events at the apartment, including appearance of Freud*: Ernest Jones, *The Life and Work of Sigmund Freud*, Volume 3, 218–19. (Subsequent endnotes citing this biography will read "Jones" followed by the volume number.)

2 *"Herr Professor"* and *"In spite of this"*: Martin Freud, *Sigmund Freud: Man and Father*, 210–11. (Subsequent endnotes citing this biography will read Martin Freud.)

3 *"shabbily dressed"* and *"Why not"*: Ibid., 207–8.

3   *"Wouldn't it be"*: Gay, 622.

4   *"aggressive cruelty"*: Sigmund Freud, *Civilization and Its Discontents*, 40–42.

5   *"Now, ah, we"*: John Gunther, *The Lost City*, 327–28.

6   *The main members*: Sources on each of them, along with full "to die in freedom" quote, are provided in subsequent chapters.

9   *"so seductive"*: Gunther, *The Lost City*, 68.

9   *It wasn't until* and *rest of Waldheim affair*: Andrew Nagorski, *The Nazi Hunters*, 266–88.

Chapter 2: "Laboratory of the Apocalypse"

12   *"Insofar as"*: Peter Kurth, *American Cassandra: The Life of Dorothy Thompson*, 60.

13   *"Vienna is"*: Arthur Schnitzler, *My Youth in Vienna*, ix (foreword by Frederic Morton).

13   *"his portrait of"*: Peter Gay, ed., *The Freud Reader*, introduction, xvii. (Subsequent endnotes citing this book will read *Freud Reader*.)

13   *"Psychoanalysis simplifies"*: Molnar, xxv.

13   *Coining novel concepts*: Sigmund Freud, *An Outline of Psycho-Analysis*, 13–16.

13   *He was born"* and *other early biographical details, including quotes*: Peter Gay, *Freud: A Life for Our Time*, 3–54; Jones, Volume 1, 1–26.

14   *"always hopefully"*: Jones, Volume 1, 2.

14   *"Then came"*: Gay, 8.

14   *"I never felt," "Deep within me,"* and *comments to Fluss*: Ibid., 9

15   *Under Emperor Franz Josef*: Ibid., 16–17; Jerry Victor Diller, *Freud's Jewish Identity: A Case Study in the Impact of Ethnicity*, 35–36.

15   *Although anti-Semitism* and *Jews as percentage of Vienna's population*: https://www.bh.org.il/jewish-spotlight/austria/modern-era/demography/.

15   *"I was at," "to study," "appreciable disappointments,"* and *rest of comments about Jewish background: Freud Reader*, 3–4.

15   *"every diligent"*: Jones, Volume 1, 6.

16   *"He grew up"*: David Cohen, *The Escape of Sigmund Freud*, 34.

16   *"to think morally"*: Anna Freud-Bernays, *Mother's Memoirs*, 3. (Unpublished translation by Hella Freud Bernays, courtesy of Randolph Bernays Randolph.)

16   *Nonetheless, Jacob*: Diller, 65.

16 *"intolerable," the rest of Freud's letter to Emil Fluss, and "A professional Jew-baiter":* Gay, 19.

17 *"In those days":* Schnitzler, 63.

17 *When he was twelve:* Jones, Volume 1, 22.

17 *"A man who":* Ibid., 5.

18 *In the summer of 1875 and trip to England:* Gay, 30–31; Jones, Volume 1, 24; Diller, 80–81.

18 *A year later and rest of Trieste stay:* Gay, 31–32; https://www.historytoday.com/archive/natural-histories/sexual-eeling.

19 *Back in Vienna and "corrected my father's":* Freud Reader, 4–5.

19 *Sigmund and Martha's and courtship:* Gay, 37–54; Jones, Volume 1, 98–138.

20 *"foolish superstitions," "If you can't," and Martha's handling of the Sabbath:* Diller, 85–86.

21 *Sigmund penned and quotes from letters to Martha, unless indicated otherwise:* Ernst L. Freud, ed., *Letters of Sigmund Freud*, 1–3, 13, 22–23, 56–57, 76, 96, 110, 184–206.

24 *The more fundamental, early coca claims, and fate of Ernst von Fleischl-Marxov:* Howard Markel, *An Anatomy of Addiction: Sigmund Freud, William Halsted, and the Miracle Drug Cocaine*, 46–50, 66–84.

27 *In 1891 and in 1896:* Gay, 74; Jones, Volume 1, 152–53.

28 *"My mother":* Martin Freud, 32.

28 *An early presentation:* Freud Reader, 8–9.

28 *"So I abandoned":* Ibid., 17.

29 *It wasn't until and Oedipus complex:* Gay, 103, 112–14.

29 *In retrospect and sales of* The Interpretation of Dreams: Sigmund Freud, *An Outline of Psycho-Analysis*, xi–xii (biographical introduction by Peter Gay).

29 *"scarcely reviewed" and "I had no":* Freud Reader, 30.

29 *in 1907:* https://blogs.scientificamerican.com/mind-guest-blog/step-aside-freud-josef-breuer-is-the-true-father-of-modern-psychotherapy/.

29 *For much of and Freud-Fliess relationship, including quotes from correspondence:* Gay, 55–61, 102.

31 *"It was not possible" and "a certain separation":* Schnitzler, 6–7, 63.

31 *"a showpiece":* Amos Elon, *Herzl*, 38–39.

31 *"He's a dirty" and rest of incident in train:* Ernst L. Freud, 78.

32 *On a summer:* Martin Freud, 70–71.

33 *"a passing fashion":* Elon, 71.

33 *Among the Jews* and *Herzl biography, quotes, and fraternity experiences:* Elon, 44–63.

33 *"with his blue"* and *"Every son":* Schnitzler, 128–29.

35 *The two never:* Avner Falk, Freud, and Herzl, *Contemporary Psychoanalysis*, Vol. 14, No. 3 (1978).

35 *"Psychoanalysis is":* Diller, 13.

35 *In the 1890s* and *Karl Lueger:* Zweig, 83–84; Brook-Shepherd, 101–3.

35 *"These Jews"* and *"himself an extra":* Elon, 163.

36 *"became the"* and *"incapable of":* George Clare, *Last Waltz in Vienna*, 26, 72.

36 *"his administration":* Zweig, 84.

36 *"I decide":* Paul Hoffmann, *The Viennese: Splendor, Twilight and Exile*, 143.

37 *"an ordinary kind":* Martin Freud, 16.

37 *on September 29, 1942:* https://www.holocaust.cz/en/database-of-victims /victim/50260-adolfine-freud/. (Some other accounts list the year of her death as 1943, but the death certificate clearly lists the date as September 29, 1942. Martin Freud reported that the cause was starvation.)

Chapter 3: "A Celt from Wales!"

39 *In 1897* and *"elevates the physician"* and *Wednesday gatherings:* Gay, 136–37.

39 *That was the same year:* Ibid.

39 *"I have obviously":* Martin Freud, 73.

40 *In* Mein Kampf and *Hitler quotes about Vienna:* Adolf Hitler, *Mein Kampf*, 3, 8, 15, 20–24, 53, 38, 64, 109, 123–25.

40 *"to become":* Ian Kershaw, *Hitler: 1889–1936, Hubris*, 26.

40 *He also went* and *other details of Hitler's visits to Vienna:* Brigitte Hamann, *Hitler's Vienna: A Portrait of the Tyrant as a Young Man*, 26–33.

41 *"Vienna was"* and *subsequent Kubizek comments:* August Kubizek, *The Young Hitler I Knew*, 126, 157, 218–21.

41 *For the first* and *entrance exam:* Kershaw, *Hitler: 1889–1936, Hubris*, 23–24; Hamann, 32–33.

42 *But other than:* Kershaw, *Hitler: 1889–1936, Hubris*, 54.

43 *"a pest, degenerate":* Hamann, 84.

44 *Getting up, Freud's routine,* and *Martin Freud's observations about his parents and family life, including quote from father's letter to Fliess about Vienna:* Gay, 157–58, 173–75; Martin Freud, 25, 45–48, 58, 132.

45 *"Our family is"* and *other Anna Freud quotes:* Anna Freud-Bernays, 4, 6, 119.

46 *"As soon as"*: "Analysts Abroad: Sigmund Freud's Travel Letters," Richard H. Armstrong review of *Sigmund Freud: Unser Herz zeigt nach dem Süden, Reisebriefe 1895–1923.* https://www.euppublishing.com/doi/pdf plus/10.3366/pah.2005.7.1.147.

46 *Freud also disliked:* https://freudsbutcher.com/psychology/7-little-known -facts-about-sigmund-freud-including-the-prescription-of-his-glasses/.

47 *"fisher of men"*: Gay, 179.

47 *"Some of the most"* and *key personalities, including Bleuler, Jung, Eitingon, Abraham, and Ferenczi,* and *"sexual trauma" and other quotes:* Jones, Volume 2, 30–53; Gay, 178–83, 197–206; https://www.ncbi.nlm.nih.gov/pmc /articles/PMC3339235/.

48 *"Even a superficial"* and *other letters:* William McGuire, ed., *The Freud/ Jung Letters: The Correspondence Between Sigmund Freud and C.G. Jung,* xvi–xvii, 8–9, 13, 16–18.

48 *When he showed up* and *Martin Freud on Jung:* Frank McLynn, *Carl Gustav Jung,* 97; Martin Freud, 108–9.

51 *"Now for"*: McGuire, 39.

52 *Born in 1879* and *Jones's early biography:* Ernest Jones, *Free Associations: Memoirs of a Psychoanalyst;* Brenda Maddox, *Freud's Wizard: Ernest Jones and the Transformation of Psychoanalysis.*

53 *"Nor was the opposite sex"*: Jones, *Free Associations,* 78.

53 *"irresistible to"*: Maddox, 30.

53 *Jones bounced:* Maddox, 31–36; Jones, *Free Associations,* 111–25.

55 *The press played* and *rest of controversy about Jones's conduct in 1906:* Maddox, 41–46; Jones, *Free Associations,* 145–47.

56 *David Eder* and *Dorothea Kann, or "Loe"*: Jones, *Free Associations,* 137–40; Maddox, 47.

56 *Another reason:* Maddox, 54.

56 *In a letter* and *Freud's responses about Jones:* McGuire, 48–49, 70, 81.

57 *At the West End* and *rest of incident there:* Jones, *Free Associations,* 150–52; Maddox, 58–60.

58 *A bemused Jones* and *Jones's interactions with Freud, travels:* Jones, *Free Associations,* 166–75.

58 *"the rat man"*: Gay, 263.

58 *"degenerate and Bohemian"* and *"They were decidedly"*: Jones, *Free Associations,* 167.

59 *"Well, here"* and *other quotes from letters between Jones and Freud:* R. Andrew Paskauskas, ed., *The Complete Correspondence of Sigmund Freud and Ernest Jones, 1908–1939,* 4, 13–28.

60 *His initial admiration* and *rest of Jones in Canada, including about Freud visit to the United States,* and *"Yes, America":* Jones, *Free Associations,* 176–200.

60 *The young Welshman:* Maddox, 71–73.

61 *"Conference Brings"* and *other details of U.S. trip:* Gay, 206–13; Maddox 76–79.

62 *"seemed like"* and *James incident: Freud Reader,* 32–33.

63 *in a letter:* McGuire, 100–101.

63 *"I am very":* Gay, 212–13.

64 *At a meeting:* Maddox, 83.

64 *"express again":* Paskauskas, 58.

64 *In early 1911* and *rest of charges against Jones:* Maddox, 90–91.

64 *In his early days:* Gay, 50.

64 *"To be slandered":* McGuire, 101.

65 *Earlier, Clarke:* Maddox, 81.

65 *The morphine* and *rest of letter to Freud and his reply:* Paskauskas, 110–12.

65 *While undergoing:* Maddox, 105.

66 *He also* and *"Be strict":* Ibid., 109.

Chapter 4: "A Long Polar Night"

63 *"was in a position"* and *"last happy years":* Jones, Volume 2, 66.

67 *At the Weimar* and *Lou Andreas-Salomé:* Gay, 192–93; https://www.bri tannica.com/biography/Lou-Andreas-Salome; Ernst Pfeiffer, ed., *Sigmund Freud and Lou Andreas-Salomé Letters,* introduction, 1.

68 *"Freud greatly admired":* Jones, Volume 2, 176–77.

68 *"The First World War":* Martin Freud, 156.

68 *"Most of you":* Maddox, 83.

69 *"I am more":* Gay, 201.

69 *"All are full":* Paskauskas, 52.

69 *"You know how":* McGuire, 153.

69 *"With Adler"* and *"I have got":* Gay, 221–25.

69 *"Recently, he"* and *other Jung-Freud letters:* McGuire, 173, 160, 101–2, 139.

70 *Moses Allen Starr:* Gay, 196.

70   *"I consider"* and *"Sexual morality"*: Ernst L. Freud, 308.

72   *The mother of* and *"What will happen"*: Deirdre Bair, *Jung: A Biography*, 158, 181, 184.

72   *Freud had never* and *"My dear boy"*: Ibid., 164.

72   *"It is a"*: Gay, 238.

73   *"only true joy"* and *"brazen candor"*: Bair, 203–4.

73   *"solver of"*: Ibid., 201.

73   *"partiality for"*: Freud Reader, 481.

73   *In 1902:* https://medium.com/mysticaltalk/carl-jung-and-mysticism-c45e 01fe50ed.

74   *"Occultism is"* and *other quotes from Jung-Freud correspondence, including "with the aid"*: McGuire, 183–84, 253–54.

74   *"Jung had"* and *"confused mind"*: Jones, *Free Associations*, 215, 165.

75   *"regressive" tendencies:* Ernst L. Freud, 299.

75   *"seems all"* and *Freud's remarks about Jung to Abraham* and *"lies, brutality"*: Gay, 235, 240–42.

75   *To this day:* https://www.nytimes.com/2004/02/08/books/l-jung-s-anti -semitism-177490.html.

75   *"No, no!"*: Bair, 119.

75   *"had a certain"*: McLynn, 352–53.

76   *"I despise"*: Bair, 418.

76   *"They would almost"*: Jones, *Free Associations*, 210.

77   *"We Freud"* and *"her feelings"*: Martin Freud, 29, 65.

77   *"Every evening"*: Anna Freud-Bernays, 9.

77   *On July 23:* https://wwi.lib.byu.edu/index.php/The_Austro-Hungarian_Ul timatum_to_Serbia_(English_translation).

77   *"Perhaps for"* and *other Freud comments about the war from July to September 1914:* Gay, 346–50.

78   *"Frankly, so far"* and *Martin Freud's war service, correspondence, and reflections:* Martin Freud, 180–86.

79   *So did:* Ibid., 39.

79   *The dream* and *seven medals and "somewhat plump"*: Helen Fry, *Freud's War*, 50–57; Martin Freud, *Any Survivors? A Lost Novel of World War II*, from preface by Helen Fry, 7.

80   *Freud's other:* Fry, 34–35.

80   *The International Psychoanalytical:* https://www.ipa.world/IPA/en/IPA1 /ipa_history/history_of_the_ipa.aspx; Gay, 350.

80 *Although direct mail* and *other Jones-Freud dealings in this period:* Jones, Volume 2, 168–206.

80 *"We are prejudiced"* and *other Jones-Freud correspondence during the war:* Paskauskas, 297–326.

81 *"All my libido":* Jones, Volume 2, 171.

81 *To Abraham:* Gay, 353.

81 *On November 25, 1914* and *"a female of"* and *"It is a long":* Gay, 192, 353–54.

82 *In his 1915 essays:* https://www.sas.upenn.edu/~cavitch/pdf-library/Freud _War_and_Death.pdf.

83 *The Wednesday evening:* Jones, Volume 2, 151.

83 *Between 1915 and 1917* and *"I am working"* and *Nobel Prize:* Gay, 362–71.

83 *"He would glance"* and *"I either":* Jones, *Free Associations,* 248.

84 *Jones was* and *attempts to enlist* and *other early war period, including D. H. Lawrence:* Ibid., 244–52; Maddox, 117–23.

84 *"The War Office"* and *"If there is"* and *"I can only":* Paskauskas, 315, 308, 312.

85 *"flowering time":* Jones, Volume 2, 179.

85 *"Fate would":* Maddox, 119.

85 *Like Freud* and *Mahler:* Jones, Volume 2, 79–80.

86 *The one who* and *Jones and Lawrence:* Jones, *Free Associations,* 251–52.

86 *He could have:* Maddox, 122–23.

86 *"She is"* and *rest of Jones-Freud correspondence about Owen, Owen's talents, "reformed character":* Paskauskas, 322, 324; Maddox, 130–37.

86 *"Singularly mature":* Jones, *Free Associations,* 254.

87 *"You see"* and *"Tomorrow"* and *"I concede":* Paskauskas, 326–29.

87 *He was busy:* Maddox, 150–51.

87 *To help him* and *Katharina Jokl:* Ibid., 151–55.

88 *in 1920:* https://psychoanalysis.org.uk/our-authors-and-theorists/ernest -jones; Gay, 393.

88 *"Both in":* Freud Reader,* 34.

88 *"To me":* Maddox, 163.

89 *The losses:* https://encyclopedia.1914-1918-online.net/article/war_losses _austria-hungary.

89 *"Vienna appeared"* and *other Kaltenborn observations:* H.V. Kaltenborn, *Fifty Fabulous Years, 1900–1950: A Personal Review,* 95–97.

89 *"Strauss waltzes":* Kurth, 61.

90 *Martin recalled* and *other Martin Freud quotes:* Martin Freud, 188–89.

90 *Tapping his* and *foreign bank accounts:* Maddox, 158.

90   *"the reconstruction":* Martin Freud, 188.
91   *"I never":* Jones, *Free Associations,* 257.

Chapter 5: "Vestal"

94   *By the summer* and *Anna Freud's trip to England:* Uwe Henrik Peters, *Anna Freud: A Life Dedicated to Children,* 21–27; Elisabeth Young-Bruehl, *Anna Freud: A Biography,* 64–70; Jones, Volume 2, 169–73.
94   *"beauties"* and *"I know from":* Young-Bruehl, 66–67.
95   *"for your kindness"* and *"She has"* and *"certainly get her":* Paskuaskas, 294–95, 297.
96   *"He seems":* Young-Bruehl, 68.
96   *"She is very"* and *ten-day journey:* Martin Freud, 180.
96   *"I have not":* Gay, 352.
97   *"She arrived"* and *He called her* and *For an assignment:* Peters, 3, 10–11.
97   *In another letter* and *occasions where Anna was left behind,* *"We like to"* and *"I want my"* and *"love and hate"* and *"the one who":* Young-Bruehl, 29, 36–37, 39, 42–43, 55–58.
99   *"charming fellow":* https://www.encyclopedia.com/psychology/dictionaries-thesauruses-pictures-and-press-releases/halberstadt-freud-sophie-1893-1920.
99   *"The death":* Ernst L. Freud, 328.
99   *"wittiest"* and *"I am taking":* Gay, 421.
100   *Ernst was a successful:* https://www.encyclopedia.com/psychology/dictionaries-thesauruses-pictures-and-press-releases/freud-ernst-1892-1970.
100   *Anna decided* and *languages and reading,* *"You see":* Young-Bruehl, 49–54.
100   *After her return* and *"One day":* Peters, 22–23.
101   *"In those days":* Robert Coles, *Anna Freud: The Dream of Psychoanalysis,* 4–5.
101   *"highly instructive"* and *hospital rounds:* Peters, 30.
101   *"Such an arrangement"* and *"We were trained":* Coles, 6–7.
102   *"Only when":* Young-Bruehl, 81.
102   *In 1922:* Gay, 436–37; Young-Bruehl, 59–60.
102   *"Back then":* Coles, 9.
102   *"blooming and"* and *"If she really":* Young-Bruehl, 110–11, 117.
103   *"very slight operation"* and *description of Freud's ordeal at the clinic:* Jones, Volume 3, 90–91.

104 *"You realize"*: Ernst L. Freud, 343.

104 *"hoping to"* and *"I realize"*: Young-Bruehl, 120.

104 *As a result* and *In interviews* and *Fichtl observations*: Detlef Berthelsen, *Alltag bei Familie Freud: Die Errinerungen der Paula Fichtl*, 27–28, 34–41, 55–56.

105 *"the Monster"*: Michael John Burlingham, *The Last Tiffany: A Biography of Dorothy Tiffany Burlingham*, 179.

106 *Long after* and *"the idea of"*: McLynn, 99–100.

106 *"Freud was"*: Max Eastman, *Great Companions*, 188–89.

107 *In December 1925* and *"At first"*: Young-Bruehl, 124.

108 *When some of* and *At the Ninth* and *"The news"* and *In 1927*: Peters, 66–71.

108 *"The audience"*: Ernst L. Freud, 397–98.

108 *"Her importance"*: Paskauskas, 677.

108 *Klein argued:* Ibid., 91–93.

109 *"I feel like"* and *She admitted:* Young-Bruehl, 129–30, 127.

109 *Hans Lampl:* https://www.encyclopedia.com/psychology/dictionaries-thesauruses-pictures-and-press-releases/lampl-hans-1889-1958.

109 *"but I am not"* and *"vestal"*: Young-Bruehl, 121, 137.

110 *"splendid and"*: Burlingham, 210.

110 *"legitimate crown princess"* and *"house arrest"*: Berthelsen, 31, 50.

110 *"One cannot"*: Young-Bruehl, 197.

110 *In 1925* and *"precious relationship"* and *other background, including expectations for her stay in Europe:* Ibid., 132–39; Gay, 540; Burlingham, 151–52.

111 *After a brief* and *"Dorothy and"* and *"naughty American"*: Burlingham, 156–59; Peters, 119–20; Cohen, 72.

112 *"hysterical or"*: Ibid., 203.

112 *In 1927* and *"the most"* and *"a charming"*: Gay, 540.

112 *Dorothy also endeared:* Berthelsen, 39; Jones, Volume 3, 141.

112 *"thoughts which"* and *rest of letter to Eitingon:* Young-Bruehl, 133.

112 *"I don't think"*: Coles, 10–11.

113 *"Our symbiosis"*: Young-Bruehl, 136.

113 *"American friend"* and *Burlingham's move to Berggasse 19:* Burlingham, 177, 205–6.

113 *"black moods," Dorothy's thoughts of returning to Robert, In 1930, farm cottage, As Anna observed,* and *In 1932:* Ibid., 207–9, 216, 223; Peters, 120.

114 *"represents an"*: Young-Bruehl, 138–39.

114 *Starting in* and *"superior interest"* and *background of school; recruitment*

of Blos and Erikson: Burlingham, 183–88; Lawrence J. Friedman, *Identity's Architect: A Biography of Erik H. Erikson,* 59–67

115 *"Anna Freud impressed"* and *"The impression":* Peter Heller, *A Child Analysis with Anna Freud,* 288, 300.

115 *"spinsterish holiness"* and *At one meeting* and *"There Freud":* Burlingham, 210.

116 *"All they"* and *"a tinge"* and *At times:* Friedman, 65–67, 79.

116 *"If the day":* Young-Bruehl, 193.

116 *"great hope"* and *"she was not"* and *"Hitler, too":* Coles, 13–15.

116 *"who took me":* Friedman, 60.

Chapter 6: "A Man of the World"

119 *"Can you even":* Will Brownell and Richard N. Billings, *So Close to Greatness: A Biography of William C. Bullitt,* 113–14.

119 *According to Biddle:* Ibid., 120.

120 *Bullitt was one:* Jones, Volume 2, 86–87.

121 *"was charming":* George F. Kennan, *Memoirs: 1925–1950,* 79.

121 *"as a member"* and *"he bore":* Orville H. Bullitt, ed., *For the President Personal and Secret: Correspondence Between Franklin D. Roosevelt and William C. Bullitt,* introduction by George F. Kennan, xv.

121 *On his father's* and *other family background:* Brownell and Billings, 8–18; Alexander Etkind, *Roads Not Taken: An Intellectual Biography of William C. Bullitt,* 3–4.

122 *"I'm going to be"* and *"Bill Bullitt has"* and *"damned liar":* Brownell and Billings, 19–21.

122 *At Yale and health crisis* and *Roswell Angier:* Ibid., 29–33; Etkin, 4; "Prof. R.B. Angier at Yale for 35 Years," *New York Times,* June 26, 1946.

123 *Bullitt tried* and *Harvard Law:* Brownell and Billings, 34–36.

124 *Bullitt helped* and *rest of Bullitt's trip with his mother, including "I was naïve":* Ibid., 36–41; Etkin, 4–5.

124 *Upon Bullitt's return* and *In late 1915* and *dispatches from Ford's peace mission:* Brownell and Billings, 41–49.

125 *In March 1916* and *"Whichever way"* and *European working honeymoon:* Ibid., 49–61; Etkind, 6–9.

126 *"laden with"* and *other quotes from Ernesta's diary:* Ernesta Drinker Bullitt, *An Uncensored Diary from the Central Empires,* 3, 7–8, 26, 152, 160. (Bul-

litt's wavy brown hair is mentioned by Orville Bullitt in the biographical foreword in *For the President.*)

127 the *"sharpest"* and *"wrecked her"*: Brownell and Billings, 63, 65.

127 *"I have a lot," "if they can," "You've made," "The unhappy,"* and *Colonel House:* Ibid., 64–67; Etkind, 11.

129 *Wilson made* and *Fourteen Points:* https://www.britannica.com/event/Fourteen-Points.

129 *"The Russian 'Terror,' " "I wish,"* and *Bullitt proposed:* Brownell and Billings, 67–69.

130 *Since the fall* and *Never bashful* and *rest of Bullitt's account of Wilson on the ship:* Patricia O'Toole, *The Moralist: Woodrow Wilson and the World He Made,* 305, 334–37; Brownell and Billings, 74–77.

131 *On February 18, 1919* and *Bullitt mission to Russia, return to Paris,* and *resignation:* Orville Bullitt, 3–14; William C. Bullitt, *The Bullitt Mission to Russia,* 14–15; Brownell and Billings, 82–95.

132 *In a letter:* William C. Bullitt, *The Bullitt Mission to Moscow,* 36–37.

133 *"many parts of":* Brownell and Billings, 98.

133 *Returning from Paris* and *Bryant pitched:* Ibid., 105–6.

133 *"Only peasants"* and *"I hate frigid"* and *"You'll never":* William C. Bullitt, *It's Not Done,* 201, 208–9, 98.

134 *Twice married* and *"The only way":* Mary V. Dearborn, *Queen of Bohemia: The Life of Louise Bryant,* 52–53, 202.

134 *By then* and *Mussolini exclusive* and *"followed her":* Ibid., 208–9.

134 *When she started working* and *"the ecstasy":* Brownell and Billings, 110–13; Virginia Gardner, *"Friend and Lover": The Life of Louise Bryant,* 236–37.

135 *Bryant had led:* Dearborn, 207.

135 *Bullitt played* and *"big Jew":* Etkind, 71; Dearborn, 234–35.

135 *Initially, Bullitt's sales:* Etkind, 56.

135 *"Lord, what a night":* William C. Bullitt, *It's Not Done,* 56.

136 *"I live":* Gardner, 246.

136 *In 1925* and *suicidal thoughts:* Etkind, 78.

136 *"Anyone who":* Gardner, 256.

136 *Writing to* and *"I didn't suppose":* Ralph G. Martin, *Cissy: The Extraordinary Life of Eleanor Medill Patterson,* 217.

136 *By 1928* and *In the proceedings* and *Dercum's disease:* Dearborn, 260–70; Gardner, 267, https://rarediseases.org/rare-diseases/dercums-disease/.

136 *According to* and *"An embarrassing":* Gardner, 255.

137   *There were* and *"really ill"*: Dearborn, 213.

137   *On May 4, 1930*: Jones, Volume 3, 150.

137   *"Somberly he said"* and *rest of Bullitt's account*: Sigmund Freud and William C. Bullitt, *Thomas Woodrow Wilson: A Psychological Study*, foreword by William C. Bullitt, vii–x.

138   *Nearly a decade* and *"psychoanalysis should"*: Gay, 554–55.

138   *"In the language"*: John Maynard Keynes, *The Economic Consequences of the Peace*, 25.

138   *By 1932* and *But at that point*: Etkind, 81–83.

139   *Wilson is portrayed* and *quotations from it*: Freud and Bullitt, xi, 137, 147, 205–6, 211, 219.

140   *Max Eastman* and *his visit to Freud*: Max Eastman, *Heroes I Have Known*, 261–73.

Chapter 7: "No Prudishness Whatsoever"

141   *Marie Bonaparte biographical details (unless otherwise indicated)*: Celia Bertin, *Marie Bonaparte: A Life*.

141   *"Marie Bonaparte embarked"*: Rudolph Maurice Loewenstein, ed., *Drives, Affects, Behavior*, preface by Ernest Jones.

142   *"The impression"* and *"Look"*: Bertin, 153–54.

142   *"My wife"*: Ernst L. Freud, 368–69.

143   *From 1929* and *diary mentions of Bonaparte*: Molnar, 48.

143   *To outsiders* and *family history, childhood, adolescence, and suitors (including quotations)*: Bertin, 3–77.

148   *In the summer* and *marriage* and *early affairs*: Ibid., 82–111.

150   *Marie noted* and *"great passions," frigidity, Halban's operation*: Ibid., 111–41.

151   *Long before* and *Laforgue and Freud, Laforgue background*: Ibid., 145–59; https://www.encyclopedia.com/psychology/dictionaries-thesauruses-pictures-and-press-releases/laforgue-rene-1894-1962.

152   *As Freud's biographer* and *Freud's recurring dream* and *"energy devil"*: Gay, 541–43.

154   *"All my life"*: Bertin, 176.

155   *"Under father's"*: Martin Freud, 202–3.

155   *Martin grew*: Fry, 35.

155   *"Mme Freud"*: Bertin, 174–75.

155 *Marie's consultations* and *Loewenstein, Lindbergh, Paris Psychoanalytic Society, In 1929, incest:* Ibid., 166–84.

158 *Their most serious* and *handling of Fliess correspondence:* Ibid., 196–97; Gay, 613–14.

Chapter 8: "Violent Pain"

161 *Max Schur was* and *rest of Schur's first interactions with Freud:* Max Schur, *Freud: Living and Dying,* 1–2, 305–7.

162 *Three years later* and *Marie Bonaparte's role* and *Schur was more* and *"There was nothing"* and *"Promise me"* and *"In the shortest":* Ibid., 2, 407–8.

163 *Trying to justify:* Ibid., 352–53.

164 *As Deutsch's wife* and *"most deadly secret":* https://www.theatlantic.com /health/archive/2014/09/how-sigmund-freud-wanted-to-die/380322/.

164 *When Jones later:* Jones, Volume 3, 93.

164 *"Promise me":* Ibid., 2, 407–8.

164 *"In the shortest":* Ibid.

164 *"Schur was":* Ibid., 145.

165 *"I feel that"* and *dispute over bill* and *Schur's first task:* Schur, 409–10.

165 *Famously, one* and *"a piece of":* Gay, 233.

166 *In the 1890s* and *"cardiac misery," letters to Fliess,* and *Schur conclusion:* Schur, 40–51.

166 *"The radiation":* Ibid., 357.

166 *When Schur consulted* and *visits to Pichler in 1926:* Ibid., 5, 389.

167 *Although he ascribed* and *"Freud's condition"* and *"a model patient":* Ibid., 410, 413.

167 *"Mindful of":* Ernst L. Freud, 396–97.

168 *"I could recognize"* and *"Specially noticeable," Pichler notes* and *Freud letters to Eitingon on smoking:* Schur, 410–13, 424–27.

168 *"I began smoking"* and *"It was Freud's"* and *masturbation:* Ibid., 61–62.

169 *On one occasion:* Peter Schur presentation, "The Freud–Schur Connection," February 1994, Vienna Psychoanalytical Association (courtesy of Peter Schur).

170 *William Bullitt* and *"accomplished as":* Schur, 423.

171 *"I am not":* Jones, Volume 1, 309.

171 *"On xx 192x":* Box 48, Sigmund Freud Papers, Manuscript Division, Library of Congress, Washington, D.C., https://www.loc.gov/resource/mss 39990.04818/?sp=4.

171 *"Well, I really"* and *"Your old Freud"*: Schur, 207, 301.

172 *"Freud cannot"*: Ibid., 233.

172 *"Some years ago"*: McGuire, 104–6.

172 *"The superstition"*: Schur, 313.

172 *"By the way"*: Ibid., 105.

173 *"I cannot face"* and *Although the operations* and *Both his father* and *Writing to Ferenczi*: Ibid., 259, 343, 356, 377.

173 *"You will not"* and *"Why?"*: Pfeiffer, 192–93.

174 *"I am still"*: Schur, 429.

174 *Death was "natural"*: https://www.sas.upenn.edu/~cavitch/pdf-library /Freud_War_and_Death.pdf.

175 *"I was expected"* and *"Thou owest"*: Sigmund Freud, *The Interpretation of Dreams*, 226.

175 *In his 1927 publication: Freud Reader*, 693.

176 *"If you want"* and *"I could not"*: Schur, 299, 302–3.

176 *"You are going"* and *Peter Schur story*: "Three Coins from Freud" by Peter Schur, *Harvard Medicine*, Autumn 2013 (https://hms.harvard.edu/maga zine/handed-down/three-coins-freud); Jones, Volume 3, 179.

Chapter 9: "Political Blindness"

179 *In Germany*: https://www.historylearningsite.co.uk/modern-world-history -1918-to-1980/weimar-germany/weimar-elections-1928-to-1932/.

179 *Germany's president* and *"We have hired"*: Andrew Nagorski, *Hitlerland: American Eyewitnesses to the Nazi Rise to Power*, 94.

180 *"My language"*: Gay, 448.

180 *"I would advise"*: Jones, Volume 3, 98.

181 *"You believe"* and *"Berggasse 19"*: Eastman, *Heroes I Have Known*, 264, 269–70.

182 *"The one to"* and *her sessions*: H.D., *Tribute to Freud*, 3–4.

182 *Joseph Wortis* and *his recollections of Berggasse 19* and *early meetings*: Joseph Wortis, *Fragments of an Analysis with Freud*, 15–28, 55–56, 76, 87, 104–8, 164–65.

182 *This was also* and *butcher shop*: https://www.psychologytoday.com/us /blog/freud-s-world/201809/did-freud-eat-kosher-without-knowing-it.

186 *"The uncertainty"*: *Freud Reader*, 197–98.

187 *"Psychoanalysis was"*: William L. Shirer, *Twentieth Century Journey: The Start, 1904–1930*, 436.

187 *Jones spotted* and *"Most unfortunately"*: Gay, 453.

187 *In 1922, Wells's first meeting with Freud in 1931:* Jones, Volume 3, 160.

188 *"If the trouble"* and *"To analyze"*: H. G. Wells, *The Secret Places of the Heart*, 18–25.

188 *At the end* and *Freud's comments about meeting Einstein:* Jones, Volume 3, 131.

188 *In fact, Einstein* and *"It's at times"*: Walter Isaacson, *Einstein: His Life and Universe*, 365–68, 417.

189 *"most insistent"* and *rest of Einstein-Freud exchange on war: Why War?* (1932, Einstein's letter to Freud and Freud's response).

189 *"As guardians"* and *The exchange* and *"the tedious"*: Jones, Volume 3, 171, 175.

192 *Sándor Ferenczi* and *Freud letter to him, Freud to Eitingon*: Ibid., 163–65, 171.

194 *Eitingon, the son* and *father's bankrupcy:* https://www.encyclopedia.com /psychology/dictionaries-thesauruses-pictures-and-press-releases/eitin gon-max-1881-1943.

194 *The facility's interior:* Volker M. Welter, *Ernst L. Freud, Architect: The Case of the Modern Bourgeois Home*, 56.

194 *Between 1920 and 1930:* Gay, 462–63.

195 *As a result* and *Freud advice to Eitingon:* Diller, 201.

195 *In April* and *"What saved"*: Jones, Volume 3, 167–69.

196 *"A nation"*: Ibid., 151.

196 *In 1932:* https://www.encyclopedia.com/psychology/dictionaries-thesau ruses-pictures-and-press-releases/freud-oliver-1891-1969.

196 *"Zionism has"*: Gay, 598.

196 *Afterward, Chaim Koffler* and *Freud response to him*: https://blog.nli.org .il/en/freud_on_zionism/. In his biography of Freud, Gay quotes the same letter (p. 598) claiming that it was written to Einstein. The copy held by the National Library of Israel leaves no doubt that it was addressed to Koffler.

197 *On January 27, 1933* and *"There is no"* and *emigrates to Palestine:* Jones, Volume 3, 182–83.

198 *"You must be"*: Paskauskas, 715.

198 *Non-Aryan doctors* and *Eitingon's resignation:* Geoffrey Cocks, *Psycho-therapy in the Third Reich: The Göring Institute*, 90.

198 *"We are having"* and *"Psychoanalysis is"* and *help for Abraham's widow:* Maddox, 215–16.

199   *On the evening* and *"The soul"*: William L. Shirer, *The Rise and Fall of the Third Reich: A History of Nazi Germany*, 241.

199   *"Against the soul-destroying"*: Schur, 446.

199   *"What progress"* and *"This must"* and *"life in Germany"*: Gay, 592–93.

200   *"In our circles"* and *rest of exchange with Bonaparte, exchange with Ferenczi*: Jones, Volume 3, 175–78.

201   *"With us"*: Pfeiffer, 200.

201   *"As a humane"* and *other Zweig comments*: Zweig, 389–90, 419, 450.

202   *The result was* and *suicide note:* https://www.newyorker.com/maga zine/2012/08/27/the-escape-artist-3; https://web.nli.org.il/sites/nli/en glish/collections/personalsites/archive_treasures/pages/stefan-zweig.aspx.

Chapter 10: "The Austrian Cell"

203   *"Despite all"* and *"We too"*: Paskauskas, 716, 725.

204   *"Our people"* and *"The world"*: Jones, Volume 3, 176, 181–82.

204   *Despite the loss:* https://encyclopedia.ushmm.org/content/en/map/ger man-territorial-losses-treaty-of-versailles-1919.

205   *"The situation"*: Gunther, *Inside Europe*, 313.

205   *The capital* and *1927 events*: Brook-Shepherd, 254–62.

205   *Most of the city's 175,000*: *The Vienna Jewish Sourcebook: A Centropa Reader*, Volume 2, 9.

206   *"The Austrians"*: Ibid., 254.

206   *Germany and Austria:* Gunther, *Inside Europe*, 314.

206   *Austria stumbled* and *unemployment rate*: Gay, 591.

206   *In* Mein Kampf: Hitler, 16.

206   *"By the end"*: Gunther, *Inside Europe*, 320.

207   *In May 1932* and *Dollfuss and Schuschnigg sagas, including 1934 battles* and *Dollfuss assassination:* Brook-Shepherd, 263–94; Gunther, *Inside Europe*, 316–54.

207   *"Dollfuss really"*: Clare, 148.

208   *A curious incident:* Gay, 448–49.

209   *As he wrote:* Pfeiffer, 205.

210   *"it is probably"*: Ernst L. Freud, 419–20.

211   *"The murder"*: Clare, 157.

211   *"the few remaining"* and *"a fairly amiable"* and *Boehm's meeting with Freud, "Quite enough!"* and *confiscation of books:* Jones, Volume 3, 186–88.

NOTES

211 *But on September 15:* https://encyclopedia.ushmm.org/content/en/article/the-nuremberg-race-laws.

211 *The following month* and *Jacobson* and *"Urgently advise":* Maddox, 224–25.

212 *"fairly amiable"* and *"Quite enough!":* Jones, Volume 3, 186–88.

212 *The last remaining:* Cocks, 90–91.

212 *Jacobson remained:* https://www.nytimes.com/1978/12/13/archives/dr-edith-jacobson-81-years-old-a-psychoanalyst-and-professor.html.

213 *"I gather"* and *letters to Arnold Zweig, Lou Andreas-Salomé,* and *Thomas Mann:* Ernst L. Freud, 423–26.

214 *On May 26, 1935:* Paskauskas, 743.

215 *"Freud was"* and *"No, the times"* and *"the rumors":* Jones, Volume 3, 198–202.

215 *A stream of* and *letter from 197 writers and artists:* Ibid., 205–6.

216 *"My most personal":* Ernst L. Freud, 426.

216 *Ever since* and *Freud on Michelangelo's Moses: Freud Reader,* 522–41.

216 *In a letter:* Ernst L. Freud, 421–23.

218 *"To deny"* and *Freud's theories:* Sigmund Freud, *Moses and Monotheism,* 11, 29–35.

219 *In a letter* and *boycott:* Schur, 459.

219 *"He forgot"* and *"It would seem":* Ibid., 444.

220 *He started looking* and *applying for U.S. visas:* Peter Schur presentation, "The Freud–Schur Connection"; author interview with Peter Schur.

220 *In the summer* and *John Wiley:* https://photos.state.gov/libraries/estonia/99874/History%20stories/Bearing-Witness.pdf.

221 *Long afterward:* Schur, 496.

219 *In a letter (Bullitt to Freud):* William C. Bullitt Papers (MS 112), Manuscripts and Archives, Sterling Memorial Library, Yale University.

222 *"Austria's approach":* Gay, 616–17.

222 *"Germany has":* Clare, 169.

222 *Schuschnigg also* and *terms of agreement:* Brook-Shepherd, 302; Gunther, *Inside Europe,* 353–54.

223 *"I love it":* Ernst L. Freud, 434.

223 *As Anna explained* and *Freud's history with dogs:* Marie Bonaparte, *Topsy: The Story of a Golden-Haired Chow,* introduction to the Transaction edition, 1–26.

224 *"sublimation":* Jones, Volume 3, 141.

224 *"Dogs are children"* and *other quotes from* Topsy: Bonaparte, 55, 75, 124, 164.

224 *In a letter:* Ernst L. Freud, 436–37.

225 *"By 1936":* Coles, 17.

226 *Writing to Jones:* Paskauskas, 756–57.

226 *"Our brave":* Ernst L. Freud, 441.

Chapter 11: "Operation Freud"

227 *On March 10, 1938:* Berthelsen, 69.

227 *"We did not"* and *rest of Hitler-Schuschnigg meeting* and *subsequent events, including Schuschnigg farewell speech:* Shirer, *The Rise and Fall of the Third Reich,* 325–41; https://www.historyplace.com/worldwar2/triumph/tr -austria.htm; Brook-Shepherd, 307–10.

230 *"Wiley from":* Molnar, 229.

230 *Given the Austrian* and *dismantling of barriers:* Brook-Shepherd, 323.

230 *"The worst"* and *"swept along"* and *Wiley:* William L. Shirer, *Berlin Diary: The Journal of a Foreign Correspondent, 1934–1941,* 95–98.

231 *"Quick, Paula"* and *rest of Martin Freud's account of March 12:* Martin Freud, 205–6.

231 *"province of":* Shirer, *The Rise and Fall of the Third Reich,* 347.

232 *Freud responded* and *"We are going"* and *"Knowing how":* Jones, Volume 3, 218–21; http://murals.wbtla.org/destruction-of-the-second-temple--the -survival-of-judaism.html.

232 *As Martin Freud:* Martin Freud, 48.

233 *He talked with* and *Jones's trip to Vienna, raid of apartment on March 15, talk with Freud,* and *return to London, including Bragg and Hoare:* Jones, Volume 3, 218–23.

233 *"The city behaved":* Clare, 230.

233 *Burlingham was* and *arrangements with Wiley:* Burlingham, 260; Cohen, 163.

234 *Martin Freud* and *his account of March 15:* Martin Freud, 207–13.

237 *"We'll be back":* Berthelsen, 71.

237 *"Dear me"* and *Martin's return to Berggasse 19:* Martin Freud, 210–11.

238 *Jones countered* and *Lightoller case:* https://www.history.co.uk/article/the -second-officer-who-survived-titanic-and-saved-130-lives-at-dunkirk.

238 *"I never left":* Gay, 624.

238 *"Fear Freud":* Sigmund Freud Papers, Manuscript Division, Library of Congress, https://www.loc.gov/resource/mss39990.04911/?sp=3.

238   *He called:* Etkind, 81.

238   *"In accordance":* Sigmund Freud Papers, Manuscript Division, Library of Congress, https://www.loc.gov/resource/mss39990.04911/?sp=5&r=-1.03, -0.03,3.06,1.445,0.

239   *"If Wiley":* Ibid., https://www.loc.gov/resource/mss39990.04911/?sp=4&r =-0.969,0,2.939,1.387,0.00.

239   *With Bullitt's encouragement* and *official car with American flag* and *"The Princess":* Cohen, 163.

240   *She stayed* and *"did the near"* and *"Success!":* Molnar, 231–32.

240   *Fichtl, the housekeeper:* Berthelsen, 79.

242   *"They feared"* and *Schur's account:* Schur, 498.

242   *"Her situation":* Martin Freud, 212.

242   *"Anna with Gestapo":* Molnar, 232.

242   *From her sickbed:* Burlingham, 260–61.

242   *The ever-vigilant:* Gay, 625.

243   *By at least:* Young-Bruehl, 227.

243   *Edith Laub:* https://www.wsj.com/articles/edie-locke-refugee-from-na zis-edited-mademoiselle-magazine-11601647202?mod=searchresults _pos1&page=1.

243   *"Within minutes":* Clare, 211.

244   *When Egon Friedell* and *500 suicides* and *"From March 12":* Gay, 621–22.

244   *At a Vienna polling* and *Shirer on plebiscite:* Shirer, *The Rise and Fall of the Third Reich,* 350.

244   *"The treatment of":* https://www.smithsonianmag.com/history/what -drove-sigmund-freud-write-scandalous-biography-woodrow-wilson -180970042/.

245   *Known as trustees* and *"improperly acquired":* Cohen, 13–14.

245   *On March 15* and *"Jewish pigs":* Ibid., 14, 164–65; Schur, 498–99.

246   *The son of* and *other Sauerwald biographical details:* Mitchell G. Ash, ed., *Materialen zur Geschichte der Psychoanalyze in Wien 1938–1945,* chapter by Christiane Rothländer, "Die Liquidation der Wiener Psychoanalytischen Vereinigung 1938 und der Raub des Vermögens der Familie Freud," 49–143; https://www.thejc.com/lifestyle/features/how-a-nazi-saved-sigmund -freud-1.13679; Schur, 498–99 (including Sauerwald's comment to Anna); Jones, Volume 3, 222–23; Cohen, 80–82.

246   *"I believe":* Ash, 82.

247   *But a recent study:* Ash, Rothländer chapter, "Die Liquidation der Wiener

Psychoanalytischen Vereinigung 1938 and der Raub des Vermögens der Familie Freud."

247 *The Municipal:* Wiener Stadt und Landesarchiv (Municipal and Provincial Archives of Vienna); letter to the author, June 29, 2021.

248 *During the initial* and *Martin's actions and comments:* Martin Freud, 214–17.

249 *In a letter:* Cohen, 181–82.

249 *"Anna is untiringly":* Molnar, 235.

249 *"Because of the":* https://www.jewishvirtuallibrary.org/adolf-eichmann-re port-on-activity-in-vienna-august-1938.

250 *Bonaparte also:* Bertin, 200.

250 *"She was hiding"* and *"The Princess":* Berthelsen, 80–81.

250 *Along with Bonaparte:* Cohen, 183.

250 *"I am writing":* Ernst L. Freud, 442–43.

251 *Bonaparte and Bullitt* and *Freud assets and flight tax figures,* and *earlier departures, On June 2:* Cohen, 167; Molnar, 236–37; Gay, 625.

253 *"I Prof. Freud"* and *"I can heartily":* Jones, Volume 3, 226.

253 *"The policeman"* and *train trip to Paris:* Berthelsen, 83–86.

253 *At the last minute* and *Schur operation and departure:* Max Schur, 502; Peter Schur, "The Freud-Schur Connection."

254 *"She looked after":* Molnar, 237.

Chapter 12: "This England"

255 *As Fichtl recalled* and *details of Paris, Channel crossing,* and *early days in London:* Berthelsen, 86–89; Molnar, 237–39; Jones, Volume 3, 227–29.

256 *As Freud wrote to Eitingon* and *"The feeling of triumph":* Ernst L. Freud, 444–46.

258 *"Our reception was"* and *rest of letter to Alexander:* Ibid., 447–48.

259 *Jones confirmed:* Jones, Volume 3, 232–33.

259 *But on June 10* and *visit to Lün,* and *June 23 visit* and *Times report:* Molnar, 240–42.

260 *"Good company!":* Schur, 507.

260 *"In all those years"* and *rest of Zweig memories, Dali meeting:* Zweig, 446–50; Molnar, 244.

261 *"I really owe":* Jones, Volume 3, 235.

261 *When the philosopher* and *rest of Isaiah Berlin visit:* Michael Ignatieff, *Isaiah Berlin: A Life,* 91.

NOTES

262 *The legendary couple* and *account of Leonard and Virginia Woolf's visit and impressions:* Leonard Woolf, *Downhill All the Way: An Autobiography of the Years 1919 to 1939,* 168–69.

263 *On July 28, 1938,* and *house and furniture description* and *Freud's correspondence:* Molnar, 244–48; Welter, 150–54.

264 *"Everything is here":* Berthelsen, 94.

264 *"Everything here"* and *"now that"* and *"The latest horrifying":* Ernst L. Freud, 452, 455.

265 *"You should have":* Burlingham, 269.

265 *On November 10:* Molnar, 251

266 *In the summer* and *fate of four sisters:* https://www.holocausthistorical society.org.uk/contents/jewishbiographies/sigmundfreudandhissisters .html; Freud Museum London, catalogue of exhibition "Leaving Today: The Freuds in Exile 1938," 108–9; Martin Freud, 16. As noted previously, some sources put Adolfine's year of death as 1943, but her death certificate is dated September 29, 1942.

266 *While Anna continued* and *fifteenth International Psychoanalytic Congress:* Molnar, 245.

266 *When William Bullitt:* Etkind, 83.

267 *Only a few days* and *"The book torments":* Molnar, 240.

267 *Writing to the German* and *letter to Arnold Zweig:* Schur, 506.

267 *In his actual text* and *"Formerly I lived"* and *"The religious argument":* Sigmund Freud, *Moses and Monotheism,* 92–93, 203–4.

267 *On July 15* and *"Moses finished":* Molnar, 242–43.

268 *"You no doubt"* and *"We Jews":* Jones, Volume 3, 237.

269 *Stefan Zweig visited:* Zweig, 450–51.

269 *Six days after* and *Max Schur in Paris and London:* Author interview with Peter Schur; Peter Schur, "The Freud–Schur Connection"; Max Schur, 501–10.

270 *"This operation was"* and *other letters to Bonaparte:* Ernst L. Freud, 451, 455, 458.

270 *On December 7* and *"At the age":* Molnar, 252.

271 *Yet he still managed:* Ibid., 259.

271 *"Father loved":* Martin Freud, 218.

271 *In a letter to H. G. Wells* and *failure of Wells's effort:* Freud Museum London, catalogue of exhibition "Leaving Today," 96–97.

271 *By not immediately* and *U.S. visas* and *Schur trip to U.S.:* Peter Schur, "The Freud–Schur Connection"; Max Schur, 522–24.

273   *"I found Freud"* and *Orthroform:* Schur, 525–29; https://pubs.asahq.org
      /anesthesiology/article/127/3/407/17788/New-Orthoform-for-Old-Freud
      -Insoluble-Numbing-for.

273   *By August* and *remaining period and death, including eulogy:* Schur, 526–29;
      Jones, Volume 3, 245–48.

274   *In those earliest days:* Berthelsen, 98.

275   *"I believe that":* Young-Bruehl, 239.

275   *"I cannot even":* Molnar, 264.

Afterword

277   *"to us he":* W. H. Auden, *Collected Poems*, 273–76.

277   *Anna Freud* and *Dorothy Burlingham:* Burlingham, 271–91; https://psycho
      analysis.org.uk/our-authors-and-theorists/anna-freud, https://www.new
      worldencyclopedia.org/entry/Anna_Freud, https://www.verywellmind
      .com/anna-freud-biography-1895-1982-2795536.

278   *Jonathan Tobis:* Tobis email to author, August 7, 2020.

279   *Ernest Jones* and *International Psychoanalytical Association:* https://www
      .ipa.world/IPA/en/IPA1/officers_past_and_current/ipa_officers_past_and
      _current.aspx.

279   *"It is not":* Jones, Volume 1, xi.

279   *Jones managed to* and *his handling of the biography:* Maddox, 259–79.

279   *"I am simply":*Maddox, 265.

280   *Marie Bonaparte* and *Twentieth Congress quotes:* Bertin, 202–65.

281   *William Bullitt:* Etkind, 180–237; Brownell and Billings, 247–332.

283   *In his 1946 book* and *"After the next":* William C. Bullitt, *The Great Globe
      Itself: A Preface to World Affairs*, vii.

283   *Anton Sauerwald:* Schur, 498–99; Cohen, 11–15, 234–41; Wiener Stadt und
      Landesarchiv (Municipal and Provincial Archives of Vienna), letter to the
      author, June 29, 2021.

284   *Max Schur:* Peter Schur, "The Freud-Schur Connection"; https://www.ency
      clopedia.com/psychology/dictionaries-thesauruses-pictures-and-press-re
      leases/schur-max-1897-1969; Max Schur, 1–16.

BIBLIOGRAPHY

Archival Sources

Library of Congress, Washington, D.C.
Manuscripts and Archives, Sterling Memorial Library, Yale University, New
    Haven, CT
The National Library of Israel, Jerusalem
Royal Society of Medicine Library & Archives, London
Wiener Stadt und Landesarchiv (Municipal and Provincial Archives of Vienna)

Unpublished Sources

Anna Freud-Bernays, *Mother's Memoirs*, translation by Hella Freud Bernays
    (courtesy of Randolph Bernays Randolph).
Peter Schur presentation, "The Freud–Schur Connection," February 1994, Vienna
    Psychoanalytical Association (courtesy of Peter Schur).

Publications

Ash, Mitchell G., ed. *Materialen zur Geschichte der Psychoanalyse in Wien
    1938–1945.* Frankfurt a. M.: Brandes & Apsel, 2012.
Auden, W. H. Edward Mendelson, ed. *Collected Poems.* New York: Vintage In-
    ternational, 1991.
Bair, Deirdre. *Jung: A Biography.* Boston: Little, Brown, 2003.

Berthelsen, Detlef. *Alltag bei Familie Freud: Die Erinnerungen der Paula Fichtl.* Hamburg: Hoffman und Campe, 1987.

Bertin, Celia. *Marie Bonaparte: A Life.* San Diego: Harcourt Brace Jovanovich, 1982.

Bonaparte, Marie. *Topsy: The Story of a Golden-Haired Chow.* New Brunswick, NJ: Transaction Publishers, 1994.

Brook-Shepherd, Gordon. *The Austrians: A Thousand-Year Odyssey.* New York: Carroll & Graf, 1998.

Brownell, Will, and Richard N. Billings. *So Close to Greatness: A Biography of William C. Bullitt.* New York: Macmillan, 1987.

Bullitt, Ernesta Drinker. *An Uncensored Diary from the Central Empires (1917).* New York: Doubleday, Page & Company, 1917 (Kessinger's Legacy Reprints).

Bullitt, Orville H., ed. *For the President Personal and Secret: Correspondence Between Franklin D. Roosevelt and William C. Bullitt.* Boston: Houghton Mifflin, 1972.

Bullitt, William C. *The Bullitt Mission to Russia.* Washington, D.C.: U.S. Senate Committee on Foreign Relations transcript, September 12, 1919.

———. *The Great Globe Itself: A Preface to World Affairs.* New York: Charles Scribner's Sons, 1946.

———. *It's Not Done.* New York: Harcourt, Brace & Company, 1926.

Burlingham, Michael John. *The Last Tiffany: A Biography of Dorothy Tiffany Burlingham.* New York: Atheneum, 1989.

Clare, George. *Last Waltz in Vienna.* London: Pan Books, 2002.

Cocks, Geoffrey. *Psychotherapy in the Third Reich: The Göring Institute.* New York: Oxford University Press, 1985.

Cohen, David. *The Escape of Sigmund Freud.* New York: The Overlook Press, 2012.

Coles, Robert. *Anna Freud: The Dream of Psychoanalysis.* Reading, MA: Addison-Wesley, 1991.

Dearborn, Mary V. *Queen of Bohemia: The Life of Louise Bryant.* Boston: Houghton Mifflin, 1996.

Diller, Jerry Victor. *Freud's Jewish Identity: A Case Study in the Impact of Ethnicity.* Rutherford, NJ: Farleigh Dickinson University Press, 1991.

Doolittle, Hilda (H.D.). *Tribute to Freud.* New York: New Directions, 2012.

Dunn, Dennis J. *Caught Between Roosevelt and Stalin: America's Ambassadors to Moscow.* Lexington: University Press of Kentucky, 1998.

Eastman, Max. *Great Companions: Critical Memoirs of Some Famous Friends.* New York: Farrar, Straus & Cudahy, 1959.

———. *Heroes I Have Known: Twelve Who Lived Great Lives.* New York: Simon & Schuster, 1942.

Edmundson, Mark. *The Death of Sigmund Freud: The Legacy of His Last Days.* New York: Bloomsbury USA, 2007.

Elon, Amos. *Herzl.* New York: Holt, Rinehart & Winston, 1975.

Etkind, Alexander. *Roads Not Taken: An Intellectual Biography of William C. Bullitt.* Pittsburgh: University of Pittsburgh Press, 2017.

Fest, Joachim. *Hitler.* San Diego: Harcourt Brace Jovanovich, 1992.

Freud, Ernst L., ed. *Letters of Sigmund Freud.* New York: Basic Books, 1960.

Freud, Martin. *Any Survivors? A Lost Novel of World War II.* Stroud, Gloucestershire: The History Press, 2010.

———. *Sigmund Freud: Man and Father.* New York: The Vanguard Press, 1958.

Freud, Sigmund. *Civilization and Its Discontents.* Mineola, NY: Dover Publications, 1994.

———. *The Interpretation of Dreams.* New York: Basic Books, 2010.

———. *Moses and Monotheism.* London: The Hogarth Press, 1939.

———. *An Outline of Psycho-Analysis.* New York: W. W. Norton, 1989.

Freud, Sigmund, and William C. Bullitt. *Thomas Woodrow Wilson: A Psychological Study.* London: Weidenfeld & Nicolson, 1967.

Friedlander, Saul. *The Years of Extermination: Nazi Germany and the Jews, 1939–1945.* New York: Harper Perennial, 2008.

Friedman, Lawrence J. *Identity's Architect: A Biography of Erik H. Erikson.* New York: Scribner, 1999.

Friedman, Susan Stanford. *Analyzing Freud: Letters of H.D., Bryher, and Their Circle.* New York: New Directions, 2002.

Fry, Helen. *Freuds' War.* Stroud, Gloucestershire: The History Press, 2009.

Gardner, Virginia. *"Friend and Lover": The Life of Louise Bryant.* New York: Horizon Press, 1982.

Gay, Peter. *Freud: A Life for Our Time.* New York: W. W. Norton, 1988.

Gay, Peter, ed. *The Freud Reader.* New York: W. W. Norton, 1989.

Gunther, John. *Inside Europe.* New York: Harper & Brothers, 1938.

———. *The Lost City.* New York: Harper & Row, 1964.

Hamann, Brigitte. *Hitler's Vienna: A Portrait of the Tyrant as a Young Man.* New York: Tauris Park Paperbacks, 2010.

BIBLIOGRAPHY

Heller, Peter. *A Child Analysis with Anna Freud*. Madison, WI: International Universities Press, 1990.

Hitler, Adolf. *Mein Kampf*. Boston: Houghton Mifflin, 1971.

Hodgson, Godfrey. *Woodrow Wilson's Right Hand: The Life of Colonel Edward M. House*. New Haven: Yale University Press, 2006.

Hoffman, Paul. *The Viennese: Splendor, Twilight and Exile*. New York: Anchor Books, 1988.

Ignatieff, Michael. *Isaiah Berlin: A Life*. New York: Metropolitan Books, 1998.

Isaacson, Walter. *Einstein: His Life and Universe*. New York: Simon & Schuster Paperbacks, 2008.

Johnson, Paul. *A History of the Jews*. New York: Harper & Row, 1987.

Jones, Ernest. *Free Associations: Memoirs of a Psychoanalyst*. New York: Basic Books, 1959.

——. *The Life and Work of Sigmund Freud, Volume 1, The Formative Years and the Great Discoveries, 1856–1900*. New York: Basic Books, 1953.

——. *The Life and Work of Sigmund Freud, Volume 2, Years of Maturity, 1901–1919*. New York: Basic Books, 1955.

——. *The Life and Work of Sigmund Freud, Volume 3, The Last Phase, 1919–1939*. New York: Basic Books, 1957.

Kaltenborn, H. V. *Fifty Fabulous Years, 1900–1950: A Personal Review*. New York: G. P. Putnam's Sons, 1950.

Kandel, Eric R. *The Age of Insight: The Quest to Understand the Unconscious in Art, Mind, and Brain, from Vienna 1900 to the Present*. New York: Random House, 2012.

Kennan, George F. *Memoirs: 1925–1950*. Boston: Little, Brown, 1967.

Kershaw, Ian. *Hitler, the Germans, and the Final Solution*. New Haven: Yale University Press, 2008.

——. *Hitler: 1889–1936: Hubris*. London: Penguin, 1998.

——. *Hitler: 1936–45: Nemesis*. New York: W. W. Norton, 2000.

Keynes, John Maynard. *The Economic Consequences of the Peace*. Heritage Illustrated Publishing, 2014.

Kubizek, August. *The Young Hitler I Knew*. London: Greenhill Books, 2006.

Kurth, Peter. *American Cassandra: The Life of Dorothy Thompson*. Boston: Little, Brown, 1990.

Loewenstein, Rudolph M., ed. *Drives, Affects, Behavior*. New York: International Universities Press, 1953.

Maddox, Brenda. *Freud's Wizard: Ernest Jones and the Transformation of Psychoanalysis*. Boston: Da Capo Press, 2007.

Markel, Howard. *An Anatomy of Addiction: Sigmund Freud, William Halsted, and the Miracle Drug Cocaine*. New York: Vintage, 2012.

Martin, Ralph G. *Cissy: The Extraordinary Life of Eleanor Medill Patterson*. New York: Simon & Schuster, 1979.

McGuire, William, ed. *The Freud/Jung Letters: The Correspondence Between Sigmund Freud and C.G. Jung*. Princeton: Princeton University Press, 1994.

McLynn, Frank. *Carl Gustav Jung*. New York: St. Martin's Press, 1997.

Molnar, Michael, ed., and The Freud Museum, London. *The Diary of Sigmund Freud, 1929–1939: A Record of the Final Decade*. New York: Charles Scribner's Sons, 1992.

Mowrer, Edgar Ansel. *Triumph and Turmoil: A Personal History of Our Times*. New York: Weybright & Talley, 1968.

Nagorski, Andrew. *Hitlerland: American Eyewitnesses to the Nazi Rise to Power*. New York: Simon & Schuster, 2012.

———. *The Nazi Hunters*. New York: Simon & Schuster, 2016.

O'Toole, Patricia. *The Moralist: Woodrow Wilson and the World He Made*. New York: Simon & Schuster, 2018.

Paskauskas, R. Andrew, ed. *The Complete Correspondence of Sigmund Freud and Ernest Jones: 1908–1939*. Cambridge: The Belknap Press of Harvard University Press, 1993.

Peters, Uwe Henrik. *Anna Freud: A Life Dedicated to Children*. New York: Schocken Books, 1985.

Pfeiffer, Ernst, ed. *Sigmund Freud and Lou Andreas-Salomé Letters*. New York: W. W. Norton, 1985.

Rice, Emmanuel. *Freud and Moses: The Long Journey Home*. Albany: State University of New York Press, 1990.

Sanders, Marion K. *Dorothy Thompson: A Legend in Her Time*. Boston: Houghton Mifflin, 1973.

Schnitzler, Arthur. *My Youth in Vienna*. New York: Holt, Rinehart & Winston, 1970.

Schur, Max. *Freud: Living and Dying*. New York: International Universities Press, 1972.

Sherborne, Michael. *H.G. Wells: Another Kind of Life*. London: Peter Owen, 2012.

Shirer, William L. *Berlin Diary: The Journal of a Foreign Correspondent, 1934–1941*. New York: Galahad Books, 1995.

———. *The Rise and Fall of the Third Reich: A History of Nazi Germany.* New York: Simon & Schuster, 1960.

———. *Twentieth Century Journey: The Start, 1904–1930.* New York: Simon & Schuster, 1976.

———. *Twentieth Century Journey: The Nightmare Years, 1930–1940.* Boston: Little, Brown, 1984.

Steffens, Lincoln. *The Autobiography of Lincoln Steffens,* Volume 2. New York: Harcourt, Brace & World, 1931.

Szasz, Thomas. *Anti-Freud: Karl Kraus's Criticism of Psychoanalysis and Psychiatry.* Syracuse: Syracuse University Press, 1990.

Toland, John. *Adolf Hitler,* 2 vols. New York: Doubleday, 1976.

Wells, H. G. *The Secret Places of the Heart.* Independently published, 2020 (originally published 1922).

Welter, Volker M. *Ernst L. Freud, Architect: The Case of the Modern Bourgeois Home.* New York: Berghahn Books, 2012.

Woolf, Leonard. *Downhill All The Way: An Autobiography of the Years 1919 to 1939.* San Diego: Harcourt Brace Jovanovich, 1967.

Wortis, Joseph. *Fragments of an Analysis with Freud.* New York: Simon & Schuster, 1954.

Young-Bruehl, Elisabeth. *Anna Freud: A Biography.* New York: Summit Books, 1988.

Zweig, Stefan. *The World of Yesterday.* Lincoln: University of Nebraska Press, 2013.

PHOTO CREDITS

INDEX

INDEX

INDEX

INDEX

Vienna Psychoanalytic Society, 39,
58–59, 100, 102, 107, 114, 115, 232,
275
Viereck, Sylvester, 180
violence, human predisposition to, 191,
201, 220
virility complex, 152

Wagner, Richard, 34
Waidhofen Manifesto, 34
Waldheim, Kurt, 9–10
war:
SF's views on, 189–92
see also specific conflicts
war neurosis, 84
Webb, Sidney, 56
Wednesday evening gatherings, 39, 44,
47, 51, 58–59, 68–71, 83, 100, 102,
157
Weimar psychoanalytic conference
(1911), 67–68
Weiss, Edoardo, 208
Welczeck, Johannes von, 239
Welles, Sumner, 282
Wells, H. G., 52, 56, 120, 187–88, 215,
260, 271
Werfel, Franz, 4
Why War? (Freud), 208
Wiegand, Charmion von, 135–36
Wiesenthal, Simon, 9
Wiley, Irena, 239
Wiley, John, 220–21, 230–31, 238–39,
245, 254
Wilhelm II, Kaiser, 77
Wilson, Edith, 139, 267
Wilson, Hugh, 238–39
Wilson, Woodrow, 7, 120, 127, 128–29,
130–32, 170, 196, 220, 282

Bullitt and Freud's biography of,
266–67, 282–83
Bullitt's disillusionment with, 132–33,
137–40
SF's criticism of, 137–40
women, restrictions on, 141–42, 147–48
Woolf, Leonard, 262–64
Woolf, Virginia, 215, 262–64
Worcester Telegram, 61
World Jewish Congress, 10
World War I, 4, 11–12, 68, 78–87, 121,
125–28, 155, 161, 174, 179, 180,
189, 206, 262, 274
aftermath of, 79–80, 87, 89–91,
129–31, 179, 204, 256, 282
British vs. German view of, 81–82
Martin Freud in, 78–80
run-up to, 76–79, 94, 96, 99, 124, 149
SF's response to, 80–86
World War II, 160, 208, 266, 282, 283
onset of, 274, 278
run-up to, 265
Wortis, Joseph, 182–86, 213

"X" (M. Bonaparte's lover), 150, 156, 158

Yahuda, Abraham Shalom, 267
Yale University, 122–23
Yalta peace conference, 282
"Young Children in Wartime"
(A. Freud), 278

Zionism, Zionists, 33, 56, 196–97
Zuckmayer, Carl, 1
Zurich, 47–48, 50, 56, 72, 88, 188
Zweig, Arnold, 214, 217–18, 219, 222, 267
Zweig, Stefan, 4, 36, 201–2, 215,
260–61, 269

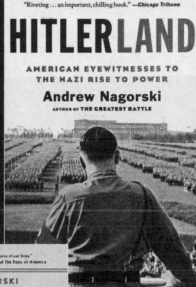